Problem Spaces

Problem Spaces

How and Why
Methodology Matters

Celia Lury

polity

Polity Press
65 Bridge Street
Cambridge CB2 1UR, UK

Polity Press
101 Station Landing
Suite 300
Medford, MA 02155, USA

ISBN-13: 978-1-5095-0793-1 (hardback)
ISBN-13: 978-1-5095-0794-8 (paperback)

A catalogue record for this book is available from the British Library.

Typeset in 11 on 13pt Sabon
by Fakenham Prepress Solutions, Fakenham, Norfolk NR21 8NL
Printed and bound in Great Britain by TJ Books Limited

For further information on Polity, visit our website:
politybooks.com

Contents

Contents

Acknowledgements

I would like to thank colleagues, friends and family near and far, including: Nerea Calvillo, Sophie Day, Michael Dieter, Sarah Doughty, Elena Esposito, Carolin Gerlitz, Christina Hughes, Eva Lash, Adam Lury, Giles Lury, Karen Lury, Henry Mainsah, Noortje Marres, Greg McInerny, Mike Michael, João Porto de Albuquerque, Maria Puig de la Bellacasa, Shirin Rai, Matt Spencer, David Stark, Martín Tironi, Nigel Thrift, Philipp Ulbrich, Matías Valderrama, Sylvia Walby, Naomi Waltham-Smith and Scott Wark. Special thanks go to Michael Castelle, who first introduced me to the idea of problem spaces; to Emma Uprichard, who kept me going; to Nate Tkacz and the three anonymous reviewers who read and commented on a draft of the book; and to Ana Gross, the co-author of Chapter 3. I would also like to thank Karina Jákupsdóttir and Jonathan Skerrett at Polity for their patience and support.

Research for this monograph was supported by an ESRC Professorial Fellowship: Order and Continuity: Methods for Change in a Topological Society, Ref No: 978-1444339598. I am grateful for this support.

Introduction:
The Compulsion of
Composition

Power is the compulsion of composition ... The
essence of power is the drive towards aesthetic
worth for its own sake. All power is a derivative
from this fact of composition attaining worth for
itself. There is no other fact. Power and importance
are aspects of this fact. It constitutes the drive of the
universe. It is efficient cause, maintaining its power
of survival. It is final cause, maintaining in the
creature its appetition for creation.

Alfred North Whitehead (1968: 119)

Ann Kelly and Lynsey McGoey (2018) suggest that we
are witnessing the emergence of 'a new empire of truth'.
Describing the significance of profound transformations in
the 'scaling, pace and symbolic power of fact-making' for
'the shifting relationships between knowledge, ignorance
and power today', they ask:

What constitutes authoritative evidence in this
political climate? To what uses is evidence put, and

what values does it carry? What obligations must be placed on the companies, such as Google or Facebook, that configure our new public spheres while profiting from the tracking and steering of online behaviour? What counts in the making of facts, and who does the counting? Which empirical tools and metrics garner sufficient political capital to guide policy during times of economic uncertainty? And, critically, how do the social sciences respond to the increasing social and political significance of data while accounting for the deepening popular scepticism of the facts that data are used to support? (2018: 2–3)

This book develops the thesis that to understand this new empire of truth and answer the questions Kelly and McGoey pose, a new concept of a problem space is needed.

So, what is a problem space?

In established methodological terms, a problem space is a representation of a problem in terms of relations between three components: givens, goals and operators. 'Givens' are the facts or information that describe the problem; 'goals' are the desired end state of the problem – what the knower wants to know; and 'operators' are the actions to be performed in reaching the desired goals. In many methodological discussions, the relation between these three components is assumed to be stable and relatively straightforward. Once givens and goals are assessed, operators – concepts and methods – can be identified and implemented, problems can be defined, analysed and solved in sequential steps: the problem space *contains* the problem. But such an approach presumes that we know the problem before we start investigating, and that it remains the same as it is investigated. And this is very often not the case: the problem is a problem, *becomes* a problem as it is investigated. If we take seriously the becoming of a problem then we cannot stick with a container conception of a problem space. Instead, we should pay attention to the constantly changing relations between givens, goals and operators in which a problem is transformed.[1] This requires an understanding of a problem space as a space of methodological potential.

To develop this understanding and consider how this potential may be realized to 'test the present' (Stengers 2019), the book outlines a compositional methodology. The distinctiveness of this methodology comes from an emphasis on the vocabulary of composition,[2] a term that Whitehead employs in the quotation above, but whose everyday definition is 'the action of putting things together'. Here it refers to the processes, the activities with which the givens, goals and operators of a problem space are put together. When the term composition is used in the visual and performing arts the emphasis is on the creativity of this action of putting things together. It is used here – in a way that it is hoped will be of interest to disciplinary and interdisciplinary researchers of all kinds – to describe a methodology in which the focus is on the ways in which a problem is put together, how it is formed and transformed, inventively (Lury and Wakeford 2012). In this process of putting a problem together, of forming and transforming, the compulsion of composition does not come from either inside or outside the problem; the problem is not acted on *in* a space but emerges *across* a problem space, from with-in and out-with.

For compositional methodology, an understanding of a problem as a form of process is fundamental, where form consists in both the problem and its limits or constraints.[3] To explicate this understanding of form, let me introduce a series of works by the artist Dorothea Rockburne: *Drawing Which Makes Itself* (1972–3). In these works, a double-sided piece of carbon paper, which I invite you to consider as analogous to a phenomenon or situation becoming a problem, is held against a wall or a floor, folded and rotated, with the edges or limits of the space it makes in these activities scored through the paper onto the wall or floor. The activities (the methods) of folding, rotating and scoring move the paper (the problem) into and through another dimension in a process of transformation. The art critic Rosalind Krauss says of these works:

> The act of scoring simultaneously deposits carbon onto the wall surface and underlines the fold of the paper itself. The resultant lines or marks are read with a striking ambivalence, for they are both on the wall and yet they are retained *within* the carbon paper that had been flipped into a new position. ... one confronts works in which the lines [that are 'out-with' the paper] arise from information that is '[with]in' the paper. (2010: 221)

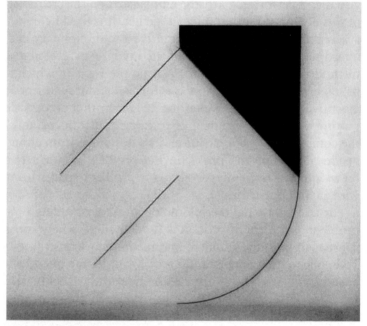

Figure 1   Installation piece: Arc
Source: Dorothea Rockburne (1973) © ARS, NY and DACS, London 2020

Acting methodically on the properties of a situation becoming a problem (trans)forms the problem. The limits of the problem are with-in and out-with it: they do not contain it, but, rather, express or encapsulate it.

The material-semiotic properties of the double-sided carbon paper mean that some acts – some methods – have expressive effects; it is a drawing that draws itself. At the same time, not only do the material-semiotic properties of the paper – the problem – have methodological potential (to be folded, to be scored, to be rotated), so too does the context in which the work is (re-)presented matter. Rockburne says the context should 'represent' the art. To do so requires that the context be (re)active:

> I was very interested in the fact that the whole room should represent the art. I painted the walls with the brightest white paint you could find. As people walked into the room, their footprints became part of the drawing. (https://www.khanacademy. org/humanities/art-1010/minimalism-earthworks/v/ rockburne-drawing)

Inspired by this work, the concept of a problem space put forward here is that it is a space of methodological potential that is with-in and out-with the ongoing trans-formation of a problem. The potential is realized in a methodology that, rather than responding only to the initial presentation of a problem, composes the problem again and again.

Compositional methodology

The activity of composing is not given in advance of a problem, but is rather ever forming and transforming across a problem space. It rarely involves just one action or operation – sensing, categorizing, conceptualizing, scaling, measuring, affecting, experiencing, varying, but involves

the doing of many together. In other words, compositional methodology presumes and exploits the fact that a
problem is not given but emerges with-in and out-with a
myriad sequence of actions or methods that (trans)forms
the problem space. Importantly, this sequencing is not
the addition of one action or method after another, but a
composition in the sense that the actions or methods are
not discrete or independent of each other. As 'it' happens,
a compositional methodology seeks to recognize and
exploit the properties of the problem on an ongoing basis.
It composes a problem by recognizing and making use of
(rather than minimizing) the constantly changing limits
that create a problem and a problem space together, identifying and operating the intensive or 'live' properties of the
problem it investigates (Back and Puwar 2012).

   Compositional methodology is, then, concerned with
form in and as transformation, a process involving
'the interweaving of data, form, transition, and issue'
(Whitehead 1968: 210) organized by the compulsion of
composition:

   It is not that which is discriminated that is most real,
   nor is it a completed, self-sustaining composition. But
   instead the compulsion of composition. (Whitehead
   1968: 133)

To adapt Rockburne's title, for compositional methodology
a situation or phenomenon becomes a problem, acquires a
form, trans-forms, as a 'problem that problematizes itself';
that is, compulsive composition is the repeated folding or
twisting of problems into forms of problematization. In
this twisting, the problem is revealed never to be simply
a problem, but also a composition of the methodological
potential of a problem space to be expressed in transformation. This is to say problems and problem spaces are
compulsively composed together.

   Let me give another example, taken from a discussion
of the development of staging models for the diagnosis

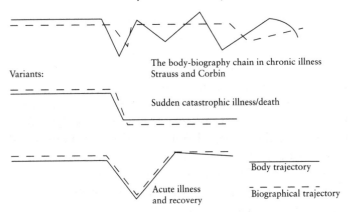

Figure 2   Model I: Body–biography trajectory
Source: Geoff Bowker and Susan Leigh Star (2000)

of tuberculosis by Geoff Bowker and Susan Leigh Star (2000). In a first model – a body–biography chain, the biographical trajectory of an individual and the trajectory of their illness are placed alongside each other.

In a second model, multiple biography/identity trajectories are introduced, as a way of recognizing the multiple dimensions of an individual's life, complicating the understanding of the course of illness in relation to the person who is ill.

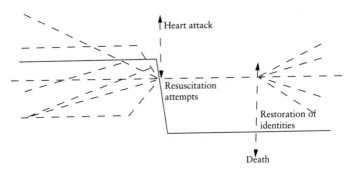

Figure 3   Model II: Multiple identity trajectory
Source: Geoff Bowker and Susan Leigh Star (2000)

In both these models, the problem space is a container space. However, in a third model, the external linear time of the classification system is folded into the model: continuities, discontinuities and layers are introduced into the problem space. In the action of folding the epistemic limit of the classification system across the trajectories, the model becomes expressive; that is, the model acquires inventive methodological potential in the folding of 'the outside' of the problem into the 'inside'. It is encapsulated. As Bowker and Star put it, there is a topology–typology twist: 'The topology created by the body–biography trajectory is pulled against the idealized, standardized typology of the global classification of tuberculosis, itself a broken and moving target' (2000: 190).

To return to the vocabulary introduced in the discussion of Rockburne, this model involves the action of folding the external limit of the classification system into the problem. That is, the method of folding changes the problem even as it persists, creating new methodological potential in the process of transformation. In other words, it is not just a problem that is defined in transformation, but the problem and the problem space, as they are compulsively composed together.

In what follows it will be suggested that compositional methodology is concerned with the way in which

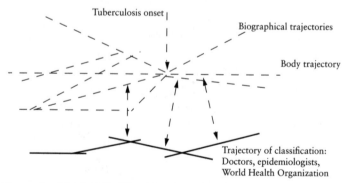

Figure 4   Model III: Classification trajectory
Source: Geoff Bowker and Susan Leigh Star (2000)

a problem emerges in the relation between two moments; that is, with the addressing of a method or methods to a specific problem, and the capacity of what emerges in their use to change or transform the problem (Rheinberger 1997). As Nina Wakeford and I (2012) argue, it is the relation between these two moments that makes methods answerable to a problem, and provides the basis of the self-displacing movement or auto-spatialization of a problem. We further argue that the inventiveness of methods is a consequence of the articulation of their double force: their constitutive effects and their capacity to contribute to the generative circulation of the problem. Here I suggest that a compositional methodology acknowledges and exploits the fact that the double force of auto-spatialization does not operate to create a space that contains the problem, but, rather, has as its aim the composition of a problem across a problem space that is itself changing.[4] Indeed it is proposed that it is the accomplishment of some kind of continuity and connection in the transformation of a problem that secures epistemological value.

Becoming topological

What the discussion above implies, and the example from Bowker and Star illustrates, is that compositional methodology does not employ a container understanding of problem space but is, rather, concerned with the *becoming topological* of problem spaces (Lury, Parisi and Terranova 2012). What might this mean?

Topology is commonly described as a mode of analysis that arises from the study of spatial properties that remain invariant under transformation. It is thus a mode of analysis that is concerned with how continuity and change can take place together. Importantly, while it might seem, from this definition, that topology describes spatial properties that exist outside of or are independent of time, just as the concept of the problem space proposed here does not presume a conception of space as container, nor does it assume a container conception of time. As Steven Connor says, 'Because topology is concerned with what remains invariant as a result of transformation, it may be thought of as geometry plus time, geometry given body by motion' (http://www.stevenconnor.com/topologies). The claim that problem spaces are 'becoming topological' is an acknowledgement of the ways in which the compulsive composition of a problem makes time and space in relation to each other in the organization of continuity in transformation.[5]

While some other discussions of methodology employ the vocabulary of topology, the usefulness of the vocabulary of topology for the analysis of social and cultural life has been much debated (Law and Mol 1994, 2002; Thrift 2008; Lury, Parisi and Terranova 2012; Shields 2013; https://culanth.org/fieldsights/series/topology-as-method), with some advising caution on the grounds that topology as an approach has been significantly developed in – and should be confined to – mathematics (Phillips 2013). In developing his geographical analysis of topologies of power, John Allen (2016) disagrees. To do so, he draws on Ian Hacking's interpretation of the transposition of mathematical terms to other domains. In a discussion which acknowledges the complexities of borrowings between disciplines as well as the variety of uses to which knowledge is put, Hacking says:

> It is not so clear whether we are discovering that the second domain has the same structure as the first domain, or whether we are sculpting the second domain so that it comes out shaped like the first. Probably both sorts of things happen. (Hacking 2014: 175 in Allen 2016: 5)

Allen says that he is not bothered with policing the borrowings between disciplines, but instead prefers to mobilize a cross-disciplinary understanding of topology

– that is, a concern with a form of relations that remains continuous in transformation – and that is the approach adopted here (see also https://www.theoryculturesociety. org/interview-with-celia-lury-luciana-parisi-and-tiziana-terranova-on-topologies). Following this approach, and as above, a compositional methodology addresses the becoming topological of problem spaces by exploring the continuity in (trans)form(ation) of problems across problem spaces. Indeed, it aims to describe and interrogate how the making of such continuities enables epistemological values to be established. However, with Hacking's analysis in mind it is important to remember that, like the drawing that requires a support to make itself, so does the becoming topological of problem spaces require a (material-semiotic) support. No methodology can operate in the abstract, and so the book is concerned not only with the composition of problem spaces but also with epistemic infrastructure.

The term 'epistemic' is used to signal that what is at issue in this new empire of truth is the nature of understanding, interpretation, explanation, justification and belief rather than knowledge as such.[6] As Karin Knorr Cetina puts it:

> Epistemic cultures are cultures of creating and warranting knowledge. This is what the choice of the term 'epistemic' rather than simply 'knowledge' suggests' ... [i]t brings into focus the content of the different knowledge-oriented lifeworlds, the different meanings of the empirical, specific constructions of the referent (the objects of knowledge), particular ontologies of instruments, specific models of epistemic subjects. (2007: 363–4)

Alongside 'epistemic', the term 'infrastructure' highlights the ways in which knowledge-making requires and installs material supports in the world, what Knorr Cetina calls knowledge settings, the 'whole sets of arrangements, processes and principles that serve knowledge and unfold with its articulation' (2007: 361–2), including 'buildings, bureaucracies, standards, forms, technologies, funding flows, affective orientations, and power relations' (Murphy 2017: 6).

An aspect of concern for a compositional methodology in this regard is the material-semiotic capacities of such supports. In short, the use of the term composition in this exploration of compositional methodology is also designed to draw attention to the heterogeneous composition – the mixing, the composting, the mess (Law 2004) – of the material-semiotic processes and entities involved in the making of problem spaces. And while the term 'infrastructure' might seem to imply that the supports of methodological practices are fixed, static and easy to identify, this is not the understanding proposed here. Instead there is an emphasis on what Haraway calls the 'extraordinary range of contexts' (1991: 197) of knowledge production, what Bowker and Star describe as boundary infrastructures (2000) and what Mackenzie calls 'the unfurling, unstable opacity of contemporary infrastructures' (2016: 380; see also Harvey et al. 2016).[7]

In recognition of this unstable opacity, this book explores a variety of changes occurring in the epistemic infrastructure that make methodology a matter of public as well as academic concern. These include processes of explicitation and literalization as well as transformations in the material semiotics of problem spaces, in cognition and in the role of the observer. Other kinds of change include challenges to the Western-centric terms and character of many methodological debates, and the shift from an epistemic culture of representation and representativeness to one of participation and transparency. However, the principal concern of this book will be with the methodological implications of platformization (Poell et al. 2019), that is, in very general terms, 'the process of constructing a somewhat lifted-out or well-bounded domain as a relational intersection for different groups' (Mackenzie 2019: 1994). The well-bounded domains of interest here are those designed to support the making of epistemic claims by different actors or communities of practice (Lave and Wenger 1991).

Platformization is an ugly neologism, but it is used here to acknowledge both the proliferation of (methodological) platforms and the way in which platforms are not usually discrete or self-contained but are interconnected in a variety of ways, often coming to be embedded in the epistemic infrastructure. Indeed, the ugliness of the term directs attention to the fact that the distinction between platforms and infrastructure is not easy to draw. As Plantin et al. (2016) observe, it is now not uncommon that platform-based services acquire characteristics of infrastructure, while both new and existing infrastructures are increasingly being built or reorganized on the logic of platforms. This logic is important, so it will be argued, because platforms have the capacity to bring together – and modify – the changes in the epistemic infrastructure just outlined, although they by no means contain or exhaust them. They do so through the ways in which they enhance specific formal properties of circulation (Appadurai 2013), specifically those associated with recursion, and in doing so facilitate specific ways to identify and create continuity in the transformation of problems in relation to changing contexts. It is argued that in this way platformization reconfigures the potential afforded by relations between a problem and a problem space, expanding the methodological possibilities of the double force of methods, by creating a boundary infrastructure (Bowker and Star 2000). In doing so, it will be argued, platforms mutate the topologies of knowledge of problem spaces.

The structure of the book

As indicated above, the book aims to address the shifting relationships between knowledge, ignorance and power by developing the concept of problem space. It does this by exploring the inter-relationship of problem spaces and the contemporary epistemic infrastructure in which the composition of problem spaces takes place. To explicate the significance of this inter-relationship, the book is divided into: this Introduction, three Parts, and a Conclusion. Each of the Parts starts from a different point of view on the inter-relationship between problem space and infrastructure, allowing for a shifting – parallax – analysis of the possibilities afforded to a compositional methodology today. Such a structure, while complicated, is necessary since as Martin Savransky so nicely puts it:

> ... problems have an existence of their own, a mode of existence that is never just immanent to thought, but to a historical – which is to say, processual – world; as such, they can never be reduced to a matter of human psychology, epistemology, or methodology. Problems, in other words, are not that which a certain mode of thinking or knowing encounters as an obstacle to be overcome, but that which sets thinking, knowing and feeling into motion. (2018: 215)

The first Part has only one chapter. It introduces the heuristic of problem spaces through a discussion of five rather disparate writers – John Dewey, Herbert Simon, Donna Haraway, François Jullien and Arjun Appadurai. The aim is to situate compositional methodology, understood as the inter-linking of the formation and transformation of a problem across a problem space, in relation to established methodological approaches.

The second Part has three chapters (Chapters 2, 3 and 4). Chapter 2 describes some of the most significant changes in the contemporary epistemic infrastructure and the new possibilities they afford for configuring problem spaces. Chapter 3, co-authored with Ana Gross, considers some of the ways in which variation in price is measured, including the Consumer Price Index. This discussion of methods in practice highlight the methodological possibilities of some of the changes described in the previous chapter. This chapter also introduces the idea that these changes are being accelerated by a process of platformization, and begins to describe the implications of this process for the composition of problem spaces. Chapter 4 further develops the idea that we are witnessing the platformization of the epistemic infrastructure through a detailed discussion of the four understandings of platform identified by Tarleton Gillespie (2010): architectural, political, computational and figurative.

Focusing on compositional methodology, the third Part comprises two chapters (Chapters 5 and 6). Chapter 5 introduces some of the challenges – what I describe as the double troubles – associated with the methodological possibilities stemming from platformization including: the natively artificial character of the empirical; the multiplicity of the epistemological object; and the genus of cognitive syndromes that, following Gregory Bateson (1972), are described as transcontextualism. Chapter 6 situates compositional methodology in relation to the account of Mode 2 knowledge production developed by Helga Nowotny, Michael Scott and Michael Gibbons and others (Gibbons et al. 1994; Nowotny et al. 2001), noting shared concerns as well as differences in emphasis by drawing on the concept of the interface. This concept is deployed to develop the argument that contemporary science is neither external nor internal to society, adding to the analysis of the topological characteristics of today's problem spaces. As part of a consideration of the accountability and autonomy of knowledge production, it also paves the way for the proposal that methods are being operationalized as part of a cultural imaginary of knowability, and highlights the dangers of the gamification and weaponization of methods. The chapter contrasts knowability and answer-ability and ends by outlining an ethics for a compositional methodology in terms of care, and the values of response-ability.

The Conclusion looks back at and reflects on the book's account of contemporary topologies of knowledge and power.

Some general comments

Before embarking on this journey, it may be helpful to make a couple of observations about some of the assumptions that inform the book. The first is that the book's understanding of compositional methodology deploys an understanding of methods as practices. In some ways, such an understanding seems too obvious to need stating: in everyday as well as methodological uses, a method is a procedure or process for attaining an object, a way of doing things. But in some accounts, methods are only discussed before or after they are put to work – described in textbooks as a set of techniques to be learnt and then applied or in articles and monographs as completed actions that led to findings.[8] Rather than adopt this approach, the book emphasizes the doing or practice of methods to make visible the work that goes into the accomplishment of epistemological values. As Andrea Mubi Brighenti puts it, while being regulatory ideals, these accomplishments are also 'peculiar creations, ... bounded and contingent practices aimed to stabilize certain courses of action and interaction patterns' (2018: 24). Recognizing that epistemological values emerge from the doing of methods as material-semiotic practices enables a recognition of the composite nature of methodological exploration; for example:

Calculation thus appears as not merely mathematical or metrical in nature, but rather as a composite work made of different stages including objectification, separation, individualization, comparison, association, transformation, disembedding and distribution. (Brighenti 2018: 24)

As the book proceeds, what becomes apparent (hopefully) is that this doing, the compulsion of composition, comprises not only the intended actions of researchers, but also the actions and operations that are proposed, engaged, activated and (sometimes) automated in the epistemic infrastructure. And such actions and operations are themselves embedded in distributed activities that are not necessarily, indeed are not often, guided by epistemological concerns.

In this regard, the book speaks to and engages with discussions of the performativity of methods, the double social life of methods (Law, Ruppert and Savage 2011; Law and Urry 2003; Giddens 1987) and social epistemology (Collier 2005) as well as learning from studies of how science is done alongside more conventional accounts of methodology. It has been profoundly shaped by the longstanding feminist debates on epistemology and methodology, which are shown to have anticipated many concerns only recently identified in other debates. It also draws on the understanding of methods as interruptions I developed with the co-editors and contributors to the *Routledge Handbook of Interdisciplinary Research Methods* (Lury et al. 2018). There we describe methods as *gerunds*; that is, as the active present tense form of verbs that function as nouns. Put rather grandly, the *Handbook*'s concern is to emphasize the role of methods in the activation of the present: the determination of a situation as a problem; that is, 'a state of things in which something that will perhaps matter is unfolding amidst the usual activity of life' (Berlant 2008: 4). A further source of inspiration is recent work on digital media, including on platforms, interfaces, data and circulation.

In drawing on and developing these ideas, the book describes the use of as many kinds of methods as possible. I do not find much value in, for example, opposing quantitative or qualitative methods or restricting my examples to one or the other; nor do I wish to fetishize either 'the' scientific method or 'the' hermeneutic method,

de-construction or constructionism. The aim is to explore
the possibilities for the accomplishment of epistemological
values as they emerge in the use of a diversity of methods.
In this regard, I follow John Dewey who says:

> We are trying to know knowledge. The procedure
> which I have tried to follow, no matter with what
> obscurity and confusion, is to begin with cases of
> knowledge and to analyze them to discover why and
> how they are knowledges. (1922: 60)

To this end, the book also deploys examples and ideas
relating to the use of methods in professional, lay and
academic practices. This is not always the case in academic
discussions of methodology but it seems especially
important at a time of platformization, since platforms
are often the site of tensions in collaborative forms of
knowledge production (Rabinow et al. 2008), between,
for example, the academy and its outside(s), across public
and private organizations, with objects that may be more
or less objective (Knorr Cetina 1997) and with subjects
who may or may not be citizens, able to act as individuals
or only be recognized as informants or data points.

The interest in the use of methods inside and outside
academia does not, however, assume equivalence between
the various practices described. Instead the aim is to
recognize that at a time when scientific registers are
losing some of their traditional hold over the deployment
and interpretation of experimental interventions, epistemological considerations must contend with alternative
repertoires of evaluation (Lezaun, Marres and Tironi
2017), and to acknowledge some of the many ways in
which relations between academic and non-academic uses
of methods are currently being negotiated.

Noortje Marres (2012a) describes some of the complications associated with these changes and the associated
redistribution of expertise when she identifies three positions
in contemporary methodological debates in the discipline

of sociology. The first is the equation of sociological and social methods, an approach in which the latter are characterized by the (sometimes unacknowledged) naturalization or appropriation of social science methodology. I do not adopt this position: as will become clear I think it is important to acknowledge the two-way exchange that happens between academic and non-academic methods while acknowledging their different concerns. The second position is the marked opposition of sociological and social methods: an opposition between disciplinary and public problems which is developed in various forms of academic critique. In relation to this second position, while I do not want to diminish the importance of critique, neither do I want to start by assuming the terms of exchange as those of opposition or that academic practice is invariably 'better'. Marres' third position is to refuse any fixed identity for either sociological or social research and to avoid presuming the nature of the differences between them. In relation to this position, which is the one she adopts, methods are unstable, undetermined and interested; that is, methods are a way of equipping a situation to be a problem. I adopt this third position, and, like Marres, view methods as sites of engagement. Indeed, it is because I agree with Marres when she says that method development is a way to engage critically and creatively with wider analytical apparatuses that problem spaces are approached through a dual focus on methodology and the epistemic infrastructure. While it is becoming harder and harder to loosen the knots in which the strands of epistemic and social control have become entangled, this does not mean that their entanglement in the new empire of truth can be ignored (Herberg and Vilsmaier 2020).

− Part I −
Problem Spaces

– 1 –

What is a Problem Space?

> Would anything change if sensible things were
> conceived of as 'across' space, rather than 'in' space?
>
> Mel Bochner (2008: 74)

Five approaches relevant to the elaboration of concept of a problem space are introduced here. A first pairing juxtaposes the methodology proposed by John Dewey, an early twentieth-century advocate of pragmatism with the approach to the 'artificial sciences' developed by Herbert Simon, one of the mid-twentieth-century founders of cognitive science. The second pairing is feminist theorist Donna Haraway and French sinologist François Jullien. The fifth approach is that of the anthropologist Arjun Appadurai. These final three authors all write at the end of the twentieth and the beginning of the twenty-first century.

The five are not introduced here because they are the 'best' exponents of problem spaces (as far as I am aware only Simon uses the term). Why I bring them together, despite their very different vocabularies and concerns, is that, in their discussions of methodology, all of them focus on the process of making or composing problems;

that is, for none of them are problems pre-given. They are all also concerned with the surrounds, environments or contexts – the spaces – in or with which problems emerge; indeed, that they do not assume space to be a container for problems is the primary reason for their selection. Instead they consider sensible things – situations transforming into problems – as emerging in movements 'across' space, as the artist Mel Bochner puts it. At various points in the presentation of their approaches their contribution to an understanding of a compositional methodology is highlighted.

Approach 1: Dewey
First, the pragmatist John Dewey, for whom the process of inquiry emerges in the transformation of an indeterminate situation into a problem understood as a unified whole:

> Inquiry is the controlled or directed transformation of an indeterminate situation into one that is so deter-minate in its constituent distinctions and relations as to convert the elements of the original situation into a unified whole. (1938: 108)

As Matthew Brown (2012) observes, this is a radical conception of inquiry. Inquiry is not a process of thought that takes place in the mind of an inquirer for Dewey, but a process of transforming a situation. As the Introduction outlined, this emphasis on the transformation of a situation becoming a problem is at the heart of compositional methodology.

But what does Dewey mean by situation? As Brown notes, there is certainly scope for a range of interpretations (see also Savransky 2016) as is clear from this long extract from Dewey's *Logic: Theory of Inquiry*:

> I begin the discussion by introducing and explaining the denotative force of the word situation. Its import may perhaps be most readily indicated by means

of a preliminary negative statement. What is designated by the word "situation" is not a single object or event or set of objects and events. For we never experience nor form judgements about objects and events in isolation, but only in connection with a contextual whole. This latter is what is called a "situation." I have mentioned the extent in which modern philosophy had been concerned with the problem of existence as perceptually and conceptually determined. The confusions and fallacies that attend the discussion of this problem have a direct and close connection with the difference between an object and a situation. Psychology has paid much attention to the question of the process of perception, and has for its purpose described the perceived object in terms of the results of analysis of the process. I pass over the fact that, no matter how legitimate the virtual identification of process and product may be for the special purpose of psychological theory, the identification is thoroughly dubious as a generalized ground of philosophical discussion and theory. I do so in order to call attention to the fact that by the very nature of the case the psychological treatment takes a singular object or event for the subject-matter of its analysis. In actual experience, there is never any such isolated singular object or event; an object or event is always a special part, phase, or aspect, of an environing experienced world – a situation. The singular object stands out conspicuously because of its especially focal and crucial position at a given time in determination of some problem of use or enjoyment which the total complex environment presents. There is always a field in which observation of this or that object or event occurs. Observation of the latter is made for the sake of finding out what that field is with reference to some active adaptive response to be made in carrying forward a course of behavior. One has only to recur to animal perception, occurring by means of sense

organs, to note that isolation of what is perceived
from the course of life-behavior would be not only
futile, but obstructive, in many cases fatally so. (1991:
72–3)

So, for Dewey, the very distinction between object or
problem and situation is not to be assumed; instead
an object or problem is always part of a situation, a
background or surrounding. That situation is not a single
object or event; it is a contextual whole. This explication
helps, to some degree, but what might Dewey mean
by 'contextual whole': the immediate surroundings of a
phenomenon, or the whole world? The interpretation that
is of most relevance for a compositional methodology
is that proposed by Brown; that is, for the purposes of
inquiry, a situation can be taken to mean those aspects
of the surrounding or whole world that preserve the
'connection and continuity' present in the experienced
world while providing limiting conditions for generalization' (Dewey 1991: 7–8 in Brown 2012: 269).

What I take from this is that the establishment of
connection and continuity in the process of inquiry should
be the aim of compositional methodology, and the basis
for the making of claims of epistemological value. Or to
put this another way: a process of inquiry informed by
compositional methodology aims to transform an indeterminate situation into a determinate situation, preserving
connection and continuity while also operating limits
for generalization. In the terms introduced in the last
chapter, this involves acting on or operating limits, with-in
and out-with a problem, to enable generative circulation
across a problem space.

An original situation, Dewey argues, is 'open' in the
sense that its constituents do not 'hang together'; it has
a 'unique doubtfulness[1] which makes that situation to
be just and only the situation it is' (1938: 105). Such
ontological 'trouble' or perplexity is not a deficit for
Dewey but a provocation. To begin with, 'The way in

which a problem is conceived decides what specific suggestions are entertained and which are dismissed; what data are selected and which rejected; it is the criterion for relevancy and irrelevancy of hypotheses and conceptual structures' (1938: 110). Inquiry, then, proceeds in terms of relations of correspondence between the observation of facts and the suggested meanings or ideas that arise. One does not automatically precede the other; rather, they operate in conjunction with each other, their inter-relationship displaying a kind of syncopated rhythm as the path of inquiry emerges.

Ideas, Dewey says, are 'anticipated consequences (forecasts) of what will happen when certain operations are executed under and with respect to observed conditions' (1991: 109). Neither facts nor ideas are self-sufficient or complete in themselves:

> Facts are evidential and are tests of an idea in so far as they are capable of being organized with one another. The organization can be achieved only as they interact with one another. When the problematic situation is such as to require extensive inquiries to effect its resolution, a series of interactions intervenes. Some observed facts point to an idea that stands for a possible solution. This idea evokes more observations. Some of the newly observed facts link up with those previously observed and are such as to rule out other observed things with respect to their evidential function. The new order of facts suggests a modified idea (or hypothesis) which occasions new observations whose result again determines a new order of facts, and so on until the existing order is both unified and complete. In the course of this serial process, the ideas that represent possible solutions are tested or "proved." (1938: 117)

Inquiry thus involves developing the meaning of ideas in correspondence with observed facts: this is what is involved in the transformation of a situation into a problem in relations of connection and continuity. For Dewey, this distributed and dynamic process or path of inquiry should continue until a determinate situation, 'an objectively unified existential situation' (1938: 104) is reached.

Approach 2: Simon

Like Dewey, Herbert Simon is of the view that a problem is not given but must be created. In doing so, he introduces the concept of problem space:

> Every problem-solving effort must begin with creating a representation for the problem – a problem space in which the search for the solution can take place. (1996: 108)

He argues that, as a purposeful representation, a designed problem space is a methodological artifact that is always 'in imminent danger of dissolving and vanishing' (1996: 131). It is sustained, however, by the boundary or artificial sciences. This is the term he uses to describe the set of methodological practices by which design[2] can be refined to be beneficial to society. A key element of design for Simon is the partitioning of a complex problem into sub-problems through boundary-making. Through boundary-making, Simon says, problem-solving can often be accomplished through the use of relatively simple recursive operations such as those performed by bundles of algorithms. He uses the analogy of a pair of scissors to describe boundary-making or partitioning: he writes: 'Human rational behavior ... is shaped by a scissors whose blades are the structure of task environments and the computational capabilities of the actor' (1990: 7).

Simon's ideas lend themselves to be taken up in an instrumental – means–ends – fashion. His advocacy of the method of optimization, for example, is often interpreted as involving the recursive use of three classes of processes: search rules, stopping rules and decision rules, in relation to predetermined goals. However, while Simon's proposals were intended to have clear practical implications (like Dewey, Simon was concerned with the transformation of situations), he explicitly argues against the use of pre-determined goals in problem-solving. Indeed, not only does he stress the multiplicity and variety of satisfactory rather than optimum solutions (satisficing), he also emphasizes the contingency of the process of reaching a solution and describes negotiating the process of reaching a variety of solutions in terms of style.

> Variety, within the limits of satisfactory constraints, may be a desirable end in itself among other reasons because it permits us to attach value to the search as well as its outcome – to regard the design process as itself a valued activity for those who participate in it. (1996: 130)

He argues that problem-solving systems should not merely assemble solutions but must rather 'search for appropriate assemblies' (1996: 124).

Simon further argues for the importance of discovering new representations of problems, rather than merely deploying existing framings of a problem, even while acknowledging that the process of discovery is poorly understood. In describing this process, the terms 'situation' and 'relevance' (both of great importance to Dewey) creep in:

> Focus of attention is the key to success – focusing on the particular features of the situation that are relevant to the problem, then building a problem space containing these features but omitting the irrelevant ones. This single idea falls far short of a theory of representation change but takes a first step toward building such a theory. (1996: 109)

He argues that it is only the practice of search guided by 'the most general heuristics of 'interestingness' or novelty [that] is a fully realizable activity' (1996: 162), and says, 'A paradoxical, but perhaps realistic, view of design goals is that their function is to motivate activity which in turn will generate new goals' (1996: 162). Indeed, he proposes that 'One can envisage a future ... in which our main interest in both science and design will lie in what they teach us about the world and not in what they allow us to do to the world' (1996: 164). He provides here a way of thinking about how methodology might direct the continuity-in-transformation of problems to realize epistemological values.

The times of problem spaces

At a basic level, both Dewey and Simon say that a problem is not simply found but must be composed or represented,[3] and then represented again.[4] Both thus understand what I am calling the composition of a problem in terms of a process of re-presentation, understood as presenting – or perhaps better, situating – the problem again and again as part of a methodologically informed process. Dewey proffers the drawing of a line of inquiry as an overarching term, while Simon uses the term design. For both, the process of re-presentation is an active practice in which a problem is repeatedly composed or put together anew. For both, the composition of a problem across a problem space involves repetition of one kind or another and is thus a process in which temporality is of profound importance.

Indeed, both Dewey and Simon show that the methodological process I am calling composition always involves the operation of 'an alternation in time' (a term I adopt and adapt from the anthropologist Maurer, 2008; see Tooker 2014). Neither believes it sensible or appropriate to restrict the temporality of composing problems to a linear sequencing or staging of re-presentation.

Instead, both consider composition to involve engaging with the non-linear organization of uncertain or indeterminate temporal relations across a space. In other words, for neither Dewey nor Simon is the indeterminacy of the relation between a problem and its situation or environment to be eradicated by containing it in space or time; rather, it is the stimulus for the inventiveness of the process of inquiry or design. Both thus recognize the methodological potential of problem spaces. However, while Dewey and Simon share an emphasis on the importance of a non-linear temporality for the expression or realization of methodological potential they differ in their understanding of what is involved: for Dewey, indeterminacy is understood in terms of the existence of solutions as possibilities in the present, and for Simon it is to do with the inevitability of contingency in the composition of a problem; that is, contingency becomes a resource because problems can always be other than they are.

To start with Dewey: he argues that, in the pursuit of inquiry, a solution must be a mere possibility in the process of problematization, not 'an assured present existence' (1938: 118). This point is of central importance to him: it is what leads him to argue that a problem is never static or fixed, but emerges in constantly changing relations to a situation that is itself constantly changing. He asserts, 'To mention the temporal quality of inquiry is not simply to assert that inquiry takes time, but that the subject matter of inquiry goes through temporal modifications' (1991: 125). As Paul Rabinow puts it, for Dewey, 'Thinking was itself a temporal experience or, to be more precise, thinking was a temporal experiment':

> From the standpoint of temporal order, we find reflection, or thought, occupying an intermediate and reconstructive position. It comes between a temporally prior situation (an organized interaction of factors) of active and appreciative experience, wherein some of the factors have become discordant

and incompatible, and a later situation, which has been constituted out of the first situation by means of acting on the findings of reflective inquiry. The final solution thus has a richness of meaning, as well as a controlled character lacking in the original. (Dewey in Rabinow 2009: 16)

To find a way to acknowledge and incorporate modification, or modulation, in the process of inquiry Dewey identifies specific roles for facts and ideas as described above. To be able to exploit the transformative relation between ideas and facts, Dewey insists upon the importance of 'formulating [facts] in propositions: that is, by means of symbols'. This is important both because unless they are so represented they will 'relapse into the total qualitative situation' and because, if facts are not 'carried and treated by means of symbols', they lose their provisional character, and in losing this character they are categorically asserted and 'inquiry comes to an end'. In other words, symbolic logic – what might also be called conceptualization – plays a vital role in Dewey's formulation of the process of inquiry, since it is what enables the researcher to identify and exploit the temporalities of possibility in a given situation in practice:

> Experimental operations change existing conditions. Reasoning, as such, can provide means for effecting the change of conditions but by itself cannot effect it. Only execution of existential operations directed by an idea in which ratiocination terminates can bring about the re-ordering of environing conditions required to produce a settled and unified situation. (1938: 118)

Simon's concern with temporality is different to that of Dewey. What is fundamental to Simon's understanding and to his adoption of the term 'design' is the notion of artificiality. Phenomena are artificial for Simon if, 'they are as they are only because of a system's being molded, by goals or purposes, to the environment in which they live' (1996: xix). Simon continues: 'If natural phenomena have an air of 'necessity' about them in their subservience to natural law, artificial phenomena have an air of 'contingency' in their malleability by environment' (1996: xi). A variety of points might be made about this distinction between natural and artificial phenomena, one of the most important of which returns us to the criticism previously noted concerning the tendency towards instrumentalism in Simon's approach.[5] He himself notes a concern as to whether artificial phenomena could or should be the subject of science, given their goal-directed nature and the consequent difficulty of disentangling description from prescription, what is from what could or should be. However, he says that this is not the 'real difficulty': what concerns him instead is how empirical propositions can be made at all about systems that, given different circumstances, might be quite other than they are. In other words, it is not so much the moral or normative aspects of sciences of the artificial that preoccupy Simon, but the problem their contingency – the unavoidable possibility of their being otherwise – poses for reason.

In different ways then, temporality is fundamental to both Dewey and Simon's acknowledgement that a problem (space) can always be other than it is. And as is true for Dewey, symbolic logic is important for Simon in this respect. He too stresses that the emphasis on the symbolic is not to be understood as an exclusive emphasis on the virtual or ideal. Thus, he says that symbol systems need to be 'physical'; that is, they 'must have windows on the world and hands too'. The computer, for example:

> ... must have means for acquiring information from the external environment that can be encoded into internal symbols, as well as means for producing symbols that initiate action upon the environment.

Thus it must use symbols to designate objects and relations and actions in the world external to the system. (1996: 22)

In short, both Dewey and Simon signal the importance of the temporality of the composition of a problem space by emphasizing the dynamism of iterative relations between symbolic representation and action or methodologically informed intervention in the (material semiotic) composition of problem spaces. The importance of this concern for compositional methodology is taken up below in the discussion of the formal properties of circulation and in later chapters in a consideration of recursion.

However, while both writers emphasize the symbolic, they have very different understandings of its relevance, with Dewey emphasizing the metaphorical potential of symbols for theory and concept formation, and Simon focusing on symbolic logic, based on abstract formulas, which he seems to see as somehow transparent to thought in ways that bypass the ambiguities of (the metaphorical dimensions of) language. While neither is especially concerned with the variety of registers and modes of signification involved in the making of problem spaces, Chapter 2 will suggest transformations in the material semiotic modalities of epistemic infrastructures is one of the things that is changing the possibility of composing problem spaces.

Thinking context

A second important aspect of inquiry that both Dewey and Simon address is the role of cognition. In each case, the understanding of cognition put forward is not restricted to the thinking of an isolated human subject but is, rather, linked to the situated nature of a problem, or the (changing) relation of a (changing) problem to a (changing) context, system or environment.

Dewey argues that there is 'nothing intellectual or cognitive' in the existence of indeterminate situations: although they are the necessary condition of cognitive operations or inquiry 'in themselves they are precognitive'. Despite this statement (which might seem to presume that cognition is only to be found in the human subject), the issue of how the distinction between cognitive and pre-cognitive is related to indeterminate situations is a little more complicated in pragmatist philosophy than it may first appear. As Rabinow remarks:

> Neither the primary locus nor the yardstick of [the practice of inquiry] are to be found in the subject. Dewey makes this point through a striking, if ambiguous, formulation: "It is the needs of a situation which are determinative" (1916: 70). We can gloss his claim by saying that thinking is a temporally un-folding, situated practice, the function of which is to clarify and to realign a problematic situation. The site of the trouble and the resolution is the problematic situation. Intervention is judged successful when it yields a reconstructive change through meeting the needs of a situation. (Rabinow 2009: 16–17)

In this way of thinking, a context or environment is not necessarily without cognition itself: indeed, for some pragmatists, the activity of selection can be exercised by a context or environment. Charles Cooley, for example, proposes that in technological societies environments are increasingly organized by communication and information technologies, which extend the environment of a phenomenon across sites, conferring on environments a 'one-among-many' mode of existence. He notes that communications technology 'permits [the social actor] to form his own environment by retaining what suits him from a variety of material' (Cooley 1897; see Lury and Marres 2015). Indeed, he further says that the selection mechanisms that structure experience may be located beyond the individual and operate infrastructurally. On the one hand, 'the man of today [is] less dependent on the environments that happen to be nearest him'; on the other, 'a million environments solicit him' (Cooley 1897: 23): in short, mechanisms of selections are equally operative within the environment. For a compositional methodology, the organization of relations between a problem and environment in the composition of a problem is not understood as the choice of researchers alone, but may also be informed by the environment. Mechanisms of selection demarcate an environment of experience *and* a situation, an 'environmental occasion' as it were, both with-in and out-with which a problem may be variously re-presented or transformed.

Writing after the rise of the computer, it seems obvious to Simon that cognition is not merely a solely human means of problem-solving, but is also a possible characteristic of the non-human. The limits of what he calls bounded rationality are not understood in terms of human cognition alone, but are the properties of a problem in changing and two-way (but not necessarily symmetrical) relations in complex cognitive environments.[6] And such environments are not inert, or unchanging; indeed, they may be characterized by different kinds of distributed cognition.

For both Dewey and Simon, then, the relation of a problem to a context or environment not only changes in time but is cognitively distributed; for both, a notion of problematization that insists upon a stable, once-and-for-all distinction between a problem and a single environment is inadequate. This insight is acknowledged in Dewey's use of the concept 'pattern of inquiry', since patterning typically involves a parallax effect of figure-ground, allowing the two-way relation between figure and ground, an object (or problem) and its environment(s), to be surfaced as part of an inquiry. Relatedly, the emphasis on the iterative relation between representation and intervention that follows from Simon's use of the term of design leads him to emphasize the importance of the interactivity of interfaces to the artificial sciences. Indeed, for Simon, the interface is the primary epistemic tool of the artificial sciences:

> An artifact can be thought of as a meeting point – an "interface" in today's terms – between an "inner" environment, the substance and organization of the artifact itself, and an "outer" environment, the surroundings in which it operates. If the inner environment is appropriate to the outer environment, or vice versa, the artifact will serve its intended purpose. (1996: 6)

The value of the concept of interface for understanding the relation between science and society is the focus of discussion in Chapter 6.

Approach 3: Haraway

The third approach presented here is that of feminist writer Donna Haraway who offers a nuanced account of the concept of situatedness (1991). Contributing to and building on feminist debates on epistemology, Haraway argues for an understanding of objectivity – a value she wants to retain as an ideal – as constituted in situated knowledges.[7]

Responding to feminist debate, in which it is argued that knowledge always emerges from a standpoint, Haraway writes of the impossibility of innocent 'identity' politics and epistemologies. In place of emphasizing the identity of the researcher in her understanding of situated-ness she proposes that, 'Splitting, not being, is the privileged image for feminist epistemologies of scientific knowledge':

> 'Splitting' in this context should be about heterogeneous multiplicities that are simultaneously necessary and incapable of being squashed into isomorphic slots or cumulative lists. This geometry

pertains within and among subjects ... Here is the
promise of objectivity: a scientific knower seeks the
subject position not of identity, but of objectivity;
that is, partial connection. (1997: 193)

But Haraway's approach is also not to be confused with
'the death of the subject, that single ordering point of
will and consciousness', but rather is a process of 'generative doubt' that follows 'the opening of non-isomorphic
subjects, agents, and territories of stories unimaginable
from the vantage point of the cyclopean, self-satiated eye
of the master subject' (1991: 192).

Haraway's resistance to, or at least complication of,
standpoint is not a proposal for a view from nowhere or
'above'. The only way to find a larger vision, she says, 'is
to be somewhere in particular':

The science question in feminism is about objectivity as positioned rationality. Its images are not the
products of escape and transcendence of limits, i.e.
the view from above, but the joining of partial views
and halting voices into a collective subject position
that promises a vision of the means of ongoing finite
embodiment, of living within limits and contradictions, i.e. of views from somewhere. (1991: 196)

For Haraway, 'feminist embodiment resists fixation
and is insatiably curious about the webs of differential
positioning' (1991: 196). Significantly, she argues that it is
not only humans that know, and describes the importance
of acquiring 'the ability partially to translate knowledges
among very different, and power-differentiated communities' in an earth-wide network of connections that
includes the objects of knowledge as 'knowers' themselves.
Perhaps most well-known is her concern with knowing
with animals, most notably with companion species such
as dogs (Haraway 2003; see also Motamedi-Fraser 2019).
Haraway's knowledge is not only situated however: it

is also post-plural, a term also associated with another feminist writer, the anthropologist Marilyn Strathern (1991). Haraway cautions against the 'easy relativisms and holisms built out of summing and subsuming parts'. She refuses 'to resolve the ambiguities built into referring to science without differentiating its extraordinary range of contexts' (1991: 197) while Strathern says of her own practice:

> [The book] *Partial Connections* was an attempt to act out, or deliberately fabricate, a non-linear progression of argumentative points as the basis for description … Rather than inadvertent or unforeseen – and thus tragic or pitiable – partitionings that conjured loss of a whole, I wanted to experiment with the 'apportioning of size' in a deliberate manner. The strategy was to stop the flow of information or argument, and thus 'cut' it. (2004: xxix)

This is a rather different understanding of cutting or partitioning to that outlined by Simon above, in which cutting divides a problem into parts that can be solved independently and then put together again as a whole. For Strathern and Haraway, cutting is (perhaps counterintuitively) a way to acknowledge patterning as a way to make connection and continuity. What they add is the importance of recognizing that this continuity is only ever partial, and is emergent in the practice of situatedness (of splitting). In consequence, Haraway stresses the importance of seeking 'perspective from those points of view, which can never be known in advance, which promise something quite extraordinary; that is, knowledge potent for constructing worlds less organized by axes of domination' (1991: 192).[8]

In addition to splitting, Haraway introduces figuration as a method to do this, a practice to put alongside Rockburne's drawing that draws itself, Dewey's line of inquiry and Simon's notion of design. Describing herself as 'a person cursed and blessed with a sacramental consciousness and the indelible mark of having grown up Irish-Catholic in the United States', she puts forward an understanding of the figure as an image, a sign that is the thing in itself: in her work the figures of the cyborg, the OncoMouse, or the cat's cradle are a way of acknowledging an 'implosion of sign and substance, a literalness of metaphor, the materiality of trope, the tropic quality of materiality' (Haraway and Goodeve 2000).

For Haraway, 'Figurations are performative images that can be inhabited. Verbal or visual figurations can be condensed maps of contestable worlds' (1997: 17). The practice of figuration is to 'somehow collect up and give back the sense of the possibility of fulfillment, the possibility of damnation, or the possibility of a collective inclusion in figures larger than that to which they explicitly refer' (Haraway and Goodeve 2000). Methodologically speaking, figuring involves the activation of methodological potential in a process that is neither teleological nor mechanistic, both of which conceive as problemetization as going in one direction only, from givens to goals, but instead is a becoming-with.

In describing figuration in this way, Haraway might be seen to call up what Hayden White, in a commentary on the literary theory of Erich Auerbach, describes as figural causation, a concept that speaks to the potential of a figure for progressive fulfilment (Erfüllung), a kind of 'anomalous, nondetermining causal force or ateleological end' (White 1991: 88): 'the later figure fulfils the earlier by repeating the elements thereof, but with a difference' (White 1991: 91). However, in discussions of the practice of string figuring, Haraway seeks to distance herself from the Judeo-Christian temporalities of salvation or damnation. In contradistinction, she identifies three key features of string figuring or sf as methodological practice:

> First, promiscuously plucking out fibers in clotted and dense events and practices, I try to follow the

threads where they lead in order to track them and find their tangles and patterns crucial for staying with the trouble in real and particular places and times. In that sense, sf [string figuring] is a method of tracing, of following a thread in the dark, in a dangerous true tale of adventure, where who lives and who dies and how might become clearer for the cultivating of multispecies justice. Second, the string figure is not the tracking, but rather the actual thing, the pattern and assembly that solicits response, the thing that is not oneself but with which one must go on. Third, string figuring is passing on and receiving, making and unmaking, picking up threads and dropping them. sf is practice and process; it is becoming-with each other in surprising relays; it is a figure for ongoingness. (2016: 2)

In developing this understanding, she emphasizes that string figures 'are not everywhere the same game': as she says, 'Like all offspring of colonizing and imperial histories, I – we – have to relearn how to conjugate worlds with partial connections and not universals and particulars' (2016: 12).[9]

Approach 4: Jullien
The fourth approach introduced here is not that of the French author François Jullien himself but is, rather, his account of the Chinese concept of *shi*, sometimes translated as potential, a set-up, disposition, position or circumstance.

Jullien (2004) describes *shi* as 'a tendency that stems from a situation' and 'which, once set off, cannot be arrested'. (In my use of Whitehead's vocabulary, it is compulsive.) Jullien observes that the concept of *shi* initially emerged in the realm of Chinese military strategy and politics but evolved to have a much broader philosophical meaning. He explicitly contrasts it with the Western practice of fixing one's eyes on a model, a practice in which, he suggests, efficacy is conceived in terms of abstract, ideal forms, set up to be projected onto the world as a goal to be attained. In contradistinction, *shi* is associated with a concept of efficacy that 'teaches one to learn how to allow an effect to come about: not to aim for it (directly) but to implicate it (as a consequence), in other words, not to seek it, but simply to welcome it – to allow it to result' (2004: vii).

Jullien's focus on *shi* as propensity allows him to reconfigure traditional Western philosophical concerns: 'the fact is that, beneath the question of efficacy, another gradually surfaces: not the question of being and knowing, which is constantly raised by metaphysics, nor that of action, which is its ethical corollary, but the question of the conditions of effectiveness' (2004: viii). He continues:

> To move on from the question of efficacy, which still bears the imprint of voluntarism, to that of efficiency, which implies an underlying fund of immanence, we need to attempt a shift. A shift in two senses of the term: a shift away from our normal thinking habits, a move from one framework to another – from Europe to China and back again – which will undermine our representations and get our thoughts moving; and also a shift in the sense of shifting the impediment that is preventing us from perceiving what we have always blocked out of our thinking and, for that very reason, have been unable to think about. (2004: viii)

This is a point of difference with Dewey, whose ethics of thought is also concerned with efficacy. As Stengers summarizes, while for Dewey, the 'question of the truth ... is not situated in the true/false alternative, but poses the question of its efficacy', she also notes that this efficacy is understood in terms of 'its possible power of breaking through indifference and of engaging and obliging one to choose' (2009: 10). However, in acknowledging Dewey's use of the term 'choice' she distinguishes his understanding from that of rational choice and adds, 'It is no longer a worldly choice – what should one choose to be or do in this world? – but a choice for the world to which it is a matter of contributing. This choice doesn't only imply a world in the making; it affirms a world whose components are themselves indeterminate, whose 'perfectibility' depends on the jumper's trust that he may connect with 'other parts' that may become an ingredient in its fabric' (2009: 11).

In Jullien's understanding of Chinese thought, context or circumstances are no longer something unpredictable, to be controlled, eliminated or excluded in experimental conditions. Instead, because of their variability, circumstances can be turned to advantage by the propensity emanating from the situation. Jullien writes:

> Now circumstances are no longer conceived only (indeed, at all) as "that which surrounds" (*circumstare*), that is to say, as accessories or details (accompanying that which is essential in the situation or happening – in keeping with a metaphysics of essence). Instead, it is through those very circumstances that potential is released, the potential, precisely, of the situation. (2004: 22)

Within this antagonistic process there is constant interaction: '"the potential of the situation is whatever profits from that which is variable"' (Wang Xi, quoted in Jullien 2004: 22). Jullien concludes:

> The whole of Chinese thought about efficacy reverts to a single act: that of "returning" to the fundamental "basis," that is to say, the starting point of something that, as a condition, subsequently carried forward by the evolution of things, will gradually impose sway of its own accord. In such circumstances, an effect is not merely probable, as it is in a constructed relation of means to an end, but will unfailingly result, spontaneously. (2004: 45)

As he concludes, the 'way' (the *dao*), as conceived traditionally in China, 'is a far cry indeed from our Western
method (*methodos*, which is a "way" to be "pursued" that
leads "toward" something)' (2004: 33).

The methodological potential of the situation

These two approaches are as different to each other as
the first two, but they are paired here to indicate some
resources to further develop the understanding of problem
space as a space of methodological potential. As indicated
in the Introduction, conventional understandings of
problem space deploy a concept of space as a container
for a problem, setting limits that act to fix an inside and an
outside, what the right or wrong context or environment
for a problem might be, sometimes even implying that
context or situation can be rendered inconsequential
('context independence'). The two approaches described
here offer instead ways to think about the co-emergence
of a problem and a problem space in terms of a dynamic
practice of situating. Haraway describes situatedness of
knowledge not in terms of a fixed position or standpoint
but, rather, as position-ing in webs of connection created
in a process of splitting. In the practice of splitting, she
says, there is a possibility of novelty and continuity in
knowing. Figures are a symbolic condensation of that
potential. Jullien says that 'Potential is circumstantial'
(2004: 22) and suggests that, if we were to follow the way
of the *dao*, 'instead of setting up a goal for our actions, we
could allow ourselves to be carried along by the propensity
of things' (2004: 16). Both thus describe the situation
– situating or situatedness – as creating conditions for
something like methodological potential, although they
have different understandings of what that might mean.

The differences are of course revealing. Jullien uses

potential and propensity more-or-less interchangeably, although the two terms are typically distinguished (in diverse ways) in Western philosophy. This interchangeability is related, it seems, to the ways in which Chinese cosmology allows for structure and change, statics and dynamics to be thought at the same time. 'Translators', Jullien observes 'translate [shi] indifferently as "positions" or as "movements". It is, however, precisely both at the same time' (2004: 105). In calligraphy, he says, shi is the position of the brush, and the stroke, the movement of the brush. That much contemporary Western philosophy and social theory is concerned with the difficulties of how change and continuity may be thought at the same time – with relations between the possible and the real, the virtual and the actual, with whether, how and under what circumstances potential may be actualized, how potential is different from propensity and how both are to be distinguished from capacity – is, I suggest, a sign of both shared concerns in these approaches and continuing differences between Western and Chinese thought.[10]

Approach 5: Appadurai

The fifth approach introduced here is that of the anthropologist Arjun Appadurai, who, in an early influential approach to the globalization of knowledge, described the complex scaling dynamics of the disjunctures and differences of global flows, including flows of ideas, people, technology, media and money (Appadurai 1990). In a later work (2013), he provides a set of terms that allows for the exploration of the specificity of different kinds of flows:[11] this specificity arises, he says, from the inter-relationship of the circulation of forms with forms of circulation. The exemplars of forms he provides include novels and comics, but might also include problems, since they too are a 'family of phenomena, including styles, techniques and genres, which can be inhabited by 'specific voices, contents, messages and materials' (2013: 66). He says:

The flow of these forms has affected major world-historical processes such as nationalism. Today, however, the flow of forms also affects the very nature of knowledge, as whole disciplines, techniques and ways of thinking move and transform in the process. (2013: 64)

His term 'forms of circulation' refers to kinds of movement or mobility, and thus draws attention to the properties of specific kinds of circulation, including scale, speed, and reach, and the organization of disjunctures of difference or internal differentiation. The methodological value of Appadurai's focus on the inter-relationship of the circulation of forms and forms of circulation has been revealed in many studies of the social life or biography of things (for a discussion of this as a method see Kopytoff 1986; Lash and Lury 2007; Law, Ruppert and Savage 2011; Coleman 2019). Consider, for example, Susan Erikson's study of new forms of philanthropic venture capitalism in global health (2015). By following the money, she shows how, in the form of its circulation, philanthropic money reveals different registers of value in global health. She says:

Asking "Who knows what?" and "What benefits whom?" opens up all manner of difference and differential stakes in well-being – financial and corporeal – and provides analytical traction on both new systems of advantage and recent intensifications of old systemic global inequalities. (2015: S307)

For a compositional methodology, a concern with the inter-relationship of forms of circulation and the circulation of forms provides a way to think about the capacity of what emerges in the use of methods to change or transform the problem in a process of generative circulation or generalization. It also provides a way to think about alterations in the epistemic infrastructure. Appadurai himself suggests that the twenty-first century is witnessing new tensions between circulating cultural forms and the emergent, partially culturally formed circuits associated with 'the explosive growth in highly advanced tools for storing, sharing, and tracking information electronically both by the state and its opponents' (2013: 62). He says: 'This dual structure of global cultural forms also generates what we may call the 'bumps' or obstacles in regard to many cultural flows' (2013: 64). Some of these bumps and obstacles will be discussed in later chapters.

Across

This chapter has outlined five approaches to methodology, informing vastly different traditions of thought. Each provides an understanding of space that is not that of a fixed container; instead, each provides a way to think about how a problem is happening – is distributed – not in but across many places at a time and in many times at a place.[12] The approaches introduced here are thus all of value to the development of the concept of problem space because they provide vocabularies by which to understand the form of problems as emerging in relations of continuity and transformation across a problem space.

Along with their understanding of the importance of relations across rather than in time and space, what also unites these authors – and makes them useful for an understanding of problem spaces – is that they link their understanding of method (if Jullien would allow the term) to more-or-less explicit understandings of potential. And in doing so, their understandings contribute to an understanding of methodological potential as constituted in the operation of limits with-in and out-with problem spaces. The importance of the necessity of the preservation of continuity and connection in a situation becoming a problem while establishing limits for generalization for Dewey, Simon's insistence on the constitutive possibilities of contingency, the understanding of *shi* as potential

or propensity in a situation described by Jullien, the
non-isomorphic possibilities of splitting for the creation of
knowledge identified by Haraway, Appadurai's concern
with the inter-relationship of the circulation of forms with
forms of circulation all provide resources for a compositional methodology. However, while drawing on and
departing from all five approaches, I end this chapter by
emphasizing one aspect of Appadurai's approach.

In the introduction, it was proposed that problem
spaces should be seen in terms of the twisting of problems
into processes of problematization. More precisely, it
was suggested that the compulsion of composition could
be understood as the articulation of a double force: the
constitutive effects of methods and their capacity to
contribute to a problem's generative circulation. In the
chapters that follow, I develop this claim by drawing
on Appadurai's account of the importance of the inter-
relationship of the circulation of forms and forms of
circulation. This relationship, I propose, is a way to
understand the becoming topological of problem spaces
to afford methodological potential. The crucial point
that Appadurai's analysis adds to an understanding of
the methodological potential of a problem space is that
not only do different kinds of problems have different
capacities to make use of properties of circulation but also
that different forms of circulation have different capacities
to support the circulation of problems.

In the chapters that follow, recent changes in the epistemic
infrastructure are described, with special attention paid to
how such changes configure the compulsion of composition.
The argument to be developed is that the properties of
these new kinds of circulation are transforming topologies
of knowledge, providing new opportunities for methodological invention and these topologies are, in turn (in the
torque as it were) transforming forms of problem, shifting
relations between knowledge, ignorance and power.

— Part II —
The Epistemic Infrastructure

− 2 −

The Parasite and the Octopus

The parasite doesn't stop. It doesn't stop eating or drinking or yelling or burping or making thousands of noises or filling space with its swarming and din … it runs and grows. It invades and occupies.

Michel Serres (2007: 253)

We are an octopus. With one hand we grab research. With another hand we grab training. We want everything … We are searching for a new way to live.

Wang Jun in Winnie Won Yin Wong (2017: S110)

In this chapter, I describe some of the changes happening in the epistemic infrastructure today, outlining their significance for a methodology concerned with the composition of problem spaces. These changes are many and various; they operate at different scales, and have different histories, but also inter-relate in complex ways. They create a changed environment for a parasite, an octopus (as the examples above suggest), the survival of 'the creature's appetition for creation', as Whitehead put it in his description of the compulsion of composition.

As Edwards et al. (2013) say, there have been 'enormous transformations ... over the last twenty years in our systems for generating, sharing, and disputing human knowledge'. Edwards et al. focus on 'Changes associated with Internet technologies – such as social media, "big data," open-source software, ubiquitous computing, and Wikipedia'. Such technologies, they say:

> ... have altered the basic mechanics by which knowledge is produced and circulated. Remarkable new knowledge practices have emerged, captured under the language of crowdsourcing, cyberinfrastructure, personal informatics, citizen science, open access, MOOCs, and dozens of other terms that wouldn't have shown up in the Wikipedia pages of a decade ago; academic studies of some of these phenomena have become virtual scholarly fields unto themselves. Knowledge institutions like universities, libraries, and government agencies (and increasingly private entities like Facebook, Google, and Twitter) have begun to adjust, opening up vast stores of anonymized data to analysis and exploitation, engaging users and publics in new ways, and in some cases rethinking logics and practices that have been decades if not centuries in the making. (2013: 1)

While such changes are undoubtedly important and are addressed below, this chapter describes other transformations in the epistemic infrastructure.

The first set of changes identified are processes of explicitation and literalization while the second set are associated transformations in the semiotics of problem spaces and cognition. A third set of changes are those to do with alterations in the role of the observer, including a variety of ways in which the constitutive role of the observer is acknowledged. The fourth set are challenges to the Western-centric terms and character of many methodological debates, and includes both critiques of epistemic privilege and proposals for more inclusive ways of knowing. The final set of changes are those associated with a shift from an epistemic culture of representation and representativeness to one of performance and participation. These changes interact with each other in different ways in different situations as the next chapter illustrates. The aim in introducing them here – in what is an incomplete list – is to show how the possibility of composing the complex and changing relations between the givens, goals and operators of problem spaces are becoming more various than in the past, introducing new methodological opportunities at the same time as producing new dilemmas.

1. Explicitation and literalization

A variety of writers from different disciplines have pointed to what they consider to be some of the general principles of the 'Western' or 'modern' quest for knowledge. The philosopher Peter Sloterdijk draws attention to an imperative of *explicitation*; that is, a 'rephenomenalization of the aphenomenal that answers the modern need to perceive the imperceptible' (2009: 32). His discussion of this term reveals the fundamental issues he believes are at stake:

> If one wanted to say ... what the 20th century ... contributed ... to the history of civilization, answering with three criteria could suffice ...: the praxis of *terrorism*, the conception of *product design*, and concepts of *the environment*. Through the first, interactions between enemies were established on postmilitary foundations; through the second, functionalism was able to reintegrate itself in the world of perception; through the third, the phenomena of life and knowledge were entwined to depths hitherto unknown. Taken together, these three criteria indicate the acceleration of explication of the revealing inclusion of latencies and background data in manifest operations. (2009: 41)

Bruno Latour expands on Sloterdijk's notion of explicitation, emphasizing the importance of relations of
knowledge of and with the environment:

> [H]istory was never about "modernization" or
> about "revolution," but was rather about another
> phenomenon ... "explicitation." As we [sic] moved
> on, through our technologies, through our scientific
> inquiries, through the extension of our global empires,
> we rendered more and more explicit the fragility of
> the life support systems that make our "spheres of
> existence" possible. Everything that earlier was merely
> "given" becomes "explicit." Air, water, land, all of
> those were present before in the background: now they
> are explicitated because we slowly come to realize that
> they might disappear – and we with them. (2007: 2–3)

The anthropologist Marilyn Strathern invokes the term
literalization to describe contemporary Euro-American
ways of knowing, by which she means 'a mode of laying
out the coordinates or conventional points of reference of
what is otherwise taken for granted' (1992: 5), while Rey
Chow follows Foucault in suggesting that:

> ... it has become increasingly inadequate merely
> to 'know' something in its empirical form or even
> through the artificial signs that 'order' them. More
> and more pressing is the need to explore the condi-
> tions of possibility, the terms on which knowledge
> itself is produced. As claims to boundary-free
> knowing become untenable, modern knowledge in
> turn becomes self-reflexive; cut off from its previous
> kinship to the world, knowing is, ever more so, an
> attempt to know how knowledge itself comes into
> being. (2006: 3)

Sloterdijk argues that the process of explicitation is accelerating, but in his discussion of the parasite the philosopher

Michel Serres (2007) suggests that the process is not new and has never been easy to contain.

Perhaps the most obvious contemporary instance of 'becoming explicit' or 'becoming literal' is datafication, a process that is often discussed in purely technical terms but sometimes intersects with proposals for the necessity of post-phenomenological approaches in complex and interesting ways. Datafication is commonly linked, for example, to what has been called a data revolution (Kitchin 2014); that is, the proliferation of techniques for the collection, storage, correlation and analysis of material signs or traces as data, including the mining of social media, the use of tracking devices, and biometric and environmental sensors and the development of data science, data journalism, data brokerage, data analytics and data informatics, not only inside but also outside the academy (Helmond 2015; Ruppert, Isin and Bigo 2017; Borgman 2019). While Sabina Leonelli (2015) describes data as material artifacts which are mobilized in relation to specific contexts of knowledge production, datafication is a process in which more and more phenomena come to be expressed in a format that can be analysed and processed by computers. As such, it includes the expansion of data to include words, sounds and images as well as numbers, and mechanisms by which data analytic processes are integrated, incorporated and assimilated into knowledge production, decision-making, organizational processes, algorithmic governance and individual practice (Beer 2018). Focusing on the role of algorithms in this process, Elena Esposito (2017) emphasizes that computers are no longer isolated but interconnected, and that this connection occurs by means of the web, which not only includes 'previously unthinkable data sources', but is also 'participatory'. She says:

> The participatory web invites users to generate their own video, audio, and textual contents, which they share with other users in blogs, social media, wikis,

and on countless media sites. This multiplicity of spontaneous and uncontrolled contents, with their metadata, adds to institutional content and to the data provided by pervasive sensors (the Internet of Things) to generate the increasing mass (or cloud) of data available in digital format. (2017: 251)

Rob Kitchin notes that big data is often described as being '*exhaustive* in scope', 'fine-grained in *resolution*', 'uniquely *indexical* in identification', '*relational* in nature', '*flexible*' and '*scaleable*' (2014: 68), but these methodological characteristics of 'data expansion' (that is, the expansion of the kinds of things that can be used as data and the possibility of linking diverse data sets) and 'analysability' (the use of more and different types of analysis) only emerge in the operation of 'little analytics' (Amoore and Piotukh 2015). As Amoore and Piotukh say: 'if the metaphor of big data is to continue to dominate the governing of digital life, then it cannot be understood without the little analytics that make data perceptible' (2015: 344). Following Henri Bergson, they understand little analytics as 'instruments of perception': while the vastness of big data makes it virtually impossible for human reasoning to determine what is of relevance, little analytics 'carve out images; reduce heterogeneous objects to a homogeneous space; and stitch together qualitatively different things such that attributes can be rendered quantifiable' (2015: 344).

Clough et al. (2018) use the alternative term datalogical to describe the coupling of large-scale data-bases with adaptive algorithms, and argue that it contributes to the emergence of a new onto-logic of sociality. This is a move from representation to nonrepresentation: 'the present absence in representation is displaced ... non-representation points to the real presence of incomputable data operative in algorithmic architectures parsing big data' (2018: 95). Exploring the implications of the datalogical turn for the discipline of sociology, they say:

... a post-cybernetic logic of computation ... de-systematizes the methods of collating and analyzing statistical and demographic data while decentering the human subject; the observing/self-observing human subject collapses as the basis for a data-driven project of understanding sociality. (2018: 112)

As Mark Hansen (2015) sees it, the datafication of twenty-first-century media means that media no longer store human experience as such; rather, they store the bits of data that 'register molecular increments of behavior that are never an expression of lived human experience' (2015: 40). As such, twenty-first-century media have shifted from 'addressing humans first and foremost' to registering 'the environmentality of the world itself', providing a 'worldly sensibility' prior to human consciousness and bodily based perception and – so Hansen believes – re-embedding 'consciousness in a far richer context of the causally efficacious lineages that have produced it' (2015: 8–9). For Hansen, datafication offers humanity the opportunity to make available to consciousness, 'aspects of its own causal background that it literally has no capacity to grasp directly' (2015: 52). These are the hitherto unknown depths of the entwining of knowledge and life described by Sloterdijk.

2. Representation, semiotics and cognition

The contemporary concern with literalization and explicitation described above has contributed to interest in the methodological implications of the material semiotics of representation and the advocacy of the non-representational in association with a radical empiricism (Thrift 2007). Radical empiricism is a move beyond sense- or observation-based empiricism, employing instead a focus on the processes and practices by which events or occasions come into being. Methods are said to be performative, to be understood in terms of play and experimentation. In place of (symbolic) representation as the primary epistemological vehicle, non-representational theory is concerned with presentations, practices, showings, tellings, happenings and manifestations of everyday life.[1] Rather than aiming to develop explanations that claim to go behind or beyond the phenomena described, the aim is to present descriptions that are infused with fidelity to what they describe. Dewsbury calls this stance a kind of 'witnessing', a stance that is orientated towards being 'in tune to the vitality of the world as it unfolds' (2003: 1923; see also Nash 2000). In this regard, non-representational theory speaks to and draws on a long tradition of feminist, post-colonial and anthropological studies – as well as more recent developments in animal studies – in which the body is not simply an appendage of the mind, and participation (or mimesis) is a fundamental constitutive dimension of experience (Pina-Cabral 2018).

As outlined in Chapter 1, both Dewey and Simon employ an understanding of inquiry that privileges the symbolic: Dewey argues for the importance of symbolic logic, while Simon argues for the importance of 'symbol systems', examples of which include the computer and the human mind. Both writers emphasize that signs are not abstract, self-standing entities, isolated from existential and material situations. Both understand signs as part of ongoing sign-processes, and as fluid and transactional. Dewey identifies the importance of existential operations to the pattern of inquiry, while Simon says that symbol systems need to be physical; that is, they 'must have windows on the world and hands too'. The computer, 'must have means for acquiring information from the external environment that can be encoded into internal symbols, as well as means for producing symbols that initiate action upon the environment. Thus, it must use symbols to designate objects and relations and actions in the world external to the system' (1996: 22). But neither Dewey nor Simon pays much attention to the multiple semiotic registers involved in composing problem spaces.

Dewey says that 'signs are always interpreted in actual

ongoing contexts and in terms of their functions and operations they perform', but does not develop this analysis
other than to distinguish between natural and artificial
signs, the latter being what he terms 'symbols'. Simon is
also very little concerned with semiotics: he makes only
general claims such as, 'both the computer and the human
brain are artifacts that belong to the category of physical
symbol systems' (1996: 21). Perhaps as a result he privileges a specialized kind of symbolic logic as the best way
to describe and explain the behavior of complex adaptive
systems. As part of this understanding, data are stripped
of any representational capacity other than a controlled
correspondence with what they represent. He argues that
intelligence emerges in a coupling with an environment,
leading him to focus his search on 'the production of
situations and patterns for actions' (Halpern 2015: 176),
but he does so without making use of the conceptual and
methodological resources of semiotics to understand the
relation between cognition and situation or environment.

Dewey and Simon are not alone in their emphasis on the
symbolic, or the assumption that the symbolic is the only
significant register of the semiotic for cognition. Haraway
provides an alternative and powerful explication of the
symbolic in the concept of string figuring, but despite
some of the most influential recent studies in the study
of science and technology using a variety of traditions
in semiotics to analyse scientific and other practices (for
example, Rheinberger, 1997, 2010; Latour, http://www.
bruno-latour.fr/node/562.html and Verran 2001, 2005), a
concern with semiotics is surprisingly missing from much
methodological discussion.

In my own work (Lury 2012), I draw on the semiotics
of Charles Sanders Peirce (1931–5) to argue that contemporary practices of datafication are associated with
transformations in the material-semiotic practices of
knowledge-making that can be described as 'bringing
the world into the world' (the title of an artwork by
the Italian conceptual artist Alighieri e Boetti). What is

helpful about Peircian semiotics, I argue, is the insistence that semiotics is a material process in which signification typically involves *three* kinds of sign – icons, indices and symbols – in various combinations.

More specifically I argue that the methodological uses of indexicality have historically been supported by complex sets of social relations and technologies, enabling the ground in relation to which entities are known to be stabilized and the knowledge they afford to be generalized, transmitted or circulated in specific ways, as captured by Latour in his notion of immutable mobiles (1987). Speaking in very general terms, I propose that historically such movement required the use of indices, including data and measurements of various kinds, in ways that enabled them to refer to objects as if the indices were indifferent to the objects that they indicated. Such indifferent indices enabled the fixing of co-ordinates – the ground – in relation to which problem spaces could be composed. In contrast, the deliberately designed instability and reactivity of many contemporary indexical practices, including, for example, the derivatives of the financial market, the indicators, measures and categories of behaviour and conduct employed in the joined-up databases of government, industry and business, and the search, 'like', and status updates that help comprise Facebook and Google, are not the outcome of the indifference of the indices by which they are represented. Rather, an a-live indexical relation to a dynamic (radicalizing) environment is increasingly being operationalized such that what is referred to is not kept separate from or external by the index, but is continually implicated. This process is sometimes described as ground-truth-ing, but it can also be described as a process in which deixis is expanded to function as 'about-ness' (Gross 2015).

In this process of activation, the methodological potential of indexical signs to contribute to the composition of a problem space is expanded by the introduction of dynamic feedback loops in diverse, iterative and automatic information processing systems (such as Amoore and Piotuckh's little analytics), supported by multiple material, sensory memory systems. In these ways, the indexical capacities of, for example, the data of datafication are constituted as a force that can be realized 'in myriad ways through its uptake and deployments' (Ruppert, Isin and Bigo 2017). In consequence of this expanded capacity, the potential of problem spaces comes to be recognized in terms of specific kinds of instability, indeterminacy or contingency that are not erased or minimized, but, rather, are made available to be exploited across a problem space.

Let me expand on this a little more. For Peirce, the action of indices comprises the two components that are necessarily part of any act of signifying: the sign–object relation and the sign–interpretant relation. The indexical act of signifying, he says, consists of a sign that signifies its object by using some physical or existential continuity (this is the sign–object relation), and generates a further sign to signify that object (the sign–interpretant relation). My argument, put simply, is that it is in the relay of such relations of referral backwards and forwards that data acquires indexicality (see also Pape 2008). The expanded capacity for data to do so is captured in discussions of various kinds of looping as by Hansen in his discussion of the significance of 'feed-forward' and by Fuller and Mazurov (2019) when they describe data as spoor, that is, as both trace and track, and the description by Nafus (2014) of the situations in which data is 'stopped' or 'stuck' as well as ways it can be 'unstopped'. That what Peirce calls the interpretant (the understanding, development or translation) of an index need not be a person but may be a machine or some other inanimate thing is significant in this regard, enhancing the methodological potential that the myriad ordering of inter-linked sequences of referral backwards and forwards affords for the composition of problem spaces.

In addition, by putting the two-faced index into sequences in different forms of circulation, the signifying capacity of an index can be mobilized by some little analytics not simply as the outcome of distribut*ed* cognition but as distribut*ive* cognition; that is, as cognition that has the capacity to distribute agency (Gell 1998). But what do I mean by this? In many disciplines, it has long been accepted that human actors are not always rational: that human decision-making may be irrational or non-rational, and is context dependent. It has also long been accepted that cognition is distributed. In cognitive science, for example, the model of an extended mind is deployed, in which the unit of analysis is a collection of individuals and artifacts and their relations to each other in practice. Indeed, since humans are always integrated into their environments and have co-evolved with them, it is argued that attention should always be paid to the ways in which feedback loops and associated forms of amplification between human (and animal) evolution, technical developments and social and natural environments take place. However, N. Katherine Hayles and others suggest that recent technological developments have contributed to fundamental changes in the characteristics of cognition. She says:

> Humans are equipped with two mechanisms of attention: deep and hyper attention. Deep attention has a high threshold for boredom and enables one to engage in a specific task or problem over an extended period time to develop expert knowledge; hyper attention requires constant gratification yet enables one quickly to scan significant amounts of data to gain an overview or identify certain patterns. Both forms of attention have been with us since the beginning of humankind, and both have specific advantages. Now, with the development of ubiquitously networked digital devices, however, we have created a socio-technical environment that systemically privileges hyper attention. (Pötzsch and Hayles 2014: 98)

In other work, Hayles argues for the importance of recognizing that while all thought is cognition, not all cognition is thought. Cognition, she suggests, may operate wholly independently from consciousness, as in the cases of bees and termites, or it may be part of a larger system such as a human where it mediates between material processes and the emergence of consciousness/unconsciousness. Alternatively, or additionally, it may be present in a socio-technological device such as a computer, or an inter-connected system of humans and computers.

For these reasons, Hayles argues that we need to acknowledge a range of different kinds of cognition and says, 'this framework, positing a tripartite structure of conscious thinking, nonconscious cognition, and material processes, catalyzes boundary questions about the delineations between categories as active sites for interpretation and debate' (2014: 5). For Hayles, the notion of nonconscious cognition challenges us to extend the concept of cognition beyond its traditional identification with thought, and identify its operation 'across and within the full spectrum of cognitive agents: humans, animals, and technical devices'. As she says:

> For the cognitive nonconscious … meaning has no meaning. As the cognitive nonconscious reaches unprecedented importance in communication technologies, ambient systems, embedded devices, and other technological affordances, interpretation has become deeply entwined with the cognitive nonconscious, opening new avenues for exploring, assessing, debating and resisting possible configurations between interpretive strategies and the cognitive nonconscious. (Hayles 2014: 199)

In introducing a tripartite structure, Hayles is not simply saying that cognition may be found in a computational environment as well as a human brain: she is highlighting that this environment is being newly equipped for knowledge production in specific ways.

Hayles puts forward the term 'cognitive assemblage' to capture these new complex human and non-human distributions of cognition and asks us to consider the role of sensors, not merely in collecting data but also in interacting with their environments and performing actions in the world. Once equipped in this way, she suggests, sensors should be described as 'actuators'; similarly, Laura Kurgan (2013) claims – in an analysis discussed in more detail below – that data is an informant or emissary. Building on such insights, Pelle Snickars (2017) describes a project to interrogate the recommendations provided by Spotify by using bot listeners; that is bots that are equipped to act as informants in the research. He draws on Kitchin (2014) who argues that, by posing as users, bots can more systematically engage with a system, running dummy data and interactions. Snickars says this methodology has a wide potential to perform 'humanist inquiry on big data and black-boxed media services that increasingly provide key delivery mechanisms for cultural materials':

> Using bots as research informants can be deployed within a range of different digital scholarship, so this article appeals not only to media or software studies scholars, but also to digitally inclined cultural studies such as the digital humanities. (2017: 184)

Relatedly, Mackenzie (2017) uses the term 'machine learners' to describe the agents of machine learning, without specifying whether the learners are human or non-human, or in what combination, while the figure of the 'lurker' is identified by Goriunova (2017) as a kind of conceptual persona, 'a sage of the digital era, constructing a form of "private" knowledge"'. Goriunova proposes that while lurkers may be humans, the persona of the lurker is increasingly 'fulfilled by algorithms, and its mode of knowing [not involved but performative, constative but only in a manner of probability] becomes a new mode of governance' (2017: 3917).

Perhaps what is most significant about Hayles' argument for compositional methodology, however, is that while non-conscious (computational) cognition may operate independently from consciousness, it nonetheless involves an 'intention toward', defined by its adaptive behavior and emergent capacities to process an environment that is itself in flux. Goriunova proposes that the lurker provides 'frameworks for private truth production through continuous adjustment' (2017: 3917), while Luciana Parisi says, 'Machine learning … is used in situations where rules cannot be pre-designed, but are, as it were, achieved by the computational behavior of data' (2019: 92). The implications of the possibility she describes as realized in machine learning – of elaborating a rule from data retrieval, rather than applying a given rule to outcomes – is a paradigmatic example of the significance of changes to the epistemic infrastructure for the composition of problem spaces: it 'points to a form of cognition that cannot be defined in terms of problem-solving, but will be understood as a general method of experimenting with problems' (2019: 93).

3. Observing the observed
One of the most significant transformations in the last hundred years in Western epistemologies has been the general abandonment of the idea of an external observer observing the world without being involved in its processes. This has contributed to a profound rethinking of the categories and methods of research. However, while there has been a proliferation of techniques of observation and a multiplication of indicators and measures to record such observations (Adkins and Lury 2011; https://limn.it/issues/sentinel-devices/; Dalsgaard 2016), the ways in which the recognition of the constitutive role of the observer – or observation – has been put to work in and across disciplines is very various, with cross-cutting debates emerging

on, for example, first- and second-order observation, reflexivity, situated knowledge and recursion.

Elena Esposito, for example, proposes that we now live in a second-order society: 'modern society has moved – in every field – from first-order observation to second-order observation' (Esposito 2013: 4), by which she means that (human and non-human) observation is now increasingly equipped to be the observation of the context of observation. In contrast, Clough et al. (2018) argue that, in some disciplines, the abandonment of the distinction between observer and observed has not been complete, and that many disciplinary practices are caught between first and second order modes of observation. The authors suggest that insofar as a discipline adopts an epistemological stance similar to that of first order cybernetics it accepts a homeostatic, equilibrium-seeking model that presumes a certain durability of reactions to observed stimuli, allowing for a probabilistic prediction of future patterns independent of the context of observation:

> In first order cybernetics, the researcher stands to some degree *outside* of the system that is being observed and applies technical apparatuses to convert incoming data from shifts in a stabilized system into repeatable and decipherable patterns. First order cybernetics maintains a duality between the systems to be observed and the apparatuses of observation (in the case of sociology, the apparatuses are the method of the research project). The apparatuses extend through, but are not of the systems that produce an implied dis-identification of researcher and researched … Ontologically there remains a separation between a stable researcher on the one hand and a systematized research environment of human behavior on the other.
>
> … in second order cybernetics and the critical social theories and methodologies that would arise in the 1970s and 1980s, reflexive interventions would be imagined that were meant to "correct" the

dis-identification of the observer with data resulting in the human subject being figured not only as observing but as self-observing. (2018: 99–100)

Clough et al. recognize that second-order cybernetic thinking was comprehensively translated into sociology in Nikolas Luhmann's systems theory (and more recently by Esposito as above), and some critical methodologies of a variety of kinds. However, they argue that the recognition of the role of the observer was less systematically followed through in other approaches – less systematically, both in the sense of comprehensively and rigorously, and in the sense of not assuming a system. On the one hand, there have been approaches that sought to engage in a kind of purification of (a disembodied) observation, including practices such as highly formal experimental set-ups and data 'cleansing' (see Uprichard 2011 for a critique). On the other hand, they say, in some other – more phenomenologically inspired – approaches such as auto-ethnography, the observer him or herself is taken to be a kind of double for the boundary: '[t]hat is to say, the boundary between system and environment is taken as an effect of the observer observing, including observing him- or herself observing' (2018: 101).

Clough et al. summarize:

A common discourse in debates over theory and methodology in the social sciences comes down to a conflict between those who would argue for a more positivist empiricist and scientistic social science and those who argue for a more reflexive one that includes taking account of the observer or insisting on his or her embodied self-consciousness being made visible. (2018: 101)

Their analysis suggests, however, that these positions – which are often opposed – have more in common than might initially appear:

They both rely on the figure of the human subject, and the insular, thermodynamic system. In both cases, the role of the observer is one of calculated disturbance and translation. In sociology, the lessons of the second order have been taken up primarily as a simultaneous acknowledgement of one's presence in the field of observation via "reflexivity" and then the dismissal of this presence's importance to the overall project of drawing and articulating human relations. In the wake of critique, the championing of reflexivity often has taken the form of a defensive insistence on the capacity and obligation of the researcher to "speak for" the researched. (2018: 101)

They further suggest that the 'constant resuscitation of the false dichotomy of observed and observing, along with that between quantitative and qualitative, micro and macro levels has hamstrung much of sociology' (2018: 102). This is a powerful analysis, but it downplays the ways in which the recognition that observation cannot be securely located outside or beyond what is observed has also led to considerable innovation, both in sociology and other disciplines, perhaps most significantly in interdisciplinary research, including feminist, black, indigenous, post-humanist and post-colonial arguments for situated knowledge.[2]

Indeed, the recognition of the constitutive effects of observation has contributed to a concern with the performative effects of methods. So, for example, John Law and John Urry (2003) describe the enactment of social worlds by methods, Nigel Thrift (2005) argues that methods co-produce the social world, while John Law, Evelyn Ruppert and Mike Savage (2011) describe what they call the double social life of methods. By this phrase they mean, first, that methods are social because they are constituted by the social world of which they are a part, and, second, they are social because they play a part in constituting that social world. Methods are of and in the world; they are ways in which a situation becoming a problem recursively refers to a description of itself.

Of course, the recognition of the constitutive or performative effects of methods of observation has not only been taken up by individual academic researchers but also by public and private organizations, including universities, with the result that the observation of observation has come to be linked to new modes of academic and other governance, especially in the public sector, where it is sometimes described as transparency but is often experienced as surveillance. For example, Nowotny et al. note 'an important shift in the regime of control ... [whereby] control is now exercised indirectly and from the 'inside' ... [through] ever more elaborate systems of peer review, more formal quality control systems, and other forms of audit, assessment and evaluation' (2001: 115; see also Power 1999).

Relatedly, Marilyn Strathern notes that the proliferation of forms of audit is designed to shape the ways in which the observer is included in the world he or she observes. She writes:

> New practices of audit demand that organizations know how to describe – more than that, to do social analyses of – themselves. Reflexivity and self-referentiality have become bywords of organizational cultures and research cultures alike. ... [As] organizations are evaluated as systems which embody standards and the standards of performance themselves are shaped by the need to be auditable ... [and] audit becomes a formal 'loop' by which the system observes itself. (2003: 3, 10)

As Annelise Riles points out, this means that many organizations not only observe themselves, but also become users of observations of themselves (in part through the indication of newly equipped indices as described above): they become literally 'self-referential' (2000: 12). Perhaps most visibly, this reflexivity has contributed to the rise of rankings (Espeland and Sauder 2007, 2016), which currently operate a curiously seductive mode of organizing very many social and economic domains.

For Laura Kurgan however, acknowledging and working with changes in the distribution of the capacity to observe is not only a reconfiguration of authority and expertise, but also allows for new kinds of inquiry. While she is by no means oblivious to the ways in which Google, Apple and Facebook exploit the critical role that their services have come to play in many people's everyday lives, she argues that changes in the distribution of the capacity to observe amount to more than the removal of expertise from academics or state-enabled researchers and the intensification of forms of audit and surveillance. In the book *Close Up at a Distance*, she explores the implications of the fact that satellite imagery – once exclusively the domain of military and government intelligence organizations – is now made available and deployed by many people in everyday activities:

> For many of us, maps now are as omnipresent as the more obvious utilities (such as electricity, water, gas, telephone, television, the Internet), functioning somehow like 'extensions' of ourselves, to co-opt Marshall McLuhan's famous definition of media. (2013: 14)

These 'extensions' have capacities that can be used in a variety of ways: 'Identify an area', Kurgan directs the reader, 'zoom in and examine the specific conditions. Zoom out and then consider both scales at the same time. The resulting image is no longer hard data. It is a soft map that is infinitely scalable, absolutely contingent, open to vision and hence revision' (2013: 204).

In this and other approaches (Day and Lury 2017), the multiplication of contexts, kinds and subjects of observation is understood in ways that do not imply an ordering in terms of hierarchy of observation, but observation as alongside, in parallel or 'with' the observed. Kurgan, to continue with this example, seeks to exploit the 'secondary' capacities of data as part of what she calls the para-empirical. She says, 'All data ... are not empirical, not irreducible facts about the world, but exist as not quite or almost, alongside the world; they are para-empirical' (2013: 35). In other words, like 'paramilitary' or 'paramedic', the para-empirical acknowledges that data are not simply the outcome of observation – as a representation, for example – but rather operate *'alongside the world'* (my emphasis).

> My claim is not that this plunges us into some abyss of uncertainty, though, or makes it impossible to function in the real world. On the contrary, it is only the condition of accepting this condition of data, in para-empirical condition, that we have any chance of operating responsibly in or on the world. (Kurgan 2013: 35)

In consequence of this understanding, she proposes a practice of engagement, of intervention, alongside, or in parallel with, data that is understood to be an 'informant', an emissary of reality. In this practice, 'an image (and/or the associated data used to construct or contextualize it) is not left to "speak for itself" but is rather used to "offer a reflection on what can be done with it"' (2013: 34).

In related reflections on the contemporary data environment, Mark Hansen suggests that we should not see such developments as simply extending human capacities of observation – or sensing as he prefers to say. Drawing on analyses of earlier technologies, including the development of chronophotography by Etienne-Jules Marey, he points to the importance of the autonomy attached to the machinic element by Marey in his inquiries into movement. He writes: 'Marey's aim is not to develop technical prostheses that extend the range or efficacy of human perception and experience; his aim, rather, is to develop machinic sensors *that possess sensory domains of their own*' (2015: 54). His proposal is that Marey's graphic and chronophotographic technologies open new dimensions of experience 'that operate *alongside* perceptual consciousness in the form of external or environmental data about its own past behaviour' (2015: 55). Relatedly, Mackenzie and Munster (2019) describe the emergence of what they call 'platform seeing'; they say, 'Seeing – as a position from a singular mode of observation – has become problematic since many visual elements, techniques, and forms of observing are highly distributed through data practices of collection, analysis and prediction.' They suggest that the visual as a paradigm for how to see and observe is being evacuated, and that space is now occupied by a different kind of perception: 'This is not simply "machine vision"', they say, 'but a making operative of the visual by platforms themselves' (2019: 6).

In other critical practices, the inside and outside of observation, the position of observed and observer, become entangled – sometimes deliberately, sometimes by accident, contributing to the emergence of a whole variety of 'inconsistent' entities created by the asymmetrical mutual observation of observers. In a discussion of metadata, for example, Tom Boellstorff (2015) shows how search terms, which he considers to be a prototypical example of 'metadata', can become 'data' in some social practices. One example he provides is the analysis of searches (as in GoogleFlu) to track possible influenza outbreaks. Another example occurred when LGBT activists responded to the heterosexist stance of former Pennsylvanian congressman Rick Santorum by consistently using his name as part of a search string for sexual fluids, temporarily pushing a 'spreadingsantorum.com' website to first place in Google's results for the term 'santorum'. In instances like these, Boellstorff argues, phenomena typically classed as meta-communication act as forms of communication.

In his discussion, Boellstorff draws attention to the

history of the term 'meta', noting that the prefix 'contains an unacknowledged tension between laterality and hierarchy'. He says:

> Throughout the twentieth century use of the *meta-* prefix expanded, including metaknowledge, metaindexicality, even metaculture. Yet the prefix has retained a fundamental instability. On the one hand it is used hierarchically: this is the framework of a zero-degree referent (e.g. language, knowledge, or data), and then 'meta' phenomena that lie above or below. On the other hand (sometimes by the same author) the *meta-* prefix is used laterally – so that, for instance, metalanguage is language *about* itself. (2015: 96; my emphasis)

As examples discussed in later chapters will show, it is this tension between the lateral and the hierarchical, the accomplishment of an about-, around-or across-ness, and the operation of limits that are with-in and out-with, that characterizes the situation – or situatedness – of observation in today's problem spaces and contribute to the composition of their methodological potential.

4. The geo-politics of methodology

The discussion above began by noting the Western-centric nature of the claims being made for explicitation and literalization. Recent years have also seen – although perhaps too often in parallel rather than in dialogue – renewed calls for the recalibration of the geographies of knowledge practices. In some accounts, the required recalibration is understood as one of many processes of globalization, while in others globalization is itself one of the universalizing terms that a geo-politically aware methodology should contest. As Walter Mignolo says:

> Once upon a time scholars assumed that the knowing subject in the disciplines is transparent,

disincorporated from the known and untouched by the geo-political configuration of the world in which people are racially ranked and regions are racially configured. From a detached and neutral point of observation (that Colombian philosopher Santiago Castro-Gómez describes as the hubris of the zero point), the knowing subject maps the world and its problems, classifies people and projects into what is good for them. Today that assumption is no longer tenable, although there are still many believers. (2009: 159)

To consider some of the issues at stake, consider the apparently benign requirement for academics to make the data they collect as part of publically funded research 'open' (Research Councils UK 2013; Nature Publications 2014; White House Office of Science and Technology Policy 2013; World Health Organization 2014). This seems at first glance to be irrefutably a good thing since it would appear to offer everyone, everywhere, equal access to data, thus increasing accountability and enhancing the possibility of people other than those who collected it having access to data. However, as Levin et al. (2016) point out, this 'one-size-fits-all' view of openness sidesteps key questions about the forms, implications, and goals of openness for research practice (see also Tkacz 2014 for a discussion of the genealogy of 'openness'). Too often, the requirement for open access reinforces existing differences between public and private or commercial knowledge practices as there is no such obligation on those collecting data outside the public sector to make the data they collect available to the public or other researchers. Those working for private companies have access to open (public) data, but academics – and citizens – do not automatically have access to privately collected data, even when this is data that is collected from them (the public). In addition, these subjects are not necessarily aware of how their actions (their 'participation') is captured, stored and analysed as data (Krikorian and Kapczynski 2010; Couldry and Meijas 2019; Ricaurte 2019). Indeed, even if the requirement for data to be open is met, the material supports for data storage and analysis available to the studied population may be minimal, less technically developed than that available elsewhere in the world, ensuring that not all subjects are able to reflect on the data they co-produce.

In short, the drive to open up data can intensify the unequal practices by which populations in some parts of the world become the objects of research by researchers in other parts of the world, without the possibility of becoming subjects of research. Indeed, it is argued that, while there are 'algorithmic states of exception' (McQuillan 2015) that do not necessarily map onto the North–South dichotomy, as well as asymmetries within specific national or regional spaces (Shah et al. 2016), the rise of big data means that development interventions in the Global South are becoming the mere 'byproduct of larger-scale processes of informational capitalism' (Taylor and Broeders 2015: 229 quoted in Milan and Treré 2019: 320). Michael Parker and Patricia Kingori summarize the 'collaboration' involved in global health research as tending to 'reproduce relationships and conditions which disproportionately favour high-income countries and institutions':

> Publication authorship, the named principal inves-
> tigators and grant holders for funding applications,
> staff remuneration policies, tax exemption for foreign
> researchers and the ownership of samples and data
> have all been presented as areas where current
> inequalities undermine equal partnerships and collab-
> orations. (2016: 2)

Milan and Treré point to the undue significance attached to 'Western epistemic centres' in processes of datafication, 'especially those considered the interpreters and story-tellers of technological development': 'The different, the underprivileged, the silenced, the subaltern, and the "have nots," whose presence outdoes geographical boundaries, often remain in the blind spot' (2019: 320). To counter this inequality, they propose that what is needed is an emphasis on what is 'new, distinct, and inconsistent with "mainstream" theories'. They ask, 'What questions, concepts, theories, methods would we embrace or have to devise if we are to "decolonize", metaphorically and not, our thinking?' To address these concerns, they outline five conceptual operations: moving past the 'universalism' associated with existing interpretations of datafication; understanding the South as a composite and plural entity, beyond the geographical connotation; developing a critical engagement with decolonial approaches; bringing agency to the core of analyses; and embracing the imaginaries of datafication emerging from the Souths, foregrounding empowering ways of thinking data from the margins.

Before the rise of datafication and associated debates, one of the most powerful formulations of the importance of the geo-politics of knowledge was proposed by Paulo Freire who argued for a pedagogy of the oppressed (1970). He opposes what he calls a banking model of education (that treats the student as an empty vessel to be filled with knowledge) with the possibility of treating the learner as a co-creator of knowledge. This is the approach adopted by João Porto de Albuquerque and André Albino de Almeida (2020) to address the ambivalence between empowerment and instrumentalism they identify as integral to many of today's citizen sensing initiatives. They argue that it is not enough to address the issue through an epistemological lens, since it magnifies some specific aspects of the citizen-sensing practices related to the sensed objects, data and citizens and diminishes other aspects, including those related to the role of researchers and their relationship with citizens. Instead, they prefer the terminology of pedagogy. Drawing on Freire, they are critical of the kind of citizen sensing that employs a pedagogy of answers, preferring instead a pedagogy of questions that is concerned with the constitutive tensions of a mode of engagement that is practised as pedagogy.

To address the gap between the globalization of knowledge and the knowledge of globalization, Arjun Appadurai (2013) argues for the necessity of enhancing 'the capacity to aspire'. Significantly for the aims of this book, he says 'the most serious problems are not those to be found at the level of theories or models, but those involving method: data gathering, sampling bias, reliability of large data sets, and comparability of categories across national data archives, survey design, problems of testimony and recall, and the like' (2013: 274).

Morgan Ndlovu (2018) describes the need for and the problems with a pan-African university. He says that the major question that universities in Africa confront is 'whether they are "African universities" or merely Westernized universities on the African continent'. He notes that even though some of the universities in Africa were developed by nationalist-led post-colonial governments, their epistemic foundations remain Eurocentric:

> The recent wave of student protests at universities in South Africa, where the call was for the "decolonization" of universities, the lowering of fees, the cultivation of a sense of belonging among students, and the Africanization of the curriculum, clearly indicated that the university institution in Africa is increasingly seen as sustaining the synchronic power structure of coloniality. (2018: 101)

Ndlovu argues that the most difficult challenges stem from epistemological entrapment: 'the epistemic foundation of knowledge is the engine that leads to the crisis of "repetition without change"' (2018: 105). However, while acknowledging diverse histories of colonialism, and their uneven effects, he suggests that in Africa, 'the process of colonial domination did not totally annihilate and exterminate indigenous African ways of thinking, knowing and patterns of expression, but merely subalternized and inferiorized them in the global cultural order' (2018: 107). Ndlovu concludes that establishing a decolonial university is the starting point towards aligning the epistemic location of African subjects with their social location.

Walton Mignolo (2009) calls for epistemological disobedience. He argues that 'euro-centred epistemology' succeeded in creating the idea of universal knowledge by concealing 'its own geo-historical and bio-graphical locations' (2009: 160) and identifies various dimensions of the privilege that follows this. These include: creating classifications as well as being part of them; the privilege of being able to publish – and be read by others – in the author's native language; and being able to exploit literal laboratories in the sciences and metaphysical laboratories in the social sciences. Whether and how what I describe later as the platformization of the epistemic infrastructure is continuing or interrupting exploitation in both literal and metaphysical laboratories is one of the most significant aspects of the emergence of what Kelly and McGoey call an 'empire of truth'.

Mignolo identifies two kinds of epistemological disobedience to Euro-centred epistemology: de-Westernization and decolonial. De-Westernization works within a capitalist economy, but proposes that 'the rules of the game and the shots are no longer called by Western players and institutions'. An example is provided by the emergence of the world's largest genomics sequencing and bioinformatics institute in the world, BGI (华大基因/*Huada jiying*). Founded in 1999 by four Chinese scientists, the Institute was established with the goal of getting China to contribute one per cent to the American-led international Human Genome Project. By 2010, BGI was estimated to produce 25 per cent of the world's genomic sequencing data (*Boss Town* 2011 in Won Yin Wong 2017).

Winnie Won Yin Wong (2017) describes this development as an example of a knowledge economy employing reverse engineering, and observes that BGI's complete domination of the genomics sequencing field was made all but complete when in 2013 it purchased the San Diego-based firm Complete Genomics, its biggest competitor. The success of the institute followed the move of its headquarters from, 'oppressively regulated Beijing to freewheeling Shenzhen':

> In the process, it secured a reported US$1.58 billion credit line from the China Development Bank ... BGI also reportedly received a land grant in the newly created district of Yantian through the personal support of Shenzhen mayor Xu Zongzheng, who was soon after removed from office and convicted of corruption (for which he began in 2011 serving a suspended death-penalty sentence). (2017: S106)

Describing the complex, multi-scalar epistemological brokerage this involved she describes Shenzhen – known as the city of fakes – as 'a site of stratifications where every legitimate thing has numerous counterparts on the black, gray, and even "blue" markets, a place where the boundary between the licit and the illicit is erased by the magnitude of production':

> Districts, neighborhoods, street-level offices, villages, and towns have been continually created in the city's short 36-year history even as the administrative powers of these multiple layers of government have changed before they could even be documented ... With each reterritorialization, a new experiment in labor, land, and knowledge management was put into action ... The stratifications of distance, privilege, and access to knowledge enabled by the city's internal boundaries draw attention to the changing nature of truth-value itself by providing sites of production in which rumor, legend, and hype are manufactured alongside scientific facts. (2017: S105)

Calling up an understanding of the mobile, prehensive

intelligence of the tentacular, she quotes Wang Jun who says, 'We are an octopus' (2017: S110).[3]

Mignolo describes the second kind of epistemological disobedience – the decolonial option – as the 'singular connector of a diversity of de-colonials' (2009: 3). It has in common with de-Westernizing arguments 'the definitive rejection of 'being told' from the epistemic privileges of the zero point what 'we' are, what our ranking is in relation to the ideal of *humanitas* and what we have to do to be recognized as such' but diverges in 'one crucial and in-disputable point': 'decolonial options start from the principle that the regeneration of life shall prevail over primacy of the production and reproduction of goods at the cost of life (life in general and of *humanitas* and *anthropos* alike!)' (2009: 3). As an example, he is critical of calls to focus on the politics of 'life in itself'. He says:

> Bio-politics, in Foucault's conception, was one of the practical consequences of an ego-politics of knowledge implemented in the sphere of the state. Politics of life in itself extends it to the market. Thus, politics of life in itself describes the enormous potential of biotechnology to generate consumers who invest their earnings in buying health-promoting products in order to maintain the reproduction of technology that will 'improve' the control of human beings at the same time as creating more wealth through the money invested by consumers who buy health-promoting technology. (2009: 20)

His argument addresses the uneven and stratified politics involved in the entwining of knowledge and life described by Sloterdijk when he says that the knowledge claims invested in the politics of life in itself is directed more towards the making of disciplines than in 'human lives and life in general' (2009: 20).

A further indictment of epistemic inequality comes from Boaventura de Sousa Santos (2014, 2019), who is an advocate of global cognitive justice. He proposes that if we were to move beyond Northern epistemologies, 'another knowledge' would be possible: epistemological diversity is, he says, as great a good as cultural diversity. This fact is obscured by the ongoing suppression of knowledge systems, a process he goes so far as to describe as epistemicide. Writing with Gurminder Bhambra, de Sousa Santos observes that if 'the injustices of the present are in need of repair (and reparation), that reparative work must also be extended to the disciplinary structures that obscure as much as illuminate the path ahead' (Bhambra and de Sousa Santos 2017: 9).

Other challenges to the legitimacy of (Western) state-sanctioned forms of knowledge concern the assumption of the necessity of a secular basis to knowledge claims. Such challenges are diverse in nature. Some are associated with various forms of populism including a variety of religious fundamentalisms; others speak to divination. Others still aim to explore the significance of faith for ways of knowing (Simone 1996; Maurer 2005; Connolly 2000). Vandana Shiva (1993) proposes the term 'monocultures of the mind' to describe Western Imperial knowledge, and its totalitarian and non-democratic implementation. Bhambra develops the concept of 'methodological whiteness' (2017): a way of reflecting on the world that fails to acknowledge the role played by race in the very structuring of that world, and of the ways in which knowledge is constructed and legitimated within it. Methodological whiteness – a term that calls up (the critique of) methodological individualism – fails to recognize the dominance of 'whiteness' as anything other than the standard state of affairs and treats a limited perspective – that deriving from white experience – as a universal perspective. Alana Lentin (2019) argues for the importance of black analytics for what she calls a white context. Rey Chow identifies an epistemic scandal (2006: 13): 'the self-reflexive and (fashionably) mournful/melancholy postures of contemporary theory on the one hand, and the strange complacency of its provincial contents (its habit to tell the story only about certain languages, cultures, and histories)'. Chow further identifies what she calls the 'one-way privilege' of specialists in Western cultures who can claim 'not having enough time or not being available to know everything' (2006: 73).

The anthropologist Helen Verran offers an example that speaks to an attempted negotiation of these epistemological concerns (see Kenney 2015 for a discussion of Verran's relational empiricism). In *Science and an African Logic*, she describes her field observations as a mathematics lecturer and teacher in Nigeria, including her realization of the radically different natures of Yoruban and Western counting practices.[4] The published book describes the difficulties in acknowledging the significance of this realization. After introducing the challenges, the book is divided into three sections. Each section consists of three chapters – the first is a chapter from an earlier manuscript, the second chapter decomposes the argument and objects of the first through a critique of her unstated assumptions, and the third chapter develops an alternative account that does not rely on the same assumptions. She says, 'the sequence of chapters in each section does not constitute a redemption narrative'; rather, she 'struggles to keep the tensions' (2001: 20). In other work (2005), she describes what she perceives as an incommensurable gap between the Aboriginal and scientific traditions of knowledge involved in the management of Australia's northern savannas through the practice of firing. Nevertheless, as part of her own continuing practice, she puts forward 'a third translating domain', a method by which epistemological differences can be acknowledged and made productive. Significantly, this translating domain requires attention to the ontic. She writes:

> This move involves an ontology that is both and neither Aboriginal and scientific. But this is not a meta-ontology. It is not an ontic domain which supervenes and contains the other two. On the contrary, it

is an infra-ontology, an inside connection.[5] It takes enough of what matters ontologically to Aborigines when they are dealing with firings, and enough of what matters to scientists when they are engaged in doing their prescribed burns. Learning how to do this in on-the-ground situations is not easy because it involved working with contradictions in disciplined ways. (2005: 7)

From a different social, geographic and epistemological position, Ulrich Beck and Natan Sznaider call for what they describe as methodological cosmopolitanism as a way to challenge national perspectives and acknowledge interconnectedness. They write:

... the social sciences can only respond adequately to the challenge of globalization if they manage to overcome methodological nationalism and to raise empirically and theoretically fundamental questions within specialized fields of research, and thereby elaborate the foundations of a newly formulated cosmopolitan social science. (Beck and Sznaider, 2010: 384)

Importantly, the concept and phenomena of cosmopolitanism are not spatially fixed for them: 'the term itself is not tied to the "cosmos" or the "globe", and it certainly does not encompass "everything"' (Beck and Sznaider 2010: 383). For Beck, cosmopolitanism is not to be equated with the global (or globalization), with 'world system theory', 'world social science', or with 'world-society', since he believes these concepts presuppose basic dualisms, such as local/global, domestic/foreign, national/international, all of which have in his view become less and less useful. However, cosmopolitanism remains a widely contested term: Gayatri Spivak, for example, argues that it does not do justice to subaltern struggles, but is rather a project of world governance (2012).

Other approaches seek to avoid the dualisms of global

and local in other ways: for example, AbdouMaliq Simone (2004) focuses on the hybridity of the urban. This emphasis is not only a matter of pointing to the heterogeneity or multiplicity of urban life; rather, his concern is with hybridity as an epistemological process in itself – a means through which the particular institutions and processes associated with the urban emerge. This epistemology entails constant experimentation, experimentation that takes apart definitive boundaries between the West and its others. And this experimentation is said to be something that the subjects of research carry out as well as, sometimes alongside, sometimes in tension with, the researcher; sometimes indeed without a researcher. Drawing on this understanding, Simone describes the importance for those living in the urban South of 'composing the conditions that facilitate improvisation and dialogue among players' (2018: 7).

A further initiative addressing the geo-politics of method advocates the adoption of 'Asia as a method', an idea drawn from Takeuchi Yoshimi's lecture of the same name and put into circulation in the 'inter-Asia' context by Kuan-Hsing Chen (2010, 2012), who elaborates its potential as a local but also transborder, regional and even intercontinental frame. Tejeswani Niranjana (2015) suggests that 'Asia as methodology' might be more accurate; she writes:

> Let us assume that by methodology we mean a system of broad principles and practices. This might give us then a different handle on the problem of how to frame new research after the Cold War and after decolonization. It might be even more accurate to say 'Inter-Asia methodology' with all the illogic of that particular hyphen … Admittedly 'methodology' doesn't sound as catchy as 'Asia as method'. But if we decide to adopt the phrase 'Inter-Asia methodology' we could treat it as a system of broad principles

from which more specific methods can be derived. (Niranjana 2015)

For Niranjana, Inter-Asia methodology involves knowledge production about Asian locations premised on a kind of 'inter-referencing' (Chua 1998) that involves both the multiplication of frames of reference (Chen 2010) and comparative research. It also includes what Niranjana calls the 'pressing' of concepts; that is, the interrogation of concepts in relation to each other as part of analysis to reveal how they simultaneously implicate different Asian locations. Niranjana emphasizes that the concern is 'not to compile similar data from different Asian countries', an effort which she argues 'involves the old Area Studies legacy of knowing each place in minute detail [and] is embedded in the academic culture of the 'regional expert' (2013). In contrast, Inter-Asia methodology does not tie the responsibility of locational knowledge production to specific identities: 'We suggest that it is not a question of identity but a question of perspective' (2013).

5. (Non-)Representation and/or participation

As has been widely observed (Desrosières 1998; Porter, 1996; Hacking 2006), in the nineteenth and twentieth centuries, the (colonial) (nation) state played a key role in the development and maintenance of an epistemic infrastructure, including support for the establishment of universities and investment in the discipline and profes- sional practice of statistics, as well as establishing principles and procedures for the collection of data relating to population (see Murphy 2017 for a powerful critique of the methodological analytic of population). In these initia- tives, epistemic and political representation converged in practices of data collection, techniques of analysis and measures of representativeness. Alain Desrosières, for example, emphasizes the importance for the emergence of statistics of the creation by the state of 'a space of common measurement, within which things may be

compared, because the categories and encoding procedures are identical' (1998: 9). The legitimacy of this space
was secured through the establishment of a network 'of
stabilized connections, of routinized equivalences, and
words to describe them'.

Desrosières argues that it was this language that
provided 'the reference points and the common meaning
in relation to which the actors [of the public sphere] can
qualify and express their reactions' (1998: 333); that
is, this language provided the terms and conditions for
the looping effects of representation and intervention
described by Hacking (2012) as central to both the process
of scientific enquiry and the governmental legitimacy
of representative democracy. Crucially, this legitimacy
involved a series of mechanisms by which 'the public' in
the form of a population comprised of different groupings
of citizens was detached and reattached to data at different
moments in practices of representativeness that combined
the cultural and the political understandings of representation with the statistical. As Dominique Cardon puts it:
'Statistical categorizations have played a central role in the
intelligibility that our societies have of themselves' (2019).
In this respect, they have contributed both to political
initiatives that aimed to ameliorate inequality and to
forms of stratification in which some lives are represented
as less valuable than others (Murphy 2017).

However, while the state continues to play an important
role in defining and collecting data about the activities of its
citizens, other actors now play an increasingly important
role, transforming the relationship between problem spaces
and 'the working surface of the social' (Bennett 2007). Of
course, the common space of measurement described by
Desrosières was never the only shared space that existed.
As Jane Guyer (2004) among others has argued, alongside
the imposition of standardized and state-supported modes
of commensuration and calculation, including profession-
alized statistical skills, the use of standardized indices, and
support for the role of 'banks' (financial, biological and

historical) and other state regulated institutions such as museums and galleries as the custodians and integrators of transactional memories (Hart 2000), there has always been a parallel architecture of disjuncture. This architecture employs dynamic value scales, in which the terms of difference are accepted as partial transformations and indices of each other (rather than equivalents), and repertoires of value are always under re-creation. Nevertheless, it seems as if linkages between measure and value are currently being re-calibrated in ways that enable an architecture for a multiplication of scalings, translations and conversions in ways that do not simply exist alongside but, rather, undermine and perhaps even displace the (post-colonial) (nation) state's space of common measurement.

In some fields, there is a move by supra-national governmental bodies towards extending the common space of measurement beyond the territorial borders of the nation state. Francesca Gromme and Evelyn Ruppert (2019) describe, for example, the ESS Census Hub as a platform for the formation of data infrastructures in official statistics that enable both 'post-national' and 'de-national' enactments of Europe's populations and territories. Gromme and Ruppert draw attention to the capacity of the platform to integrate national census data in 'cubes' of cross-tabulated social topics and spatial 'grids' of maps. In the use of this platform, they say, 'old' geometries of organizing and mapping populations co-exist with 'new' topological orderings and arrangements that can mix and fold categories of population across national borders.

In other initiatives, measures are designed to capture phenomena that the (patriarchal) (colonial) (nation) state has ignored; so, for example, Shirin Rai, Catherine Hoskyns and Dania Thomas (2013) introduce the concept of depletion and develop methods to measure it to capture some of the gendered inequalities of social reproduction that are invisible in many other indicators of household life and labour. They conclude by arguing that a measure of depletion through social reproduction can be a powerful tool for understanding the consequences of non-recognition of the value of domestic work to national economies, as well as the harm that might accrue in the doing of this work at both a systemic and individual level. Sylvia Walby engages with the difficulties of mobilizing established statistical data and indicators in establishing the extent and nature of domestic violence (Walby 2005; Walby and Towers 2017). These and other initiatives exist alongside the growth of a market in metrics (Moor and Lury 2011) as part of an unprecedented 'precession of measures' (Brighenti 2018: 31):

> In the early 21st century, we are experiencing a rapid transformation of the measures in place. Certainly, the trend towards the universalization of basic physical measures, which has been underway since late 18th-century revolutionary France, has reached a seeming end-point with international standardi- zation and the deputed United Nations organization known as ISO.2. While units such as metres and kilos go seemingly unchallenged, however, many relevant measure units for contemporary life are much more controversial. What about, for instance, the produc- tivity of workers, which neoliberal management based on performance control and assessment has propelled so forcefully? Which measures are apt for human mobility (including the exceptional mobilities of refugees) that is increasingly turning into a new factor of social inequality? What about the new forma- tions of the polity, given the insufficiency of both traditional national frameworks and the established supra-national institutions? (Brighenti 2018: 26)

In addition to this multiplication of measures, the changes in the semiotics of epistemic infrastructures described above have the capacity to disturb or confuse the methodological links between representation and representativeness that were historically established by the nation state: once the two-way relations of indexicality are activated in more dynamic loopings it becomes apparent that there are no fixed co-ordinates by which to map (or ground-truth) population onto territory. At the same time, not only is the methodological value of the concept of population being tested, as the population in question is either expanded – with the support of datafication – to be all-encompassing (as in n=all) or decreased (as in n=1), but developments in the fields of AI and deep learning challenge the usefulness of older statistical techniques of representation and measures of representativeness:

> The issue of representation lies at the heart of the debate between the logic-inspired and the neural-network-inspired paradigms for cognition. In the logic-inspired paradigm, an instance of a symbol is something for which the only property is that it is either identical or non-identical to other symbol instances. It has no internal structure that is relevant to its use; and to reason with symbols, they must be bound to the variables in judiciously chosen rules of inference. By contrast, neural networks just use big activity vectors, big weight matrices and scalar non-linearities to perform the type of fast "intuitive" inference that underpins effortless commonsense reasoning. (LeCun, Bengio and Hinton, 2015: 436)

Dominique Cardon speculates that the implications of such transformations in thought will be wide-ranging (2019; see also Lury and Day 2019). He says of the rise of personalization:

> Three features appear. First, the calculation performed within the digital infrastructure customizes its operations according to each individual. Second, this personalization uses the recording of the user's behaviour as a means of verifying the relevance of the

predictions made to the user. Finally, digital recommendations seek to adapt, in real time, to the environment and context in which the user is situated. While large technical infrastructures have often been dedicated to the production of an organized and regulated space for all beneficiaries of the service, digital infrastructures seek to reconfigure the space in a personalized way for each of them. They produce differentiated environments rather than a common space. (2019)

This shift can be understood in terms of a move away from an epistemological regime given legitimacy through practices of representation and representativeness, to one in which legitimation is accomplished – or not – in practices of participation.

Barney et al. (2016; see also Kelty 2020) provide a useful account of the centrality of participation to Western societies, even going so far as to suggest that there is 'no place or time in human history where or when people did not "participate" by living together and acting in their world'.[6] However, so they argue, we are now experiencing a 'participatory condition'. This term, they say:

> ... names the situation in which participation – being involved in doing something and taking part in something with others – has become both environmental (a state of affairs) and normative (a binding principle of right action) ... It has become a contextual feature of everyday life in the liberal, capitalist, and technological societies of the contemporary West ... the fact that we have always necessarily participated does not mean that we have always lived under the participatory condition. What is distinctive about the present conjuncture is the degree and extent to which the everyday social, economic, cultural, and political activities that comprise simply being in the world have been thematized and organized around the priority of participation as such. (2016: vii)

While not assuming digital media has determined this expansion of participation as 'a relational possibility', they note that the generalization of participation is 'concomitant with the development and popularization of so- called digital media, especially personal computers, networking technologies, the Internet, the World Wide Web, and video games' (2016: vii).

It is this condition – in which the organization of 'taking part with others' provides the environment for problem spaces – that provides the context for the current methodological concern with participation. In Mike Savage's nuanced account of the history of the social sciences in the UK in the twentieth century (2010), he describes the importance of an engagement with the ordinary and the everyday, captured by an emphasis on 'the popular'. This concern with the popular was mediated by specific methods, notably the survey and the interview, and the interpretive techniques associated with cultural studies. He also identifies the importance of the tradition of Mass Observation and the various field research activities of the mid-twentieth century that sought to show how the public could research themselves through projects of observing and writing. But, so it seems, in the early years of the twenty-first century participation is coming to supplement and sometimes even displace the popular as the preferred way in which social science researches the sociality of the everyday, even as, in a return of the repressed, the popular erupts in a variety of forms of political populism that gain at least some of their appeal from a refusal of established socio-demographic ('politically correct') categories of representation. Indeed, many contemporary methodological debates are concerned with whether and how the popular and participation inter-relate (in, for example, competing understandings of the public), and whether and how this inter-relationship can really provide a useful alternative to representation and representativeness.

In many accounts, participation, or participatory method, emerges as a means of making research lead more directly to social transformation; that is, participation is linked to a vision of changing processes of knowledge production to enhance democratization, innovation and social integration. For example, the New Economics Foundation observes:

> "Consultation" and "participation" are fashionable words. Our institutions are starting to appreciate that a lack of accountability breeds a lack of legitimacy and trust. We are all starting to understand that society is now so complex that no decision will stick unless it has involved everybody with a stake in it. (https:// neweconomics.org/1998/06/participation-works)

This assertion points to a common political rationale informing the current imperative for 'citizens' to participate in knowledge-making: the need to establish trust and democratic accountability in relation to processes of decision-making. However, 'participation' is understood by different agencies in different ways, ranging from the acquisition of personal data acquired from the tracking or surveillance of 'liking' and other forms of online 'sharing' or 'use' that has been described as 'leveraging the many' (Picot and Hopf 2018) to more engaged involvement in knowledge-making practices such as citizen (social) science, collaborative research, deliberative mapping, the volunteering of data, precision or personalized medicine, participatory integrated assessment and social design and participatory development (for a critique of which see Agrawal 2002).

One influential example of participatory methods is the creation of 'competency groups' as described by Whatmore and Landström (2011, authors who are associated with non-representational theory). These are groups set up to enable civic involvement with controversies, such as flood-defence schemes in rural Yorkshire in the UK, at the same time as providing a basis from which to study such involvement. Whatmore and Landström propose that the design of experimental participation events creates new opportunities for pursuing the democratization of relations between science and politics. Drawing on the work of Isabelle Stengers, they argue that this requires the 'invention of research apparatuses that can "slow down" expert reasoning and redistribute expertise' between experts and lay people implicated in a techno-scientific issue such as flood defence (Whatmore and Landström 2011: 606). In another approach that is part of the move towards the methodological take-up of participation, Noortje Marres proposes 'material participation' (2012b). This term draws attention to the fact that while participation traditionally refers to human activity (securing the involvement of people in forms of inquiry), it need not only imply the involvement of people, but may also refer to the deployment of seemingly mundane artefacts in settings of public deliberation. In the case of the competency group discussed above, for example, one of the participants transformed the terms of debate by bringing a piece of carpet salvaged from a recent flood to the public forum.

Drawing on Dewey's understanding of 'ontological trouble', Marres describes material participation as the design of objects, devices or, more generally, material settings or environments, in such a way that publics can form and act in relation to a problem. Such devices, she argues, have the capacity to turn everyday activities 'into an index of public participation', conscripting subjects into an 'ecological public'. She further argues that experiments in participation are characterized by 'normative multi-valence': that is, they can simultaneously serve multiple agendas, such as politicization, innovation and economization. She proposes that we should not merely attempt to extend the scope of participation, to include more issues or more relevant actors, but should also look at 'the facilitation involved in the organization of public engagement exercises' (2012b: 135–6); that is, we should be attentive to how publics are connected to, and facilitated by, institutional structures.

As an advocate of material participation, Marres argues that one of its advantages is that publics can form and act in relation to a problem, without 'investing' time, money, attention, or ideology; devices of material participation can suggest 'a range of simple actions, rather than requiring citizens to grasp the complexity of environmental issues' (2012b: 80). But Karin Knorr Cetina (2007) provides an alternative view of material participation, by emphasizing the role of material objects in the knowledge cultures of consumer lifestyles, such as those associated with technology, health and fitness, music and sport. She suggests that the attachment to objects in these cultures brings into focus potentially large areas of conflict having to do with asynchronous development across divides in knowledge cultures. She points, for example, to the contrast between the pace of innovation cultures and the temporal frameworks instantiated in politics, government and associated areas:

> ... the temporalities of knowledge and expertise and the times of government frequently clash, with the latter determined by relatively fixed schedules and long procedures of collective decision-making implemented by reference to the display of legitimacy. Areas of knowledge and expertise, on the other hand, would seem to promote adaptations to the temporal requirements of objects and appear more guided by efficiency – an efficiency linked to time being seen as a major driver and generator of research and innovation value. (2007: 372)

In short, as an increasingly widespread set of practices, the participatory condition is profoundly transforming the configuration of problem spaces, not least in the ways in which it intersects with changes in the organization of the academy. As Savage acknowledges, the contemporary academy exists in a 'messy, competitive context' in which 'the roles of different kinds of intellectuals, technical experts, and social groups are at stake' (2010: 237).

Nevertheless, in all these examples, key issues are the extent to which participation is more, or less, active (participatory or participative), more-or-less informed, more-or-less intentional, and, still significant, more-or-less-representative, as is evident, for example, in discussions of sampling. There is much debate about whether and how programmes of participation (Gabrys 2016) or the 'legitimate peripheral participation' that is involved in becoming a member of a community of practice (Lave and Wenger 1991) can be made more inclusive and polyvocal, alongside a movement for responsible metrics (for example, https://responsiblemetrics.org/the-metric-tide) as well as explorations of the role of participative metrics; that is metrics that invite and exploit participation (Gerlitz and Lury 2014). While such metrics can be understood in terms of 'performance' or 'performativity', and the reactivity involved in the use of such measures, understanding them in terms of participation offers, in addition, a focus on the habitability of problem spaces, a concern that will be discussed in the Conclusion of the book.

Conclusion

As stated at the beginning of the chapter, the changes to the epistemic infrastructure described here have different histories and intersect in different places in different ways. However, in their differences, the changes all suggest that the possibilities of configuring the composition of problem spaces are being transformed, affording new opportunities for what Kelly and McGoey (2018) describe as epistemological leverage. The next chapter describes some examples of how that leverage is being exercised.

– 3 –

Indexing the Human

(with Ana Gross)[1]

Indexing, and reindexing, the 'human' to money
has changed over several centuries, through several
phases ...

Jane Guyer (2016: 182)

The last chapter outlined some of the vectors of change
in the epistemic infrastructure. This chapter outlines some
of the methods currently employed for the measurement
of variation in consumer prices including the methods
involved in: the production of the Argentinian state's
Consumer Price Index (CPI); an alternative CPI created
by The Billion Prices Project; the company Premise's
measures of food staples; and a failed attempt to produce a
personalized CPI. The creation of a CPI was chosen as an
example of how the possibilities for composing problem
spaces are changing since, as Jane Guyer (2016) so neatly
puts it, this measure indexes 'the human' to money, and
as such, provides many societies with pivotal numbers, the
numbers around which the distribution of resources turn.

The chapter ends with the proposal that we are witnessing the platformization of the epistemic infrastructure, a process that variously enables and modifies the vectors of change described in the previous chapter.

Indicators of price

The Consumer Price Index (CPI) is a widely used macro-economic indicator of the average measure of change in the prices of a representative 'basket' of consumer goods and services bought for the purposes of consumption by the reference measure of the population of a specific geographical territory. It is commonly produced by National Statistics Offices and used by governments to produce inflation figures, to regulate wage increases, to calibrate social security and pension payments, to index tax thresholds, to influence the setting of interest rates by banks, and by business to inform commercial strategy. As such, it is a paradigmatic example of the way in which methods result in epistemic artefacts that have consequences for 'the working surfaces of the social' (Bennett 2007).

CPIs are generally described as 'pure price indexes': 'pure' in this context meaning that only changes in prices between stabilized reference points are captured in the index. The methodological process of 'purification' requires the isolation of price factors in a fixed (base) period of time, a comparison with the same factors in a second period, and then an estimation of the change that occurs if everything else – such as consumers and their spending patterns, the goods and services the market offers, the condition in which products are encountered – is taken out of the equation. What is desired from this process of purification is that variation in price is detached from all other kinds of variation. Indeed, it is the task of state supported statistical CPI methodology to render other modes of variation demonstrably external to variation in price.

A complex process of classification of products is required for this to be achieved. The aim is to enable price collectors to do three things in ways that are deemed methodologically sound: to specify an actual product that is functionally and physically representative of a class of goods which is itself determined to be representative of patterns of household consumption; to specify the product in such a way that it may be identified and its price may be recorded repeatedly in different spaces within a given territory and time period; and to establish equivalences for the product such that if the product becomes unavailable or is no longer deemed representative a substitution can be made. All these things are necessary for the variation in price to be established as pure, since it is only if 'exactly the same' product is observed repeatedly that its price can be said to have varied in itself and its variation not be a consequence of, for example, changes in the qualities of the product being taken into account, commercial or political intervention, and so on.

This process of measuring variation in price further involves the iterative collection of data according to criteria of both representativeness of products and persons (representative products that representative groups in a given – usually territorially delimited – population might purchase) and representational accuracy (as defined by criteria which make the products identifiable as the same in specific contexts at the same time that those contexts are rendered unimportant or external to the observation of price). Together, the criteria of representativeness and representational accuracy support a form of symbolic representation that displays a kind of epistemological realism.[2] However, just as in other forms of realism (including, for example, the realism of novels and painting), the representativeness and accuracy of this form of realism have been the focus of political contestation, including a variety of forms of stat-activism (Bruno, Didier and Vitale 2014).[3]

In Argentina in 2007, for example, a long-running controversy regarding the production of the CPI by the national statistics office (INDEC) erupted, leading to the declaration of a National Statistics Emergency in 2016.[4] The controversy involved challenges to both the representational accuracy of the price variation it recorded and its representativeness,[5] and in doing so disputed its realism (see Daniel and Lanata Briones 2019 for a more detailed account of the political and economic context of this controversy). The challenges took a variety of forms including protestors surrounding the walls of the building in which national statisticians were employed in a symbolic embrace, while the statisticians themselves called upon the National Statistics Act to refuse a demand from the government to provide details of exactly which products were being identified as those whose prices were being observed. Their refusal – which contributed to their removal from their posts – was directed to the protection of a space of secrecy from which 'the data could first be developed and from which the figures could emerge as part of its process of entering the public sphere' (Didier 2005: 639) and demonstrated their belief that a hiatus, a 'sphere of obscurity and a structure of withholding' was required for the methodological legitimacy of the index.

In our analysis of the first years of this controversy, Ana Gross and I (2014), focused on the activities that went into the making of this index. In the case of the specific CPI we discussed, these activities included the collection of the prices of approximately 80,000 products as found in approximately 6,000 different retail outlets within the region of the Capital Federal and Greater Buenos Aires region (*INDEC Manual de Metodologia Numero* 313: 15). In this instance, as in the case of many other CPIs being produced today, the process of specification of the products whose prices are to be ascertained relies in part on an international classification system of products for household consumption expenditure known as COICOP (*Classification of Individual Consumption by Purpose*), a nomenclature developed by the United Nations Statistics Division. The specification of these products is a complex and vital process, as the goal is to attempt to observe and record the prices of a 'representative' sample of products and services in specific sites at specific times on a regular basis.

In this case, the CPI was designed to take into account nine Chapters (e.g. Food and Drink), 26 Divisions (e.g. Food), 65 Groups (e.g. Fruits), 123 Sub-groups (e.g. Fresh Fruit), 182 Products (e.g. Citrus Fruits) and 818 Varieties (e.g. Oranges). Following this classification, and once again as part of a standard CPI methodology, products are described through the listing of attributes such that they – or their substitutes – can reliably be identified in situ. This includes specifying not only characteristics of the products (for example, size or colour), but also aspects of the way they were produced, their packaging, their distribution pathway or country of origin. This complex specification, sometimes but not always, culminates in the naming of a branded product held to exemplify those attributes of the item whose price is to be ascertained.

At the same time as there is a concern with accuracy, however, there is an orchestration of opacity around the public release of information concerning such attributes, the process by which they are linked to actual identifiable products, and the location in which they may be found. This opacity is deemed necessary so that the prices of the products may be observed in a 'natural' state; that is, in the conditions in which they present themselves to consumers, protected from artificial manipulation. Until 2007 the INDEC made public inflation figures only to the level of Varieties; that is, it made public average price variation to the level of a relatively unspecific generalization: for example, Oranges. In contrast, some other countries provide figures relating to products more closely specified. So, for example, the UK Office of National Statistics (ONS) released what is defined as 'CPI's micro-data' following a Freedom of Information Act request that was filed in 2011 requesting the publication of individual item details. Since then, the UK ONS has extended the network

of attributes that make visible each of CPI's products
as part of its Open Data agenda. However, because of
other regulatory frameworks still in place, products are
often still unidentifiable (in part because brand names are
excluded from public data releases in the UK).

The following example extracted from the UK's CPI
'open data' disclosure shows the degree of specification
that ONS currently allows as well as indicating something
of the types of objects and substances of observation that
a CPI typically takes into account:

> Six bread rolls white/brown; whole sponge cake not
> frozen; home-killed beef – lean mince KG; tea bags
> 2-packets of 240; fruit juice not orange 1 L; sandwich
> – take-away cold; vending machine – fizzy drink;
> lager-pint 3.4–4.2%; wallpaper paste; door handle –
> pack for one door; duvet double tog 10–13.5; scissors
> – household; sheet of wrapping paper; watch battery
> replacement; women's casual outer jacket; 9 CT gold
> chain 18–20"/ 46–51 cm; indigestion tablets 16–24
> per pack; full leg wax (both legs); car service – local
> garage; boxed board game (not travel); beginner's
> acoustic guitar; book fiction – paperback – top 10;
> houseplant; wall hanging mirror up to 1.5 M; etc.
> (ONS, Price Quote 2012 Q4 Database)

The classificatory process thus delimits the actuality indexed
by the CPI in some detail and offers national statistics 'a
point of contact with the stuff of the world' (Lezaun 2012:
1). However, to create a representative index this classification is supplemented by the geographical specification
of the contexts in which specified, identifiable products
are to be found.

Alongside this (partial) description of the statistical
methodology involved in the production of the Argentinian
CPI Ana Gross and I also described one of the alternative methodologies that emerged at the same time as
the controversy noted above: The Billion Prices Project

(BPP; http://bpp.mit.edu). The BPP not only provided a challenge to the accuracy of the index that emerged as the percentage variation in price put forward by the Argentinian national statistics office as the capital region's CPI during this controversy but also to the production of national statistics *tout court*, since it involved the use of on-line or secondary data rather than the primary data of INDEC statisticians. Created by Alberto Cavallo and Roberto Rigobon, two Argentinian economists now based in the USA, the BPP methodology is now used to monitor the daily price fluctuations of approximately five million items sold by approximately 300 online retailers in more than seventy countries. A version of it informs the production of, among other things, a daily price index and inflation rate for many countries, still including Argentina.

The BPP originated in 2007 as part of Cavallo's PhD thesis at Harvard University which compared the online price variations for Argentina, Chile, Brazil and Colombia. Cavallo later went on to produce an alternative online inflation index for Argentina called 'True Inflation' which was accessible via a webpage and updated price variations for Argentina on a daily (that is, much more frequent than the national CPI) basis. In 2008, data collection was expanded to fifty other countries, an expansion which officially became The Billion Prices Project. What started as an academic exercise was later taken up and developed by a company that describes itself as 'the leading source of daily inflation statistics around the world', trading under the registered trademark of PriceStats (http://pricestats. com). In 2014, the BPP website referred those seeking more high-frequency inflation data across countries and sectors to PriceStats, which it described as 'the company that collects the online data we use in our research initiatives and experimental indexes'.

The BPP methodology makes extensive use of online price data, at least some of which are taken from large supermarket chains, collected using scraping software. As a method, scraping is substantially different to the procedures used to specify and find products off-line to observe their prices. It is described by BPP as a three-step process. First, there is the downloading of selected web-pages where product and price information is given. Second, the underlying code of those web-pages is analysed by software to locate each piece of relevant information: 'this is done by using custom characters in the code that identify the start and end of each variable, according to the format of that particular page and supermarket' (Cavallo 2010: 7). Third, scraped information is then stored in a database containing 'one record per product per day' (Cavallo 2010: 7).

The nature of the data collected through the method of scraping thus differs substantially from that conventionally used in the production of CPI as a national statistic: first, the data is collected on a daily rather than monthly basis; second, the data collected is relevant for a number of countries, not just one; third, the data comprises detailed information on the full array of a retailer's products, rather than being a selection specified in terms of measures of representativeness; fourth, there are no forced item substitutions – products may disappear without substitution and new products may simply be added; and fifth, the data are rendered comparable across countries, with prices recorded for the same categories of goods and time periods in different places. In short, while the BPP methodology was used at the time to confirm the popular belief that the official offline inflation figures in Argentina were inaccurate, it is far from being just a substitute methodology to produce a CPI. Indeed, precisely because the data collected would be described by statisticians as secondary – that is, not produced in response to directed (statistical) enquiry, its collection can, in principle, be more variously organized – or put to work in a greater variety of indexing activities – than can the data required to produce national statistics. Indeed, this methodological multiplicity can be used as the basis for experimentation with categories in the creation of a variety of economic indicators, as well as allowing for temporally differentiated periods and geographically diverse regions of comparison, allowing for both very short-term and long-term comparisons, within, across and between administratively defined regions. Together, these differences in the methodology of indexing enable the production of a working surface of the social in new ways, supporting the creation of a variety of measures of different kinds of relevance to different kinds of actors.

It is interesting in this respect to observe that the data collected by PriceStats is made available to others in commercial, academic and 'public' forms, defined by varying terms of access. For example, the PriceStats website says that it distributes (that is, presumably, it sells) its daily inflation statistics through an exclusive partnership with State Street Global Markets (http://www.statestreetglobal-markets.com), whose target clients include the managers of hedge funds, pension funds, and sovereign wealth funds. It also presents itself as being in partnership with the BPP, described by PriceStats as 'an academic initiative that uses high frequency price information to conduct breakthrough economic research'. Finally, PriceStats says it collaborates (once again presumably for a fee) with public institutions to improve decisions in public policy: for example, they create special indices that measure the price of specific goods across countries to 'anticipate the impact of commodity shocks on low-income, vulnerable populations'. In short, the scraped (secondary) data is used by PriceStats for diverse kinds of operations, in relation to specific kinds of clients, resulting in, for example, the production of indices of real-time global inflation, price synchronization among brands and contiguous products, price stickiness, price markups, etc. In this regard, its data has the potential to be used not only to challenge the legitimacy of the CPI as a national statistic but also to offer new opportunities for (new) economic actors.

In this example, many of the opportunities created by the new methodology contribute to the financialization[6] of variations in price, insofar as the BPP methodology provides the data for economic actors to put variation in prices of categories of products defined in multiple different ways in relation to a wide variety of macro- and micro-economic processes, not only those of interest to national and regional governments. Rather than being tied to categories produced in relation to the kinds of indexicality specified in measures of representativeness, the BPP methodology invites experiments in categorizing within data sets in relation to a wide variety of multi-scale economic and political processes. Such experimental categories do not need to be tied to either specific geographical territories or to measures of representativeness for the population of specific countries,[7] but can, rather, be created and fine-tuned in terms of the opportunities they offer for political action or economic advantage by specific actors who have diverse (and constantly changing) grounds-for-truth.

A further example of methodology to measure variation in price is offered by Premise, a company that launched its own 'real-time' inflation indicator based on 'crowd-sourced' and online data collection techniques in 2012.[8] One of the founders, David Soloff, a former investment banker describes the reasons he helped set it up by saying:

> So you have a really manual survey infrastructure that's generations old ... [and] an incredibly fast-moving set of micro economies and a hopeless gap between the two. And that was only going to widen – unless we built the infrastructure to keep tabs on what's really going on. (https://www.wired.co.uk/article/premise-app-food-tracking-brazil-philippines)

The Premise methodology was described in a newspaper report as 'a blend of Google Street View and the CPI', and as 'an alternative photo-collage project'. The proprietary data it produces is described on the Premise website as having unique sources including e-commerce websites, third-party transaction streams, and a gig economy workforce which visits 'real-world' stores in Argentina,

Brazil, China, India and the United States to 'ground truth directly'. This workforce is equipped with a mobile phone app to photograph products with a time and date stamp.

The numerical and visual data collected in this way informs the production of both a global Food Staples Index and individual country Food Staple Indices as well as indices for 'sub-components of interest such as Meat, Fruit, Vegetables, and so on'. The uses to which this data collection methodology can be put have diversified since the company's start-up, including for example, 'vector surveillance and control for infectious diseases', 'monitoring radicalization and vulnerability to violent extremism'. A recent version of the website makes much of the involvement of what they call their network of contributors to provide up-to-date, local, contextualized data; their tag-line says, 'Premise is *the* source for Ground Truth.'

The full details of the methodology Premise employs are not made publically available but a little detail was provided in early promotional material, including a discussion of the constitution of onions as a Staple Food. In this early self-description, Premise say that they track the price of the staple food of onions across hundreds of everyday markets in Mumbai, Chennai and Kolkata. According to David Soloff, the company detected, as early as June 2013, a significant increase in price per kilogram of onions by its street teams. The street teams' photographs showed the colour of the onions displayed was fading, along with a diminution in size and a visible decrease in stock, all of which were taken as signs of shortages and hoarding. Newspapers, however, didn't start reporting a spike in price until late August and there were public protests and a tripling in price of onions before the RBI, the Indian central bank, responded by changing interest rates to strengthen its currency. The currency finally got moved in early September, and prices declined 30–50 percent. In the promotional material, Soloff suggests that the Indian government could have saved itself trouble by using Premise, since the company sets a trigger for the manual analysis of price variation anytime a price moves 15 percent on a 30-day basis: 'We see the peak being talked about when it's already being resolved', Soloff said. 'We have a reliable granular read on inputs, rather than waiting for official bodies to speak about it. We've built a better mousetrap to capture data at scale.'

This case was of promotional value to Premise since the onion, as a category of food, is known to be a reliable indicator of inflation in India. From the point of view of the changes in the epistemic infrastructure described in the last chapter, this points to an interesting continuity in the geo-politics of 'large numbers'; that is, the development of methods by colonial or globalizing actors in developing, colonized or third-world countries. In discussing the development of statistical methods of sampling, for example, Savage identifies the importance of

> ... the remarkable reception given by the RSS [Royal Statistical Society] at its annual meeting of 1946 to a paper by the Indian statistician P. C. Mahalanobis, who had "had the opportunity to apply statistical methods, the scientific technique of sampling, and the design of experiments on a scale so vast as to seem to someone like himself, inhabiting a small overcrowded island, almost astronomical". (Savage 2010: 201)

As Savage remarks, India served the Royal Statistical Society[9] as the 'quintessential modern imagined nation ... especially in the context of decolonization and an emerging geopolitics organized around nation states' (2010: 201). In the example of the category of onions by Premise, India seems to have the same role now: in this case it is, apparently, a challenging test-bed for the development of methodological techniques of globalizing tendencies since – in the description given by Premise – it has 'no natural geographical boundaries [and is] riven by cultural divisions', a description which fits many other countries, including the UK and the US.

With the Premise methodology, there is no need to specify *a priori* criteria of representativeness linked to the population of a specific region or country. Instead, weightings in relation to a shifting variety of criteria of relevance, as well as experiments in contexting (Asdal and Moser 2012), can be introduced on a bespoke basis as required by Premise's clients.[10] The website says:

> The Premise Ground Truth Platform offers an alternative to traditional data collection methods such as time-intensive polls/surveys, or costly direct observation capture in the field. Applying proven growth/recruitment strategies, Premise can quickly standup a relevant contributor base, leverage our existing public network of thousands of respondents, or partner with clients to create a private respondent network to collect targeted insights. (https://www.premise.com/products)

Variations in product quality (such as the condition of the onions) need not be rendered external to the measures of variation in price that Premise produces, but instead can be folded into the problem space as visual data and made available for analysis through their photographic capture. The Premise methodology thus produces measures of variation in price in relation to a classification such as a Staple that is not pure, and is not designed to be so, but is, rather, contaminated – or animated – in a variety of practices of contexting. In this sense, the Premise methodology is a striking example that demonstrates that 'big data' does not remove context, but rather, has its own specific practices of contexting (Seaver 2015a), involving a variety of practices of scaling. '"We are not a big-data company," says Joe Reisinger, 33, [another] Premise co-founder and CTO. "In fact, we are kind of the opposite of crowdsourcing. So my job is to work out how to get the type of data that may be smaller, but with the precision that allows us to derive meaningful conclusions from it"' (https://www.wired.co.uk/article/ premise-app-food-tracking-brazil-philippines).

In many ways then, the methodology employed by Premise contributes to the assetization of knowledge (Birch and Muniesa 2020), a process involving the co-option of knowledge resources (Watkins and Stark 2018). Moreover, as Ana Gross and I note, the category of 'staple' produced in these practices seems designed to recruit political as well as economic actors as clients:[11] a staple food is a food that is eaten routinely and in such quantity that it constitutes a dominant portion of a standard diet in some populations, and thus identifies a politically significant population without the need to specify that population socio-demographically or territorially (although it can be made to do so). In 2015, Premise

> ... asked its collectors in Venezuela to photograph the lengths of queues outside supermarkets, gaps on shelves and signage that indicated rationing, to see the true effect of falling oil prices on the country's food supply. (The government was painting a rosier picture.) And it predicted the outcome of Brazil's 2014 presidential election by counting the number of posters for rival candidates on the streets of the country's cities. (https://www.wired.co.uk/article/ premise-app-food-tracking-brazil-philippines)

A further example – an attempt to build a personalized CPI – illuminates other aspects of what is involved in creating a CPI in its failure. In collaboration with an interaction designer, Dawn Nafus, a researcher at Intel Research Labs, experimented with the practice of 'critical making' (2014). Her stated aim was to build physical sensor-related software and hardware able to show sensor data in different numerical forms. One of the devices to be designed was intended to allow individuals to scan product barcodes to produce their own personal price variation index. However, the hope of generating a 'personalized' CPI, through which people could critically reflect on their individual relationship to collective spending, was soon thwarted. Although a scanning technology was made available to enable individuals to record prices, no way was found to link personal purchasing realities to the publicly available aggregations involved in making this index at a regional or national level.

In a second – more successful – case of critical making also discussed by Nafus, a different kind of problem space was brought into existence. In this case, an interaction-design initiative aimed to develop a comparative metric which could employ the sensor data that the users of the website Pachube (https://www.haque.co.uk/pachube.php) were already uploading. The data on home energy sensors, largely generated by the 'data enthusiasts' or 'activists' of Pachube, is described by Nafus as 'dead' or 'trapped' prior to the design intervention, but was brought 'to life' when the sensor users could put a visualization of their own collected data on indoor temperature alongside the outdoor temperature. In these experiments in critical making, Nafus is interested in the 'un-stopping' of the data, and in the kinds of labour that are involved in making numbers 'lively'. Her claim is that the ability of measures to index or 'point towards' a referent derives from the mobility of data as supported – or not – within a wider ecology. As in Kurgan's (2013) discussion of the para-empirical discussed in the previous chapter, she concludes by saying that data may be enabled to be an informant and generate new realities or they may be stalled and stopped in their tracks.

In this regard, it is worth noting not only that commercial entities such as PriceStats and Premise are now routinely involved in the collection of economic data, playing an increasingly significant role in the measurement of price and other economic indicators, but the sources of variation in prices themselves are being reconfigured (Muniesa 2007).

This is important as an example of the ways in which previously stable relations between data and meta-data are being challenged in the changing configuration of what was called an infra-ontology in the previous chapter. For example, prices are currently being re-personalized after a long period of de-personalization. As Liz Moor and I observe (2018), systems of 'fluctuating' pricing, 'dynamic' or 'surge' pricing are on the increase, and there are claims that fixed prices in supermarkets will be obsolete within the next few years, as retailers take advantage of electronic systems allowing them to adjust prices on an ongoing basis to reflect demand. As new pricing strategies reconfigure price as dynamic and contextually 'aware', the question of how to understand its signal in terms of representation and representativeness becomes more and more difficult to answer, while the methodological possibilities afforded by participation – of people (consumers), but also products and packaging – are on the increase. In addition, the rise of multiple kinds of currencies – cryptocurrencies and local currencies of all kinds – as well as the increase in mobile money services and the growth of the payments industry (Maurer 2012) provide challenges to the state-sanctioned and territorially grounded value of money itself, meaning that the relation between price and money is less and less a matter for the state alone.

Platformization

The case of the CPI was chosen to illustrate how the possibilities of composing problem spaces are changing today with transformations in the epistemic infrastructure. But methodologies for indexing human value have never been fixed. For example, Jane Guyer identifies 'three "modern" benchmarks for an index of human value in money terms' and proposes that 'we are perhaps now living the inception of a fourth'. The benchmarks are 'a status equation, a labour-reproductive value equation, a citizenship-value equation, and an asset-value equation' (2016: 182). It is the shift between the third and fourth benchmark that is at play in the examples above, but as Guyer notes, the methodology of the CPI at any one time seems to,

> ... refer backward and forward in time across all these human valuation frameworks, potentially including income and expenditure from property and labor, then relating to the necessities and aspirations for citizens (and thereby social peace, welfare and mobilizability in collective effort), and then implicitly projecting life courses into a future which is now in the process of reframing and turbulence under a philosophy of investment in assets, such as "the ownership society" advocated by President George W. Bush and the Cato Institute since the first years of the twenty-first century. (2016: 185)

While the examples described above support Guyer's analysis, the focus was on the methods employed in each case, not only the individual methods of classification, observation, scraping, machine learning and critical making, but also how these methods are combined, who combines them, how often, for what purpose and with what effect; that is, the emphasis was on the composition of the problem space. From this point of view, one of the key features of the shift from the third to the fourth benchmark is the challenge to earlier numerical and political links between representation and representativeness as outlined in the previous chapter. Indeed, it seems as if 'the common space of measurement' laboriously brought into existence by the state, a space 'within which things may be compared, because the categories and encoding procedures are identical' (Desrosières 1998: 9), is being radically undermined. The shift in these and many other practices is also linked to the other vectors of change in the epistemic infrastructure described in the last chapter, including processes of explicitation, an expanded role for indexicality and associated transformations in distributed cognition, as well as displaying continuities with and challenges to the established geo-politics of methodology along with a new emphasis on participation by citizens, a gig economy workforce or free labour (Terranova 2000).

How then are we to understand this shift? John Law introduces the concept of a method assemblage to describe the ways in which methods are brought together in specific arrangements – a method assemblage 'works in and "knows" multiplicity, indefiniteness, and flux' (2004: 14):

> ... they detect, resonate with, and amplify particular patterns of relations in the excessive and overwhelming fluxes of the real. This, then, is a definition of method assemblage: it is a combination of reality detector and reality amplifier. (2004: 14)

Law, Ruppert and Savage (2011) use the term method assemblage to describe sites set up to produce data while, as noted in the previous chapter, N. Katherine Hayles (2016) mobilizes the concept of cognitive assemblages to describe the arrangements in which different kinds of (conscious and non-conscious) cognition are brought together. One advantage of the concept of assemblage is that it specifies that the nature of the relations between its components' parts are not fixed or predetermined. However, the specific transformations in methodology discussed here suggest that it may be helpful to consider the ongoing shift in terms of the rise of a specific kind of assemblage – namely, a platform, and to say that we are witnessing *the platformization of the epistemic infrastructure*.

In discussing the contemporary economy, Guyer (2016) uses the term platform as an alternative to the term market, and proposes 'platform economy' as an alternative to 'market economy'. My proposal for the use of the term platform in relation to changes in the epistemic infrastructure is in part motivated by the rise of private companies with an investment in methodology such as PriceStats and Premise, as well as other aspects of the rise of a market in knowledge production, including the growth of a market in metrics. As Plantin et al. point out, there is a general trend in which digital technologies have made possible 'lower cost, more dynamic, and more competitive alternatives to governmental or quasi-governmental monopoly infrastructures, in exchange for a transfer of wealth and responsibility to private enterprises' (2016: 306). At the same time (and this is Guyer's point), it is not simply 'the market' that is transforming – or deforming – the common space of measurement established by the state: one of the responses of the Argentinian government to the controversy about the accuracy of the figures produced by the state sponsored agency of the National Statistics Agency was to propose a kind of citizen science initiative – 'To Look in Order to Protect'. As part of this scheme ordinary citizens could acquire the identity of 'verifiers' (alongside official price monitors) by checking the prices of 500 products, products whose prices were forcibly frozen by the government in a political agreement with big supermarket chains. If the prices did not conform to those agreed by government and retailers, then the verifiers could call a free telephone line to inform government officials who would then take action in 'defence' of the consumer.

And there are numerous initiatives such as those essayed by Nafus in which people engage in a variety of practices of quantification and make measures for their own purposes. Perhaps the most well-known example of this is the Quantified Self Movement (https://quantifiedself.com; see Neff and Nafus 2016), the members of which aspire to 'Self-knowledge through numbers'. In recent years, this organization has been working on

... the launch of a new nonprofit organization called Article 27, whose mission is to advance the human right to participate in science. Inspired by the achievements of the Quantified Self community, we want to do what we can to help everybody trying to learn about themselves using empirical methods. (https://quantifiedself.com/blog/human-right-to-science)

In short, like Guyer, my use of the term platformization is not simply to do with a process of marketization or economization, but is motivated by a recognition of the importance of the characteristics that she ascribes to platforms for the composition of problem spaces, namely that they are 'a combination of architecture, standard applications, and spaces for novel performances' (2016: 112). The concept, she says, provides 'a new heading that already expects tangles, junctures, cacophonies, and combinations ... of "market devices", as well as structures with durational qualities and frontiers of innovation' (2016: 114). One way to sum this up in relation to the concerns of this book is to say that platforms are mediators in the composition of problem spaces; as such, they 'transform, translate, distort, and modify the meaning of the elements they are supposed to carry' (Latour 2005: 39).

In the next chapter I take up and develop this idea of the platformization of epistemic infrastructures by considering the characteristics of platforms, and outline some of the ways in which platformization is transforming the possibilities of composing problem spaces.

– 4 –

Platforms and the Epistemic Infrastructure

Describing News Corp's purchase of MySpace in the pages of *Wired*, Jeremy Philips (vice-president) also found the term [platform] useful: 'News Corp's traditional media business has two legs: content and distribution', he says. Then he sketched a circle in between. 'That's where MySpace fits. It's neither one nor the other, though it shares aspects of both. It's a media platform, and a very powerful and adaptable one. Which is why it has such enormous potential.'

Tarleton Gillespie (2010: 351)

This chapter develops the proposal that platformization is a crucial process, harnessing – and modifying – many aspects of the vectors of change in the epistemic infrastructure identified in the previous two chapters, recomposing the methodological potential afforded by the socio-cognitive topologies of problem spaces.

Platformization

In the last chapter I outlined the understanding of platform used by Jane Guyer (2016) in her analysis of a platform economy. To develop the significance of platformization for an understanding of problem spaces I now turn to one of the earliest and most influential accounts of platforms, that provided by Tarleton Gillespie in a discussion of digital media (2010). He groups the uses of the term into four categories: architectural, political, computational and figurative. He says, 'the emergence of "platform" as a descriptive term for digital media intermediaries represents none of these, but depends on all four' (2010: 349). It is in this quadruple duty that the concept of platformization is enrolled here to describe changes in the epistemic infrastructure: while I will outline each category of use in turn, what matters for the composition of problem spaces is how they come together.

Indeed, this is what is important to Guyer, who also draws on Gillespie. She values the capaciousness and currency of the term as a way to make use of 'the full range of the analytical toolkit', facing 'straight on, the importance of locally specific entanglements of regulations, practices, rational choice, and future imagination-anticipation under rapidly shifting technological and political conditions in an interconnected world' (2016: 111). Platforms, she says, have the capacity to be changed by as well as change the activities that they support. Nevertheless, what matters about platforms, she concludes, is their durability, their dependability across whatever temporal rhythms emerge in their use.

1. The architectural
According to Gillespie, the oldest definition of platform is *architectural*: 'A raised level surface on which people or things can stand, usually a discrete structure intended for a particular activity or operation' (OED 2006 in Gillespie

2010: 349). In this use, 'platform' describes 'human-built or naturally formed physical structures, whether generic or dedicated to a specific use: subway and train platforms, Olympic diving platforms, deep-sea oil-rig platforms, platform shoes' (2010: 349). In relation to methodology, this 'raised level surface' is typically comprised of the institutions associated with macro-epistemic actors, including religious institutions, the state, funding bodies, government and associated bodies such as universities, military bodies, large-scale sites and instruments of scientific research, data-bases and national statistics offices. These established actors have recently been joined by the major technology companies, GAFAM (Google, Apple, Facebook, Amazon and Microsoft) in the West, and the so-called 'three kingdoms' of the Chinese internet (Baidu, Alibaba and Tencent) in Asia, which, so David Nieborg and Thomas Poell (2018) argue, are reconfiguring the production, distribution and monetization of many kinds of products and services, of which knowledge is but one.

Alongside religious, military and state-associated organizations 'dedicated directly to the production of knowledge, or taking on specific knowledge-related tasks in larger knowledge contexts' (Knorr Cetina 2007: 367) are the organizations of civil society (journalism, publishing houses, museums, galleries and the media as well as NGOs and charities), the R&D arms of commercial bodies in medicine, pharmaceuticals, agriculture, engineering, architecture, urban planning and elsewhere, by regulatory bodies of all kinds and marketing and advertising companies, lobbying organizations and think-tanks. As Knorr Cetina says, '… organizations outside the narrower fields of academic science … have specific epistemic roles and functions, for example observer roles, representing roles, validating roles' (2007: 367).

Different knowledge platforms are layered in different ways and connect to and disconnect from each other in diverse ways. For example, Adrian Mackenzie notes that the more than '100 Data Science Institutes [that] have been set up in North America, Europe, and UK since around 2012' are interconnected in a variety of ways: 'The traffic between higher education and data analytics in industry is intense and flows in several forms: people funding, research findings, software, and technical devices (code) and training' (2018: 13). Similarly, Hannah Griffiths (2019) identifies a range of 'underlying infrastructure or platforms' in urban planning, including test beds ('physical or virtual infrastructure that enables experimentation, development or testing of products'); living labs ('user-centred, open innovation ecosystems that use a co-creation approach to solutions or service development in real-life settings'); proving grounds ('typically comprise open-access, private realm, controlled environment facilities to enable the testing of new solutions'); test networks (open-access communication networks, typically available for non-commercial purposes, to enable the prototyping of new products and services'); and virtual demonstration platforms ('digital representations of real locations that enable collaborative, virtual experimentation, improved planning and informed decision-making') (2019: 16–17).

Most, perhaps all, of these bodies put edges or boundaries around their platforms, notably in policies of state and commercial secrecy, the use of intellectual property law (as in copyright, patent, and trademark and associated legal conventions as well as e-commerce and personal data protection legislation), proprietary (sometimes commercial) control over source code, software packages and data (through licences, contracts, Digital Rights Management tools[1] and so on), standardization, restricted access to libraries, archives and other repositories, as well as through control of terms of qualifications and training of personnel, the use of methods of evaluation and review, and sometimes the operation of various kinds of 'lock-in', through techniques as various as enforcing technical dependencies, bundling packages, and building in constraints on the movement of key actors who may be prevented by contract from taking their knowledge and clients with them when they leave an organization.

But few platforms are completely closed; indeed, cross-platform communication is critical to the making of epistemic circuits, new and old. So, for example, Knorr Cetina describes the global financial architecture in terms of relations between units of various kinds:

> ... the international financial system is an epistemic system: it rests on the architecture of observation rules and strategies, of the units that generate and process the observations (e.g. statistical offices, rating agencies, research departments of banks), and of the information flows that circulate between these units. Moreover, the epistemic system safeguards the economic system. Information rules and strategies seek to discover the 'truth' of units' states and other relevant developments in order to detect possible problem areas, anticipate ripple effects and spot signs of turns in economic cycles ...
>
> The units in the circuit do not produce a single outcome and no one may fully publish their results. Nonetheless, we are confronted with a knowledge system; it is the design of the system, for example the epistemic rights and procedures of the respective units, which is at stake in discussions of the global financial architecture. (2007: 368)

Sometimes the edges emerge in unanticipated ways, as for example, a consequence of the opacity of algorithmic processing, leading commentators such as Frank Pasquale (2015) to suggest that we live in a black box society. But not surprisingly, despite attempts to police the edges, most platforms are subject to overflows or leaks of a variety of kinds, as well as being the sites of hacking, reverse engineering, and other kinds of re-purposing. And such activities present methodological opportunities for actors other than, as well as, the proprietors or approved users of a platform. For example, Ana Gross describes data leaks as 'empirical occasions through which the contextualization of data and the devices, techniques and methods that make such contextualization possible, become visible and legible for analysis' (2015: 11–12). Fuller and Goffey say:

> The leak ... is an attempt to capture and mobilize the dynamics of unintended consequences, to enter into the domain of the accident, the double agent, confusion, and to render it fruitful. The leak, however, is never simply bivalent. For some, everything cries out for it, trying, if only by dint of time, to edge its way past the demon of the chamber of equivalence in which it is trapped, hungry for a connection, the accident of knowledge, for that or the chance to turn to dust, unnoticed and indifferent. (Fuller and Goffey 2012: 103)

Drawing on Michel Serres' figure of the parasite (2007), Aradau et al. re-conceptualize hacking as 'acts of digital parasitism': 'parasitic relations are transversal in the sense in which they introduce a "third", a surplus which modifies existing relations by working alongside or beside rather than working against them' (2019: 25–55). What or who is a host or a parasite is, however, not always easy to identify.

The defining characteristics of platforms as described in economic sociology is that they bring together two or more distinct user groups that provide each other with network benefits. But one of the major issues facing designers of such platforms is how to motivate user groups to use the platform when, as is common, the benefits of doing so are not symmetrically distributed between users. A prime example of a platform as a multi-sided market is Facebook, which in 2007 made public its API (application programming interface) to allow third parties to design PHP or Javascript widgets that users can incorporate into their profiles (Facebook 2009). YouTube is another example of the 'double articulation' of communicative mediation that occurs as social media platforms are folded within an economic logic (Langlois et al. 2009).

As Gillespie observes of YouTube, the difficulty facing platforms that are multi-sided markets are those of producing a stage on which all parties can perform:

> YouTube must present its service not only to its users, but to advertisers, to major media producers it hopes to have as partners and to policymakers. The term 'platform' helps reveal how YouTube and others stage themselves for these constituencies, allowing them to make a broadly progressive sales pitch while also eliding the tensions inherent in their service: between user-generated and commercially produced content, between cultivating community and serving up advertising, between intervening in the delivery of content and remaining neutral. In the process, it is offering up a trope by which others will come to understand and judge them. (2010: 348)

In other words, platformization does not simply introduce many sides to a market or an organization. It also transforms how sides, limits or boundaries function as operating conditions; how they connect as well as separate. In relation to changes in the epistemic infrastructure, platformization complicates how distinctions are drawn between inside and outside, and how transfers are conducted across layers. In the process, platformization reconfigures possibilities for the compulsion of composition, changing the kind of knowledge that emerges.

An example: Halpern et al. (2013) argue that with the emergence of test-bed urbanism we are witnessing:

> a new form of epistemology that is concerned not with documenting facts in the world, mapping spaces, or making representative models but rather with creating models that *are* territories. Performative, inductive, and statistical, the experiments enacted in this space

transform territory, population, truth, and risk with implications for representative government, subjectivity, and urban form. (Halpern et al. 2013: 274–5)

Knorr Cetina says of the global financial system that its organization is such that what is valued is knowledge as information:

I use the notion [of information] to suggest a specific epistemic attitude that locates relevance not on the level of underlying laws but on the level of surface events. Information reports knowledge of events and some of their causes, but this knowledge tends not to be processed further in the system with respect to the regularities and laws that govern the events. In other words, what appears to be at stake in information circuits is not truth in the sense of lasting findings but news, knowledge of relevant developments in a continually changing environment. The shift to news implies a shift in temporality away from the large amounts of time required by research and toward speed in identifying and reporting the news content. But a deeper aspect is that information-knowledge in the area discussed tends to be interpreted with respect to an expected future and used as a basis for implementing financial moves. In this process, information-knowledge gets used up: usage changes the conditions of relevance for what counts as knowledge and information. (2007: 368)

2. The political

As these examples already suggest, the second, *political*, meaning of platform emerges from the architectural meaning. '[R]eferring first to the actual stage constructed for a candidate to address an audience, from which they would articulate their political beliefs' (Gillespie 2010: 350), the meaning of the term has come to include the beliefs being articulated:

Puritan ministers in colonial New England could issue
their statement on the governance of the church as
'The Cambridge Platform' in 1648; in 2008 the US
Democratic and Republican parties could support
their respective presidential candidates by publishing
their party platforms ... . We still sometimes refer to
individual political positions as 'planks', or ask where
a candidate 'stands' on an issue, subtle reminders of
the term's legacy. (Gillespie 2010: 350)

In these examples, a term that generally implied 'a kind
of neutrality towards use – "platforms" are typically flat,
featureless and open to all – carries a political valence,
where a position must be taken' (Gillespie 2010: 350).

In relation to methodology, it is possible to see a shift
from a platform as a material support to a platform as
the facilitation of a position on that support happening at
a variety of interconnected levels. For example, Calkins
and Rottenburg suggest that 'infrastructures of evidence
... reconfigure the worths [that is, the general or widely
accepted values] at play in a situation or controversy by
enabling certain types of information to circulate, while
disabling other types from moving and becoming known'
(2016: 258). An example is documented in Uprichard
et al.'s (2008) analysis of statistical software packages.
The authors observe that, from the late 1960s onwards,
'there have probably been 50 or more [statistical software]
systems that have been utilized for teaching and research'
(2008: 606). They focus on one package which, during the
period they studied, was consistently popular: SPSS, and
describe the changes the package underwent. The package
was first put together by academics but, although SPSS
initially 'stood for the Statistical Package for the Social
Sciences, it is now no longer an acronym but a named
software *brand*', and the software's potential users are
no longer described as social scientists on the company's
website, but, rather, as 'those seeking "business solutions"'
(2008: 607). The authors further observe that while

SPSS is still concerned with some things most sociologists will recognize: market research, survey research, public health, administration and institutional research, statistics, structural equation modelling, education, government and health ... [there are many] other items ... with which most sociologists may be less familiar: marketing effectiveness, fraud detection and prevention, risk management, enterprise feedback management, business intelligence, data mining, text mining, web analytics, financial services, insurance, retail, telecommunications and, at the top of the list, predictive analytics. According to SPSS, this shift in software development was to meet an "expanding need for understanding ever–increasing volumes of data, and to support ... the widespread use of data in decision–making". (2008: 613)

The authors conclude:

... the profound and stark transformation of SPSS from a tool for empirical social research to a corporate behemoth primarily concerned with something called 'predictive analytics' ... has been fast and dramatic. (2008: 607)

Of the various stages in this transformation they identify one of the most significant as the introduction in the mid–1980s of a mainframe statistical package able to run on a PC. This development 'not only resulted in a different way of *doing* quantitative research, but in a different *kind* of quantitative research as well' (2008: 611). Indeed, while the authors suggest that a wholesale shift in concern from cause to description may over-state the change they describe, they are confident that SPSS did not broaden 'its analytical capacities randomly' (2008: 6017); that is, the platform-enhanced package took a position by displaying a certain kind of methodological valence.

Table 1 A schematic overview of changes in British quantitative sociological research

Shift	'Old Face'	Emerging 'New Face'?
Technique	• Parsimonious model building, e.g. multiple regression analysis, factor analysis, multi-level analysis, etc.	• Describing and exploring groups, e.g. cluster analysis, simulation (micro–simulation and agent–based simulation especially), correspondence analysis, QCA, etc.
Generalization	• Generalization as possible, reliable and desirable	• Move to 'moderatum generalization' which is somewhat reliable, but remains more or less enduring relative to future research and findings
Causality	• Single causes • Linear causal models • General causal 'laws' – outcome consistently explained through particular variable interactions • Faith in 'finding' causes	• Multiple, contingent causality • Configurational causality: same outcome possible through different variable configurations; different outcomes possible through same variable outcome • Complex, nonlinear and in flux • Less faith in 'finding' causes
Prediction	• Onus on predicting the ultimate single future • Considered possible	• Onus on describing multiple possible futures instead of determining one simple future • Possibility of prediction becomes questionable
Sampling	• Probability sample as best possible form of knowing population • Sample used statistically to infer sample findings to population • Statistical significance testing as key to understanding population	• Population data widely available through increased digitization of data • Statistical inference is seen as unnecessary • Probability sample used to confirm descriptions of population rather than inferring them
Interpretation	• Focus on explanation and confirmation	• Focus on description, exploration, classification, case profiling and visualization.
Variables and Cases	• Focus on the variable	• Focus on the case and describing types of cases.

The research for the study shown in Table 1 ended in 2008. If you search for information about SPSS on the Internet now, one of the top links that comes up is: https://www.predictiveanalyticstoday.com/category/buying-guides. This is a website for a company called PAT Research: 'a B2B discovery platform which provides Best Practices, Buying Guides, Reviews, Ratings, Comparison, Research, Commentary and Analysis for Enterprise Software and Services. We provide Best Practices, PAT Index™ enabled product reviews and user review comparisons to help IT decision-makers such as CEOs, CIOs, Directors and Executives to identify technologies, software, services and strategy.' It seems as if the transformation Uprichard et al. identify has continued: as part of a process of platformization, not only have the number of statistical software packages multiplied, but the political valence that Gillespie identifies is recognized and used to distinguish one package from another for commercial ends.

However, as argued in the last chapter, the political dimension of platformization is not restricted to marketization; that is, while platforms can support (multi-sided) markets they typically combine market-based and social forms of coordination, enabling heterogeneous forms of political-methodological organization. Consider Alberto Corsín Jiménez's account of 'open-source urbanism' (2014), as part of which he identifies the emergence of a right to infrastructure. There are three dimensions to this right as he sees it. One is conceptual: so, for example, projects in open-source urbanism populate urban ecologies with novel digital and material entities whose emergence destabilizes classical regulatory distinctions between public, private or commercial property forms, technologies and spaces. The second is technical: open-source urban projects are built on networks of expertise and skills that traverse localized boundaries.

Decentralized communities working in open source projects have to reach prior consensus over the methods, protocols, and standards to be applied. These decisions often generate new designs, techniques, and rules for certification. (2014: 343)

The third dimension Corsín Jiménez identifies is political: open-source projects transform the stakes in and modes of urban governance. In an open-source project, he says, a community may assume political and expert management of its infrastructure. An example is *In the Air* (http://www.intheair.es; Calvillo 2012), a visualization project that makes 'visible the microscopic and invisible agents of Madrid's air (gases, particles, pollen, diseases, etc.), to see how they perform, react and interact with the rest of the city', a 'platform for individual and collective awareness and decision-making, where the interpretation of results can be used for real time navigation through the city, opportunistic selection of locations according to their air conditions and a base for political action'. If the three dimensions are brought together, Corsín Jiménez suggests, the right to infrastructure becomes a verb, not a noun.

The process of infrastructuring makes visible and legible the languages, media, inscriptions, artefacts, devices, and relations – the betagrams – through which political and social agencies are endowed with any expressive capacity whatsoever. (2014: 357)

The new possibilities for infrastructuring and the associated redistribution of epistemic agency, including infrastructural inversion (Bowker 2016), that is, the process of making explicit and working on the epistemic infrastructure itself, is also part of the significance of political platformization for the composition of problem spaces.

3. The computational
The third, *computational*, use of platform is the explicit focus of Gillespie's article: as the epigraph to this chapter suggests, he highlights the description of YouTube and

Facebook, and even the whole of Web 2.0 by industry representatives and academics with this term:

> ... Tim O'Reilly of O'Reilly Media, whose business seems to be discursive as much as anything else, proclaimed that 'Web 2.0 is the network as platform, spanning all the connected devices; Web 2.0 applications are those that make the most of the intrinsic advantages of that platform' ... . In classic O'Reilly style, he draws a term from the computational lexicon, further loosens it from the specific technical meaning and layers on to it both a cyber-political sense of liberty and an info-business taste of opportunity. (2010: 352)

It is hard to deny that the epistemic infrastructure is significantly and increasingly technological (although the non-technological aspects of the epistemic infrastructure should not be downplayed):

> Seen from the empirical end, changes of Internet technologies and related knowledge technologies (social media, crowdsourcing, wikis, big data, open source software, open access, citizen science, MOOC, etc.) have altered the basic mechanics by which knowledge is produced and circulated, and these new forms of infrastructuring demand theoretical recalibrations. (Calkins and Rottenburg 2016: 254)

As Fuller and Mazurov put it, the technical is a significant 'intermediary and mobile scale by which other scales are articulated, traced and composed' (2019: 177). So, for example, computational platforms often assign 'the actuality, probability or likelihood of a trace-bearing relation between things and processes' (Fuller and Mazurov 2019: 174), providing the often-unacknowledged basis for many regimes of fact-making and decision-taking.

Take the case of the platformization of mapping. As Jean-Christophe Plantin and Alison Powell note, maps have been described as:

> ... closed information systems that both reflect and enforce the power of the state ... . They constitute strategic information administered by knowledge infrastructures ... such as the Ordnance Survey in the UK or the IGN in France. Maps act as strategic tools through which a state 'creates a kind of national transparency through the uniformity of codes, identities, statistics, regulations, and measures. (2016)

In recent years, however, there have been a variety of initiatives to 'open up' maps by adopting the logic of web-based platforms, including the development of GoogleMaps and OpenStreetMaps (Perkins 2003; Hind and Lammes 2016). Plantin and Powell suggest that while such platform maps combine with existing infrastructures in, for example, their reliance on open geographic data from national institutes, they nevertheless have a distinctive logic: they 'recentralize knowledge production while remaining open'. On the one hand, accessing geographic knowledge is rendered easier for platform users, while on the other the affordances of the platform allow for multiple commercial and other uses of everyday or citizen use. In these ways, they suggest, platforms are altering the relationship between knowledge and citizenship:

> ... on one hand, platforms promote an exercise of citizenship that revolves around notions of openness and participation. On the other hand, this open and participatory conception of citizenship runs the risk of appropriation and enclosure through the same platforms that promote them, hence limiting autonomy and democracy. (2016)

This case is just one example of what Adrian Mackenzie

and Anna Munster (2019) describe as the automation of visual culture associated with the rise of computational platforms. As noted in Chapter 2, they argue that transformations in the collection and accumulation of images as ensembles is having a profound qualitative and material effect, enabling the partial, situated and multiple nature of observation to be exploited in a variety of new ways.

Koed Madsen (2013) provides another example. He develops a framework to study what he calls web-vision analysis; that is, filter-driven modes of seeing embedded in computational platforms, where filters are understood to act as 'epistemology engines', delineation devices, screened visions or, in terms drawn directly from economic sociology, as distributed calculative spaces. He distinguishes between myopic vision, which is focused by the platform filter and hyperopic vision which, he says, is what can be seen by the researcher's operationalization of the filter. The first constrains the second in another example of how computational platformization configures the possibilities of research.

4. The figurative

The fourth and final use of the term platform identified by Gillespie is *figurative*. He reports the relevant OED definition as 'the ground, foundation, or basis of an action, event, calculation, condition, etc. Now also: a position achieved or situation brought about which forms the basis for further achievement' (2010: 350). In this use, the original understanding of platform as a physical stage becomes a meta-physical one for opportunity, action and insight, and the ground of action is not fixed or stable, but constantly shifting in response to that action.

In the understanding of the platform as figurative, there is a recognition of the methodological significance of the patterning of inquiry, as the relation between figure and ground is activated in dynamic practices of ground-truth-ing as well as an acknowledgement of the ability of platforms to support a diversity of processes of configuring

(Suchman, 2012) as in the case of multi-sided markets above. Some of the implications for the composition of problem spaces of the possibilities of configuring afforded by platforms are illuminated by Laurent Thévenot's (1984; 2009) concept of 'investment in form'. This term provides a way to think about what Guyer (2016) considers a key characteristic of platforms, that is, their durability across whatever temporal rhythms emerge in their use as well as drawing attention to the work that is involved in platform maintenance and operation.

By investment in form, Thévenot means, 'a costly operation to establish a stable relation with a certain lifespan', which can be performed through a 'great variety of formatting operations, from the material constraint of standardization to the moral imperative of engagement, and the obligation of conventions':

> Conforming and informing both require and are preceded by acts of giving form. This is why an 'investment in form', which might rely on different 'formats of information' [...] is the keystone that joins 'regulation' and 'objectivity'.

He suggests that the returns on such an investment, in terms of coordination, vary according to three dimensions:

> ... the temporal and spatial validity of the form, and the solidity of the material equipment involved. Once an investment has been made, it will have a 'temporal validity': that is, the period of time in which it is operative in a community of users. It will also have a 'spatial validity', which refers to the boundaries demarcating the community within which the form will be valid. This is why participating in the process of form-giving can be a means to prevent a standard from becoming external to one's own concerns, and therefore, potentially exclusionary. (Thévenot, 2009: 794)

Some of the complications this can involve are highlighted in Gromme and Ruppert's description of the implementation of an anticipatory logic in the design of a platform:

> While flexibility is desired to meet unknown future needs, inevitably infrastructures are designed in anticipation of known ones: they configure in advance data on what is relevant in relation to governing problems expressed as "needs." In doing so they can close off other possibilities, such as problems and needs not (yet) known or recognized ... But policies also anticipate their infrastructures: they are generative of demands for new data because of their implementation. (2019: 254)

A well-documented example of the investment in form that is required by the configuration of a platform is the setting up of the European Rare Diseases Platform discussed by Éric Dagiral and Ashveen Peerbaye (2016). In interview with the authors, one director of the French Muscular Dystrophy Association said, '... we wanted to function as a platform. The idea is that in order to make progress on such a topic, we need to advance in a systematic, global fashion, tackling things from all sides, provided that there is a minimum of coordination and consistency in approaches' (2016: 48). While the production of knowledge was always intended to be one of the principal outputs of the platform, it was also always to be articulated with other kinds of activities or infrastructural work, including those of patient groups. In this articulation or configuration, this (investment in) form led to the making of distinctions between knowledge and 'mere' information. Dagiral and Peerbaye say: 'Here, this kind of boundary work (Gieryn 1999) serves as a resource in strategies to embed competing visions and goals into the boundary infrastructure, define priorities, and allocate resources for carrying out different tasks related to rare disease initiatives' (2016: 46).

While it is undoubtedly the case that the positionality of those carrying out boundary work informs how likely their work is to succeed (do Mar Pereira 2018), there are also examples in which inequalities in those positions are explicitly acknowledged in the doing of the work with the aim of overcoming them. Take, for example, the People's Biodiversity Register project in India described by Moe Nakazora (2106). She describes this as an instance of reflexive infrastructural inversion in which a project team consisting of local plant taxonomists, phytochemists and an anthropologist worked together to codify scientifically the environmental knowledge of local people. She says, 'Although the initiative to database "Indian" biodiversity and related traditional wisdom may appear as a "new imperial project" ... in fact it also includes an interest in "an identity switch" of the Indian archive; that is, it entails an effort to go beyond colonialism by new database construction' (2016: 310). She describes what Thévenot would call an investment in form as an attempt to create the possibility of 'a dynamic archive that captures knowledge in motion as performance' (2016: 311) by making the meta-data – the categories of classification – amenable to rewriting by users (a practice described as parataxonomy). She suggests this ambition – to exploit the parataxonomic potential of classification – can be understood in terms of the interdisciplinary concept of 'emergence' becoming experimentally and reflexively integrated in databases: 'It is becoming part and parcel of postcolonial attempts to make databases more "democratic" and more flexible' (2016: 312). In the terms being developed here, it is an example of the meta-physical dynamics of the configurational dimension of platformization.

The emphasis given to temporalities in this fourth, figurative capacity of platforms is also significant for the changing composition of problem spaces insofar as it speaks to the staging of their 'ongoingness'. This is perhaps most easily recognized in descriptions of data collection and analysis as 'real-time', descriptions that have been deployed (and criticized) from a wide variety of perspectives (Back and Puwar 2012; see also http://www.case-stories.org/blog/2014/7/24/part-1-every-minute-of-every-day-an-experiment-in-realtime-ethnography-yasmin-gunaratnam-and-les-back, as well as calls for slow research: https://www.slowlab.net/ABOUT). Equally importantly, the figurative dimensions of platforms enable a wide variety of approaches to causality, including a variety of alternatives to previously dominant linear-causal models of prediction (Amoore 2013).

An example is provided by Adrian Mackenzie (2019) in a discussion of recent shifts in programming practice at Facebook. He suggests that there has been a significant growth in predictive programmability, which he understands in terms of an increasingly experimental interplay between processes of platformization and infrastructuralization. He quotes Facebook senior software engineer Joseph Dunn's description of a new platform within Facebook:

> We decided to build a brand-new platform, FBLearner Flow, capable of easily reusing algorithms in different products, scaling to run thousands of simultaneous custom experiments, and managing experiments with ease. This platform provides innovative functionality, like automatic generation of UI experiences from pipeline definitions and automatic parallelization of Python code using futures. FBLearner Flow is used by more than 25 percent of Facebook's engineering team. Since its inception, more than a million models have been trained, and our prediction service has grown to make more than 6 million predictions per second. (Dunn, 2016 in Mackenzie 2019: 1995)

He further suggests that opacity (not transparency) is a constitutive opportunity for such platforms rather than a proprietary limitation:

Rather than simply implementing predictive engines to drive recommendations or advertising, the flow of models suggests an experimental practice concerned with constant modification, mutation and commutation of elements of the Facebook platform. (Mackenzie 2019: 1996)

But the epistemological validity of such methodological practices is widely questioned. There are those who put their faith in models that make six million predictions per second (as the platform described by Mackenzie is capable of doing), but there is also an increasingly vocal lack of trust in expertise.[2]

As discussed in Chapter 1, causal figuration has been conceptualized in relation to literary history as a process of progressive fulfilment, and as an incitement for innovation: as such, it deploys a form of spatio-temporality that is specifically Western and both historicist and modern. In his explication of the role of Erich Auerbach's understanding of causal figuration in the conception of literary history, Hayden White writes:

... although the history of Western literature displays the plot structure of a redemption, this redemption takes the form less of a fulfillment of a promise than of an ever renewed promise of fulfilment. (1991: 88)

While understanding literary history in terms of causal figuration allowed Auerbach 'to endow [that] history with a meaning of a *progressus* toward a goal that is never ultimately realizable nor even fully specifiable' (White 1991: 88), dwindling belief in the possibility of renewing this promise is, I suggest, precisely what is at issue in the curious oscillation between theological and empirical justifications for democratic governance that Kelly and McGoey (2018) identify as a characteristic of the contemporary empire of truth.

Finally, the figurative dimension of platformization also

resonates with the use of the concept of figures by Donna Haraway (1997), that is, as performative images that can be inhabited. Most of the symbolic figures that emerge across platforms involving social media, such as #JesuisCharlie, are not the outcome of purposeful methodological design, but they may have significant epistemological dimensions, and are often subject to tests of validity. While claims of accuracy are typically widely contested (and have led to the rise of a variety of human and non-human fact-checking tools and services: see Marres 2018), they are nonetheless transforming the terms of public debate, and provide the basis for the emergence of competing vocabularies of truth.

#MeToo provides a salutatory example in this respect; it is a cognitive assemblage, a moving ratio, emerging across and outside social media, in which authenticity, belief, doubt and speculation are the always contingent outcome of a serial calibration of signal and noise, interference and (un)certainty' (Lury forthcoming), raising the question of the scale at which claims to truth can be made. While the speech of participants in #JesuisCharlie, #MeToo, and #BlackLivesMatter may not 'count' as public opinion, or be accepted as evidence in court, as they metamorphose across space these figures illustrate both the changing grounds for truth that are involved in the move from representation to participation discussed in Chapter 2, and the vertiginous implications for those captured in or captivated by such spaces.

Fundamental to the significance of the understanding of platform as figurative, then, is the issue of how figures are inhabited, including the kinds of performance, participation and pedagogy they require or invite, especially given Walton Mignolo's emphasis on the exploitation of 'literal laboratories in the sciences and metaphysical laboratories in the social sciences' (2009: 167). Understanding the figurative capacity of platforms in terms of habitability makes it possible to see, for example, that data science is populated by a variety of figures that do not always sustain life, and enables an interrogation of the way in which figures that speak to the desire for precision and totality, for prediction and prevention, for recognition and inclusiveness, animate the imaginary of big data in uneven, socially differentiated ways. Unfortunately, however, the political significance of participation or critical pedagogy in the production of such figures is often not acknowledged, although the example of the naming of the platform for the study of rare diseases and orphan drugs discussed above as Orphanet (orpha.net/; Dagiral and Peerbaye 2016), as well as a machine learning algorithm as a 'threat centaur' (Amoore 2019: 116)[3] indicates an awareness of the inter-relationship of human and non-human partners in the figures of platformization. And as movements as various as Black Lives Matter and The Quantified Self attempt to make clear it is how figures are inhabited – with what rights, obligations and responsibilities to others – that matters.[4]

Conclusion

This chapter has developed the claim that we are witnessing the platformization of the epistemic infrastructure; that is, that the epistemic infrastructure is increasingly colonized by platforms. It concludes by suggesting that platformization has implications for the composition of problem spaces insofar as it equips the epistemic infrastructure to be a boundary infrastructure, that is, '[an] infrastructure [that] serves multiple communities of practice simultaneously, be these within a single organization or distributed across multiple organizations' (Bowker and Star 2000: 313).

The proposal to be developed in the next chapter is that the diverse processes transforming the epistemic infrastructure described in Chapter 2 – explicitation, the changing semiotics of the epistemic infrastructure, the acknowledgement of the observer, the recalibration of the geo-politics of methodology, and the increasing role of participation, are being brought into relation with each other in uneven and sometimes unanticipated ways in platformization. The proposal is developed by drawing on Arjun Appadurai's account (2013) of the importance of the relationship between the circulation of forms and forms of circulation discussed in Chapter 1. His vocabulary allows for an analysis of the implications of platformization for the composition of problem spaces through a consideration of the forms of problems that emerge from the formal properties of plat-form circulation.

– Part III –
Compositional Methodology

– 5 –

More than Circular

At the initial stage, when nothing is yet determined,
one gets to know, through roundness, thanks to its
perfect adjustment to anything that may get started.
Later, once the process has begun, one proceeds in a
square way, maintaining stability.

François Jullien (2004: 128–9)

The Introduction and Part I outlined an understanding
of compositional methodology as the operation of the
potential of a problem as it emerges across a problem
space. The compulsion of composition was described as
the articulation of the double force of inventive methods,
the constitutive effects of methods and their capacity
to contribute to a problem's generative circulation. In
Chapter 2, the first of three chapters in Part II, some of
the ongoing changes in the epistemic infrastructure were
outlined. Chapter 3 gave some examples of how these
changes are being played out. Chapter 4 put forward
the thesis that we are witnessing the platformization
of the epistemic infrastructure. This chapter and the
next – together comprising Part III – aim to describe the

implications of platformization for compositional method-ology. To do this, they draw on Appadurai's identification of the importance of the inter-relationship of the circu-lation of forms and forms of circulation (2013) to describe the becoming topological of problem spaces in relation to platformization.

What is especially helpful about Appadurai's account in this regard is his insistence that circulation itself has formal properties.[1] The properties afforded to circulation by platforms, this chapter now suggests, are transforming the ways in which problems and problem spaces are composed, contributing to the emergence of new topologies of knowledge and value. In short, drawing on the four-fold understanding of platforms outlined in the previous chapter, the chapter develops the thesis that the boundary infra-structure associated with platformization now plays a key role in configuring the compulsion of composition: more specifically, by comparing model systems and platforms, it proposes that platforms act as a kind of methodological multiplier, producing novel methodological opportunities and dilemmas in the process of circulation.

This multiplication of methodological possibility is explored through a consideration of the circulatory property of recursion and the ways in which it enables 'experience or judgements about objects and events ... in connection with a contextual whole' (Dewey 1938: 72). This, you may remember, is the account of the logic of inquiry proposed by Dewey described in Chapter 1. This chapter suggests that the possibilities for recursion offered by platformization enhance the making of the 'active adaptive response to be made in carrying forward a course of behavior' that Dewey believes is involved in such a process, providing new possibilities for partial 'connection and continuity present in the experienced world while providing novel limiting conditions for generalization' (Dewey 1938: 7–8 in Brown 2012: 269).

Developing an understanding of the inter-relationship of the circulation of problems and platforms of circulation as recursive, the chapter describes the development of ways of getting to know through 'roundness' as Jullien (2004) describes. The chapter then describes some of the methodological troubles that ensue: the natively artificial character of the empirical; the multiplicity of the epistemological object; and the genus of cognitive syndromes that Bateson (1972) describes as transcontextualism. While they are distinguished here, each is often entangled with the others in the designs of an infra-ontology (Verran 2005; Corsín Jiménez 2017).

From model systems to platforms: the case of classification

I begin by comparing platforms to model systems, since such systems are said to be one of the primary ways in which facts 'travel' or circulate. For example, Michael Guggenheim and Monika Krause put forward the term to describe what they consider to be one of the most efficacious ways in which facts travel; model systems, they say, are fact-carriers. They further suggest that one of the things that makes model systems especially powerful is that they have the effect of focusing research, while enabling the pooling of resources. In this process, models will be precisely conceptualized, deliberately manipulated and standardized:

> A drosophila needs to have known, defined, and stabilized genes and known and stabilized forms of behaviour. Only once specimens are thus rendered stable, can they be summarized as a model system. Because of this feature, model systems allow facts to travel across contexts by seemingly making context irrelevant. (Guggenheim and Krause 2012: 103)

Indeed, standardization is sometimes explicitly enforced in the name of efficiency; sometimes, Guggenheim and

Krause say, research grants are more readily awarded if a certain model system is used.

While acknowledging that the term arose from a study of the discipline of biology (Creager et al. 2007), Guggenheim and Krause further suggest that the term model system subsumes 'exemplar', 'paradigmatic case', 'canonical case' and 'genre' in other disciplines.[2] All these terms describe a way to 'carry' or circulate facts (or claims to knowledge) because they allow research carried out on different occasions in different places to be considered comparable:

> Scientists working on a specific strain of drosophila can assume that there is no, or only very little, variance in the genotype and phenotype, and thus differences in research outcomes can be attributed to the research rather than the organism. (Guggenheim and Krause 2012: 103)

In this sense, model systems enable the circulation of problems to support techniques of generalization of a variety of kinds. More precisely, what characterizes the generalizing properties of model systems for Guggenheim and Krause is that they serve as: 'an object of study that ... stand[s] in for a more general class of epistemic objects' (2012: 104). Perhaps the most important methodological feature of such systems in this regard is that they allow the relationship between specimen ('the actual physical copy in front of the researcher' – for example, the life model in art, the novel in literature, drosophilia in biology, or the map in urban studies) and the epistemological object ('the object that is studied through this' – the nude, romanticism, diseases, territory) to be systematically varied in ways that enable epistemological claims to be made with confidence.

The thesis proposed here, however, is that platforms operate formal properties of circulation such that the methodological relations between an actual physical copy and the epistemological object being studied can be varied in ways that supplement the relations that have historically been developed in model systems. In short, the thesis is that platformization describes the emergence of a new configuration of the technologies, disciplinary expertise and resources in which the double force of methods is articulated, supplementing, transforming, perhaps even replacing the model system as the primary form of circulation or carrier of facts and transforming the ways in which claims to generalizability can be made.[3] To overstate the contrast somewhat,[4] whereas model systems enable facts – or more broadly, the epistemological values associated with cognitive success – to be produced and then reproduced (or circulated), platforms enable such values to be constituted *in* circulation (Wark 2018, 2019).[5]

Let me give an example of how this is happening: the changing ways in which classifications are being produced. In his discussion of the 'recombinatorics' of search, link and interact, Stark (2011) suggests that established modes of classificatory logic are being transformed through their combination with network logics. In such combinations, he says, categories come to be temporary or emergent constructs, rather than 'the already-stabilized taken-for-granteds' of the demographic categories associated with variables-based social science. These new kinds of category are derived from alternative measures, linked to forms of participation organized in circulation, that is, by complex dynamics of interactivity in which settings, actions and content are mutually adjusted and re-adjusted on an on-going basis. Stark writes:

> As a temporary container of knowledge, [the category] resembles transient, context-dependent knowledge arrangements characterized by Andy Clark as 'on the hoof' category constructions. Such short-term categories bridge together a number of possibly highly unrelated contexts, which in turn create new associations in the individual information resources that

would never occur with their own limited context.
(2011: 173)

The making of this proto-categorical pathway or bridging
adjustment across otherwise unrelated contexts is one of
the most significant accomplishments of what I am calling
platform circulation.

For Stark, the search engine is the paradigmatic
technology enabling this change in processes of classification. He says:

> In place of a hierarchical structure based on classi-
> ficatory principles, [there is] a hierarchical structure
> based on horizontal authority and network
> principles ...
>
> Search engines organized around collaborative
> filtering ... use network principles ... Here, too, the
> key idea is that the search engine does not need to
> classify your tastes ... It just needs to match your
> past choices (purchases, rankings) to those of other
> users who have made similar, though not identical
> choices. Emphatically, collaborative filtering does not
> build profiles of users based on preexisting or even
> emergent categories. Instead it builds user profiles
> from network ties ... (2011: 170)

The argument being developed here however is that it
is not simply search engines that are transforming the
possibilities of composing problems, but the process of
platformization more generally,[6] proliferating as it does
a variety of ways of connecting and contexting. And
this is because of the ways in which platforms make
more easily available certain formal properties of circulation – including, but not only, network properties – for
methodological innovation.

Indeed, if a single term were required to describe
these formal properties, *recursion* seems a more inclusive
and precise concept than network to describe how the

compulsion of composition is configured by platforms. Here it is important to note that while recursion is often identified as one of the defining characteristics of computational algorithms, it is not confined to them (as it is also important to be aware that there is more to algorithms than recursion). For example, in their discussion of recursion, Paulo Totaro and Domenico Ninno (2014) note that the concept of function 'has come to dominate the culture of the modern world, both on the theoretical and the practical level' (2014: 32). They say that at 'the practical level it has done so in the specific form of recursive functions (algorithms)' (2014: 32), but also emphasize that algorithmic or recursive logic has a much longer history than its contemporary role in computing suggests. They say:

> Although its existence and principles have been theoretically identified only recently, at the cultural level it had already been incorporated by modern human beings through the dissemination of the bureaucratic organizational model, of machines, and of all kinds of practical applications of calculation. (2014: 32).

Indeed, it is suggested here that recursion acquires cultural significance because of the ways in which it is able to amplify other practices, including notably *queuing* (architectures of ordering, waiting and allocating), *sorting* (the primary method of which is by comparison), *contexting* (operating two-way indexicality) and *capture* (closing links in the architectures of ordering, halting comparison by establishing equivalence, and stopping indexicality).[7]

What is being proposed here, then, is not that recursion is novel but that platformization enables recursion to be used in new ways for the composition of problem spaces. The most important methodological effects of the recursive properties of platform circulation in this regard are:

1. enabling problems to be transformed in more diverse ways, by supporting variation in the speed of circulation (accelerating, decelerating, interrupting, sequencing, pausing and so on) as well as varying ways to act on problems in techniques of queuing, sorting and capturing;
2. enabling problems to be transformed by multiplying possible actors and increasing the possibilities of creating populations, publics or collectivities of (participant) observation; and
3. enabling problems to be transformed by supporting a variety of modes of contexting, including multiplying the contexts in which the representation of a problem leads to intervention, enabling a problem to 'actively adapt to', be responsive, or responsible, to more than one context or environment, and so distributing and enhancing cognitive agency of a variety of kinds.

Bowker and Star say, 'infrastructure does more than make work easier, faster or more efficient; it changes the very nature of what is understood by work' (2000: 108). In the case just described above, the recursive properties of platform circulation mean that it becomes easier to create categories that operate as fractal distinctions (Gal 2002); that is, as categories that are reproduced (and transformed) by being projected onto narrower contexts or broader ones, projected onto different 'objects' – activities, interactions or spaces, for example. In other words, while fractal distinctions have always happened, the capacity to do so with methodological intent is accelerated and expanded by platformization. Recursion can both be more easily co-ordinated across (multiple) contexts in pathways or trajectories of various kinds and made more variously purposeful.

There are significant consequences for the uses of categories in both analysis and everyday life of the operation of recursion in platforms.[8] Gal says of the semiotic logic of fractal distinctions that it 'forms a scaffolding for possibilities of embedding and thus for change, creativity, and argument'. She notes, that in these nested dichotomies, 'there is always some skewing or redefinition at every iteration' (2002: 85). She further observes that although 'such calibrations are always relative positions and not properties laminated onto the persons, objects, or spaces concerned' (2002: 81), the logic matters: while the classifications that fractal distinctions introduce can be momentary or ephemeral, dependent on the perspectives of the 'participants', they can also be long-lasting and 'coercive, fixing and forcing ... distinctions, binding social actors through arrangements such as legal regulation and other forms of ritualization and institutionalization' (Gal 2002: 85; see also Fourcade and Healy 2013, 2017). As a matter of general principle, she says, 'indexical signals are difficult to discuss explicitly' (2002: 85), and the question of how they should be introduced into the composition of problem spaces, how to craft the 'fractal backbone' (Gal 2002: 86) of classification, for example, is a matter of considerable debate that has only intensified with platformization.[9]

Double trouble

It is certainly not surprising that platformization has engendered considerable methodological debate, mixing in uneven ways as it does the four characteristics of platforms identified by Gillespie: architectural, political, computational and figurative. Perhaps one of the most poignant expressions of this concern is given by the artist Hito Steyerl in a discussion of what she calls circulationism (2013). Describing her own practice, she says film editing is now:

> ... being expanded by techniques of encryption – techniques of selection – and ways to keep material safe and to distribute information. Not only making it

public, divulging or disclosing, but really finding new formats and circuits for it. I think this is an art that has not yet been defined as such, but it is, well, aesthetic. It's a form. ... Now it's not only about narration but also about navigation, translation, braving serious personal risk, and evading a whole bunch of military spooks. It's about handling transparency as well as opacity, in a new way, in a new, vastly extended kind of filmmaking that requires vastly extended skills. (Steyerl and Poitras 2015: 311)

She proposes that the question of how information is 'stored, secured, circulated, redacted, checked, and so on ... [the] entire art of withholding and disseminating information and carefully determining the circumstances' is a 'formal decision'. With circulationism, she suggests, this formal decision has a new, unstable temporality:

When I'm working with *After Effects*,[10] there is hardly any real-time play back. So much information is being processed, it might take two hours or longer before you see the result. So editing is replaced by rendering. Rendering, rendering, staring at the render bar. It feels like I'm being rendered all the time.

What do you do if you don't really see what you edit while you're doing it? You speculate. It's speculative editing. You try to guess that what it's going to look like if you put key frames here and here and here. Then there are the many algorithms that do this kind of speculation for you. (Steyerl and Poitras 2015: 312)

The condition Steyerl identifies is described by Mark Hansen in methodological terms. Drawing on Whitehead, he suggests that as more and more dimensions of the 'causal efficacy' of the sensory become, at least in principle, available for understanding there is uncertainty about how best to describe, interpret, interrogate or explain. He says:

Whitehead's 'reformed subjective principle' gives a name to the shift from an agent-centred perceptual modality to an environmental sensibility that lies at the heart of the twenty-first century media. (2015: 9)

More specifically, Hansen argues that the forms of circulation associated with twenty-first century media compound the empirical by correlating humans with sensors, other microtechnologies and environmental networks that gather data from experience, 'including our own experience, that we "ourselves" cannot capture' (2015: 64). In this way, he makes clear that his definition of media is not a restricted notion of digital media but a more encompassing notion of media as *milieu*, middle place or environment (Wark 2019; Hui 2019; Sloterdijk 2009).

The enhanced capability to gather data from experience means, Hansen says, 'that we must renounce the position of mastery we have long accorded ourselves and instead take our place within the larger environmental networks of sensibility that generate experience' (2015: 64–5). For some others, a renunciation of mastery is long overdue, and/or was never a position they occupied. Nevertheless, while the acknowledgement that mastery has its own problems has come relatively late to some, the thesis being developed here is that, as Hansen argues, many of the methodological concerns associated with platformization are to do with the role played by media as *milieux* or environments, particularly insofar as they support the recursive organization of relations between physical copies and epistemological object.[11] Three areas of concern are identified here as 'double troubles'.

1. The natively artificial character of the empirical
The first double trouble associated with platformization relates to the status of the empirical that emerges from the inter-relationship of the circulation of problems with plat-forms of circulation (Adkins and Lury 2011). This

concern is often expressed in the claim that data is 'cooked' rather than 'raw' (Gitelman 2013). An example of 'cooking' data is given by Mayer-Schönberger and Cukier, who describe datafication as what happens when information became 'usable not just for human readers but for computers to process and algorithms to analyze' (2013: 83). Another example is provided by Adrian Mackenzie when he observes that 'Even the elementary data form of the genome as DNA base pairs is a highly algorithmic construct' (2017: 154).

Even when data are recognized to be at least partially cooked, there are complications entailed in deciding whether and how they are 'well done' stemming from the implementation of the formal property of recursion. Recognizing that the 'cooked' status of the relation between measurements and the things they aim to measure has always been a methodological concern, Emma Uprichard asks:

> ... what happens when the reification of measurement and the subsequent ontological properties that measurement comes to possess, is one that drives the epistemological and methodological basis of knowing the social world in the first place? What happens when measurements are taken to matter as much if not more than the social matters we are measuring? (2018: 134)

What she is pointing to here are the dilemmas associated with the way in which measurements are increasingly integrated into the systems that measure them, and sometimes

> ... even go on to constitute the measuring systems as well. ... some of these measurements take on an *ontological status of the system* through the classifications that they then subsequently carve out. Thus, it might not be because a book is ranked to be 'world

leading' that it is necessarily ontologically so, but the fact that it is [so ranked] may make it more likely to become so. (2016: 135)

She concludes by saying that we face a curious situation where measurements may 'be increasingly *more than* properties of the systems, but intrinsic to the mechanisms generating and shaping the systems themselves. If taken to the extreme, properties of systems and the systems are both epistemologically and ontologically conflated with one another' (2016: 135). In describing the recursive use of measures, Brighenti observes a related tension between means and end. He says:

Every time measures turn into targets they end up replacing the phenomenon they were supposed to apprehend in the first place. Such a 'precession of measures' – to borrow from Baudrillard's ... famous expression, 'the precession of simulacra' – over measured objects is particularly clear in the case of the current thrust towards productivity and quality rankings. Academic scholars, for instance, are increasingly asked to be accountable to their H-index as a measure of their productivity, with the paradoxical outcome of having them spend their time and efforts in producing such accounts to the detriment of a focus on actual research. Instead of measuring their current work, the production of measures and related preoccupations turns into an increasingly larger share of their work. (2018: 31)

Brighenti demonstrates how measures and values are entangled in data, and, like Hansen, argues that measures are not simply tools but environments we live in.

Of course, as most discussions of the empirical status of data make clear, the empirical has never been 'raw'. However, in the constant relay between the role of mediator and reference described by Totaro and Ninno (2014), the platform-assisted deployment of recursion produces an empirical that is increasingly recognized to be 'natively artificial' (Fuller and Mazurov 2019). This wry but potent phrase calls up the term 'digital native' or 'born digital', a term that refers to materials that originate in a digital form rather than being converted from analogue, while also drawing on the sense of 'artificial', as used by Herbert Simon and discussed in Chapter 1; that is, as indicating phenomena that 'have an air of "contingency" in their malleability by environment' (1996: xi). In other words, while the empirical has always been contingent, contaminated and malleable by the environment, the recursive effects of platformization compound these characteristics in ways that are often hard to make apparent. In short, while the term might always have been an apt description of the empirical, perhaps 'natively artificial' has special value now given the ways in which platforms enable the activity of recursion to be played out experimentally in a huge variety of ways, across contexts, to different effects, augmenting and transforming, compounding, the infra-ontology of problem spaces.

2. The ontological multiplicity of the epistemological object

A second implication of the capacity of platforms to systematically organize variation between physical copies and epistemological object is the granting, across more and more domains, in more and more disciplines, and with the use of more and more heterogeneous methods, of the ontological multiplicity of the epistemological object, and the potential this affords for the accomplishment of epistemological values.

Let me develop this point. What is distinctive about recursion, Totaro and Ninno suggest, is not repetition as such; rather, 'The crucial point is not the repetition of the act in itself ... but that the repetition is *the aim of the action*, because it is then that the action becomes a step in a recursive process. Indeed ... the intuitive definition of recursion is that of an operation whose aim is to operate on itself' (2014: 36). The ability of recursion to inform a line of inquiry – a pathway or a trajectory of some kind – that can realize epistemological values stems, then, from the 'dual relation between its results, which always constitute a sequence, and the operator that generated them, which is instead invariant' (2014: 1). The plat-form assisted organization of this process is at the heart of the topologies of knowledge and power associated with the new empire of truth.

While considering only computational algorithms, Fuller and Goffey provide a complementary analysis of recursion. They describe it as 'the use of a procedure that involves a series of discrete steps, one of which entails the relaunch of the procedure' (2012: 75):

> An algorithmically specifiable technique for generating continua, it is a constant relaunching that aids both programmatic concision and economy, and which doesn't have to be simply stacked inside itself, as is often thought the case. Recursion may involve the launch of another procedure which in turn relaunches the first one – such as a piece of software working its way through websites by following one link then another, at each point splitting into a copy of itself carrying out the same behaviour, deleting itself once an end point in the chain of links has been reached. In this respect, recursion exemplifies a process of automatic production, of time, over time. (2012: 81)

What both definitions of recursion make apparent is the role of this circulatory property in the determination of relations of continuity and connection at the same time that what is acted on or referenced is changing. As Fuller and Goffey say:

> [While i]t may consist of a derivable pattern of activity, of self-similarity … each recursive event is

different, in terms of its scale, location in time, in the complications it may entail, and in terms of its place in relation to its nesting within other recursions or to those in which it is in turn nested. (2012: 75)

Crucially, the resulting ontological multiplicity of the situation becoming a problem that emerges in the process of recursion need not obviate the making of epistemological value claims. Although recursion inevitably means that the object is epistemically 'multiplex' (Merz 2018: 333–4), the ability to generate relations of (partial) continuity or connection while providing limiting conditions for generalization supports the accomplishment of epistemological values. Or to put this another way, in the platform-assisted operation of recursion, the process of inquiry can be organized so that the event-ive or ontologically multiple characteristics of the epistemological object can be acknowledged in ways that are rigorous as well as inventive.

Let me return to the example of the changing practices of classification described earlier to illustrate how this is possible. In their discussion of model systems, Guggenheim and Krause observe that one aspect of the problem of standardization in the discipline of sociology is that 'classifications are often part of the object to be studied' (2012: 111).[12] Consider, Guggenheim and Krause suggest, the case of petty criminals for criminology:

[As a model system, p]etty criminals come to stand in for the relationship between the legal system and society … But within the study of criminality, the notion of what petty criminality as an object is, is vastly different in different places of study, simply because the criminals in one place are different from those in another. Moreover, the notion of the petty criminal itself is not standardized within sociology since it is not a sociological notion, but a legal notion that is dependent on national and regional legal definitions particular also to different historical

circumstances. A comparative study of petty criminality has to grapple with the problem that the
systematics of the object is unstable over the cases and
renders a comparison difficult. (2012: 111)

What Stark's analysis of the transformations in classification
processes demonstrates, however, is that the difficulties
associated with standardization are being transformed,
in processes of platformization, into opportunities.[13] An
example of this is the study by Gabriel Gatti of the category
of the 'disappeared'.[14] He shows how the rapid circulation
of the category across contexts does not evacuate it of sense
or value (although it risks sensationalizing the category), but
can be employed to turn it into a tool 'for understanding (that
is, thinking about, managing, operating on) a universe filled
with places that are outside the norm, a universe of dislo-
cated identities, of sufferers, of escapees, of abandonment,
of waste, of pariahs, of precarious individuals, of the
vulnerable' (2020: 28); in short, its recursive circulation
across contexts is precisely what enables the category to
function as 'an *explanans* for the bad life' (2020: 28).

In addition, there is the possibility not only that empirical
differences in classification over time and across contexts
can be explored and investigated (Uprichard 2011) in a
process of generative circulation, but also that alternative
classifications can be introduced to identify unexpected
continuities and changes in the epistemological object
being studied. Such changes need not necessarily involve
the loss of the ability to establish causality or theorize but
offer new ways of combining description and causality
(Uprichard 2013; Krause 2016). They offer, for example,
opportunities for different kinds of abductive reasoning,
including what Schurz describes as selective abductions;
that is, abductive search strategies that can identify 'an
optimal candidate from [a] given multitude of possible
explanations' as well as 'creative abductions, search strategies that introduce new theoretical models or concepts'
(2008: 201; see also Magnani 2001).

However, while the ontological multiplicity of the epistemological object can be acknowledged and exploited in methodologically innovative ways in plat-form circulation, there are undoubtedly complications associated with these possibilities. In some discussions, there is a concern with the potential instrumentalism of the use of recursive functions to identify paths of inquiry: that is, there is a concern that description or explanation will always be subordinated to prescription. While this is certainly possible (and will be discussed in the next chapter in terms of an imaginary of know-ability), it is important to acknowledge that the use of recursive functions is not always goal-orientated, that goals can be and often are changed in the process of inquiry, and that goals need not be restricted to commercial or other gain. It is also worth addressing the changing use and understandings of functions in methodological discussions.

As Matthew Spencer notes, the falling out of favour of functionalism in social theory during the latter part of the twentieth century 'makes us wary of talking about functions, purposes, teleologies'. However, while recognizing that methodological anti-functionalism is 'a valuable empirical tool' since it limits the possibility that a practice or institution will be seen as necessary 'because it seems to serve a particular end' (2019: 319), Spencer also suggests that there are 'new ways of thinking about the purposeful in culture'. In relation to the production of knowledge, these include methods of testing, trialling, transforming, sorting, solving, ordering. He says:

> What makes these devices lively is their material instantiation of purposes, as emergent micro-teleologies of practice. That they are 'for' certain ends does not imply necessity, or that the wider whole 'works', but rather speaks of their specific ways of being actual. (2019: 319)[15]

Elsewhere (Lury 2020) I have described the micro-teleologies of methods as doings; that is as *gerunds*: active present tense forms that function as nouns. This verb form is typically the object of prepositions, the variety of which, Serres suggests, philosophy has neglected,[16] but which, I suggest, are explicitly put to work in a compositional methodology (see also Michael and Rosengarten 2012). By following the with-in and out-with of connection and context, the 'across' of translation, the 'among' and 'between' of interferences, the 'through' of the channels through which Hermes and the Angels pass, the 'alongside' of the parasite, the 'beyond' of detachment (Serres 1994: 83 in http://stevenconnor.com/milieux/), the doing of methods makes the present purposeful. That is, compositional methodology, understood as pre-position-ing problems in the doings of methods, allows functions to contribute to their becoming as 'figures of suspension and expectation', able to act as 'traps for the emergence of compossibility' (Corsín Jiménez 2014: 383).

To support the do-ing of visualizations, Greg McInerny (2018) argues, for example, for the importance of keeping hold of a conception of design space unrestricted by specific design constraints. This is 'envisaged as a hyper-volume of *all* possible visualization designs with as many dimensions as there are ways to visualize data using coordinate and mapping systems, visual encodings and formatting, scales and sizing, sampling and aggregation methods etc.' (2018: 135). As he observes, the impossibility of describing such a space 'forces us to reflect on how we define, evaluate and interpret visualizations' (2018: 135). And there are an increasing number of examples of how the micro-teleologies of do-ing, purpose, 'intent toward' (Hayles 2014), or 'mattering for' are being mobilized in this work of definition, evaluation and interpretation, the compulsive composition or auto-spatialization of problem spaces.

Take the case of the 3DH, a platform Johanna Drucker (2018) and a team of others designed to support a non-representational approach to model-*ing* interpretation in a graphical environment. Drucker observes that with a representational approach to visualization, data precede display: 'display is a surrogate produced according to automated protocols and algorithms. These cannot be altered or intervened except through rewriting their code, and the display, though interpretative and subject to interpretation, cannot be used as a means by which inter-pretation is actually modeled' (2018: 248). Her point is that while most visualizations express a model, they do not provide a modeling environment. In the alternative non-representational approach she proposes, graphical input serves as a primary means of interpretative work, while the graphical environment supports the model-*ing* of interpretation, using visual argument structures such as contradiction, ambiguity, parallax and point of view to support traditional humanistic approaches, such as close reading, and marking of texts, documents, and artifacts. She says:

> ... a non-representational approach to modeling interpretation in a graphical environment, [can] add crucial capacity to the existing methods and platforms by providing a space for direct creation and inscription of interpretative work. (2018: 248)

Another example of the operation of methods as do-ing or 'mattering for' is described by Corsín Jiménez:

> "A monumental tool," someone whispered. "Hund-reds of pages long," someone else noted. "The Processgram," a third person finally glossed, while providing a description that functioned as both nomenclature and mythical signature. It must have been 2011 or 2012 when I first heard these words, and the images they provoked have stayed with me ever since. I was mesmerized. It had never occurred to me that guerrilla architectural collectives might have developed a project management tool with a view to registering every action, every bifurcation, every

photograph and drawing and sketch, every failure and insight garnered during a community project. At once a self-made archive and a social design interface, an organizational program and an urban directory, here was a tool that architects were using for auto-constructing the city (for building social and material relations) at the same time as they auto-constructed their methods. (2017: 450)

Jiménez's concern is auto-construction, the term he uses to describe the practices of a guerilla architectural collective based in Madrid who adopt an approach that involves 'dwelling in controversy', and designing habitats for each and every problem of the inhabitants. Drawing on the work of Simone (2004), Corsín Jiménez describes auto-construction as a 'perceptual system' for the city, 'a sensory organ that functions as at once an economy of attention and an economy of resources, and that finds tentative anchorage in the city as a method for other methods' (2017: 457). Corsín Jiménez highlights the view of Manuel, a member of the collective, who says that the circulating economy of learning is the infrastructure: 'the auto-construction of the city as an infrastructure of apprenticeships' (2017: 472).

Importantly, as part of this recognition of the doubled heuristic of auto-construction as theory and method, Corsín Jiménez acknowledges that the term itself has undergone 'an important conceptual migration':

... from its original use in designating self-help housing in the global South (auto-construction as object), to more recent usages signaling the inventiveness and resourcefulness of self-organized initiatives (auto-construction as process), to my own proposal for thinking of auto-construction as a method and platform of inquiry and exploration. (2017: 453)

In doing so, he reflects on his own use of method (ethnography) as an anthropologist, and its geo-politics. He notes that auto-construction in the global South is 'often a far cry from the community projects in political autonomy and democratic experimentation that I report on' (2017: 454), but argues for the value of an ethnographic approach as part of auto-construction in Madrid on the grounds of co-habitation of methods, and the possibilities of 'partial and interdependent descriptions' (2017: 454).[17]

A final example of the articulation of methodological potential afforded by the ontological multiplicity of the epistemological object is provided by the practice of the agency Forensic Architecture (Fuller and Mazurov 2019). In the practice of this 'cognitive assemblage' or platform, model-ing is purposively used to establish the evidential status of data – a practice they describe as ground-truthing.[18] The aim or purpose might be to demonstrate how a phenomenon, a wall with bullet holes in it, 'is implicated in sets of anticipated reactions to it and prepa-rations for it'. To provide such a demonstration, bespoke models of the reactions of specific materials in a wall to bullets (comprising specific materials shaped in specific ways) fired at specified speeds from specified directions by specified guns operated by specified persons are developed, enabling Forensic Architecture to give the epistemological value of 'evidence' to the statements they make about who shot the gun and from where.

As Fuller and Mazurov note, such event-ive forms of making epistemological claims mean that 'communication between kinds of rigour is important, and plays out differ-entially and generatively in different contexts'.[19] A similar point about the epistemological values of knowledge in circulation is made by Calkins and Rottenburg in their discussion of infrastructures for evidence. They say:

> Empirical findings are aligned with different worths as they leave the biotech labs, greenhouses and trials fields to produce forms of argumentation that can convince public fora. Scientific evidence about the risks and potential of GMOs is thus mobilized and

these evidences shape and are shaped by intersecting knowledge infrastructures. (2016: 260)

In their counter-forensic practice, Forensic Architecture develop architectural-image complexes precisely to allow for communication between different criteria for rigour:

> ... the means by which an argument or set of proofs are made tends to offer different capacities of resistance to or concurrence with different forms of enquiry attuned to the matching of certain patterns or traces ... In working to develop and elicit evidence [Forensic Architecture] recognizes that any forensic interpretation and significance is part of a wider set, that of epistemic systems, such as law, media, human rights, various forms of politics, by means of which, and by virtue of the procedures proper to them, it may in turn gain the status of proof. The question of what constitutes a proof is in turn subject to a range of variable and mobile regimes, which include law, but also automated systems that monitor, filter and inspect the circulation of data. (Fuller and Mazurov 2019: 174)

In this practice, there is an explicit concern with the distribution of cognition, and the ways in which the distribution enables some kinds of actors to make knowledge claims and not others. As Fuller and Mazurov say in their discussion of the practice of Forensic Architecture:

> ... when the location of veridiction or of witnessing moves outside of being simply the property of the knowing subject, and is also found in artefacts, files, timestamping systems, and other things that must be attended to, there is a complex realignment of knowledge and action underway. (2019: 176)

Transcontextualism

A final set of challenges associated with the articulation of the double force of methods in an era of platformization are to do with the expanded indexical dynamics of today's problem spaces, and whether and how to deal with a problem's connections to its context(s): whether to seek to minimize these connections or to exploit them as part of the process of problematization.

As Guggenheim and Krause point out, sociologists and scholars from many other disciplines have mostly *not* wanted to attempt to 'disconnect the epistemological objects from their (physical and immobile) context, ... because such a disconnection, a laboratization of the object, would appear to threaten for many the interest of the object':

> Although there are both old and more recent attempts to call sociological fields laboratories, which would imply control of objects, sociologists rarely attempt such control ... Sociologists believe that the situatedness of the epistemic object forms precisely its value. (2012: 109–10).

However, as discussed in Chapter 1, how to conduct situatedness is itself a matter of ongoing methodological concern.[20] Angela Last says, 'What becomes apparent is that methods can never be divorced from their context, and if they are, the context will keep surfacing' (2018: 197), while Nick Seaver (2015a) observes; 'the importance of context is uncontroversial; the controversy lies in determining what context is'. Contrasting different approaches to the use of big data, he argues that context is 'constructed by the methods used to apprehend it':

> For the developers of 'context-aware' recommender systems, context is typically operationalized as a set of

sensor readings associated with a user's activity. For critics like boyd and Crawford, context is that unquantified remainder that haunts mathematical models, making numbers that appear to be identical actually different from each other. These understandings of context seem to be incompatible, and their variability points to the importance of identifying and studying 'context cultures'–ways of producing context that vary in goals and techniques, but which agree that context is key to data's significance. To do otherwise would be to take these contextualizations out of context. (2015a: 1101)

Across disciplines there has always been a concern with methods of contexting: the rise of methods such as multi-site ethnography in anthropology (Marcus 1995) and multi-situated analysis in digital media studies, as well as the use of comparative methods in disciplines as various as literature, biology and media studies attest to the recognition that contexts are not only enacted and relational, but also cannot be detached from forms of circulation (Dilley 1999; Meier and Dopson 2019). For example, recognizing that apps are always located within multiple infrastructural settings, Dieter et al. (2019) propose a variety of ways to investigate the tendencies of apps to be situated and to situate themselves, their reciprocal causality with contexts, and their ability to connect scales. Such an approach – a kind of infrastructural inversion – allows for an investigation of the workings of apps *and* their contexts.

The history of site-specific art practices described by Miwon Kwon (1997) illustrates some of the responses that follow from the recognition that context is relational. She identifies a shift in the 1970s from a practice that engaged the 'literal space of art, the physical condition of a specific location' to one that engaged a site understood to be 'the techniques and effects of the art institution as they circumscribe the definition, production, presentation, and dissemination of art'. As a consequence of this shift, 'The "work" no longer seeks to be a noun/object but a verb/ process, provoking the viewers' critical (not just physical) acuity regarding the ideological conditions of that viewing' (Kwon 1997: 91). Kwon describes attempts to take art (physically and conceptually) out of the museum/gallery space-system into a discursively determined site. In some of this practice, the site is not defined as a pre-condition (a circumscription in Jullien's terms): 'Rather, it is *generated* by the work (often as "content"), and then *verified* by its convergence with an existing discursive formation' (Kwon, 1997: 92). In the 1990s, there was a further shift towards what was called the functional site, under-stood as a process, or operation occurring between sites, a 'temporary thing; a movement, a chain of meanings devoid of a particular focus' (Meyer in Kwon, 1997: 95).

In making the claim above that, with platformization, epistemological values are constituted *in* circulation, I have suggested that we are witnessing changes in cultures of contexting or context-awareness. This is not the same as saying, as Antoinette Rouvroy (2013) does, that 'immanent knowledge' is 'atopic'; that is, that in circulation knowledge is not linked to any temporal or geographical anchor. Instead it is to suggest that while knowledge is always epistopic (Lynch 1993) – that it emerges from the connection of localized practices ('topics') with 'familiar themes from epistemology and general methodology' (1993: 280) – the terms of that emergence are many and varied. It is to suggest that as plat-forms of circulation proliferate so do practices of contexting and context cultures, so that, for example, while techniques such as machine learning 'produces a common space that juxta-poses and mixes complex localized realities' (Mackenzie 2017: 73) there is always more and other contexting work to be done.

With the proliferation of context cultures, however, comes a rise in the genus of cognitive syndromes that Gregory Bateson (1972) describes as transcontextualism.

By this term, Bateson refers to a variety of cognitive tangles sharing common features, which he says are a result of the 'weaving of contexts and of messages which propose context but which, like all messages, whatsoever, have "meaning" only by virtue of context' (1972: 275–6; see King 2011 for a discussion of transcontextual tangles). Examples include when 'Exogenous events may be framed in the context of dreams, and internal thought may be projected into the contexts of the external world' (1972: 200). And, while Bateson's discussion of this genre of syndromes is largely confined to the level of an individual organism (non-human and human animals are both considered), his comments have considerable relevance in relation to cognitive tangles that may emerge with platformization insofar as there is now not only an increased potential for contexts to be multiplied, and for heterogeneous cultures of contexting to collide but also that contexts are equipped to be able to be interactive.

Bateson observes that there are different ways for an individual to respond to or inhabit the transcontextual, including acquiring skills that may coalesce as habit or 'background' knowledge, minimizing encounters with the transcontextual, and actively resisting transcontextual pathways. All these options, I suggest, are visible in contemporary methodological (and everyday) practice. However, as the distinction that Boltanski and Thévenot (2006) draw between 'reality' (that is, that which appears to hold firm and be consistent) and the background, the 'world' or 'whatever happens', becomes increasingly hard to sustain, encounters of a transcontextual kind multiply, and there are likely to be context collisions as well as context collusions (Davis and Jurgenson 2014).

Solon Barocas and Karen Levy's (2019) description of equivocal measures provides an example. Equivocal measures, as they define them, are the product of multiple terms, in which the referents of the component terms are not observed directly and are likely to interact with one another as they change. They say that while such measures are methodological complications of long-standing concern to researchers, they are becoming of increasing interest to policy-makers and the public. This is because, they say, people understand such measures to be referring to different aspects of the problem (or perhaps even to different problems), and different appropriate ways to respond to the problem, from different positions or contexts. As with debates about the value of 'cleaning' dirty data, it is not always clear whether the uncertainty created by such context collisions are to be avoided or exploited.

It is not surprising, however, that such collisions are sometimes fiercely contested since the measures divide the participants sharing a problem space; what is less often recognized is the role of affect. Typically, even when affects are recognized – as doubt, skepticism, hubris, narcissism, hope and paranoia for example – they are considered epi-phenomenal, detachable from the epistemological values that are accomplished in practices of contexting. Yet, as Bateson observes it is not that emotions or affect are attached to relations but that such relations always have affective as well as epistemological dimensions. He writes:

> Psychologists commonly speak as if the abstractions of relationship (dependency, hostility, love, etc.) were real things which are to be described or expressed by messages. This is epistemology backwards: in truth, the messages constitute the relationship, and words like 'dependency' are verbally coded descriptions of patterns immanent in the combination of exchanged messages. (1972: 201)

Despite the widespread reluctance to take the affective dimension of cognition seriously, there are examples of analyses that acknowledge its significance (see Clough 2018 for example). Drawing on the practice of the artist Salvador Dali, Sloterdijk (2009) argues for the value of critical paranoia, Rosalind Krauss (1976) argues that the medium of video is narcissistic, and Sianne Ngai analyses aesthetic categories in terms of 'knowing-feeling' (2012). As noted in Chapter 1, Dewey identifies the possibility of what he calls 'a mania of doubting' while Paulo Freire (1970) mobilizes the concept of a limit situation (in German, *Grenzsituation*), drawing on the use of the term developed by the philosopher and psychiatrist Karl Jaspers, who considered fright, guilt, finality and suffering as some of the key limit situations arising in everyday life. Drawing on this insight, Freire argues that the encounter with the form of a limit situation could be a way for knowledge and emotion to inform action, or praxis (see also Moreno Figueroa 2008).

Sometimes affect is personalized in discussions of methodology but it also circulates in problem spaces as a collective ethos, characterizing whole cognitive assemblages, as when the financial system is said to be in crisis. Indeed, pathological consequences have been identified for machines as well as humans when they become 'trapped' in patterns. So, for example, some computational algorithms are said to suffer from apophenia (boyd and Crawford 2012; Pasquinelli 2019). This term was coined by neurologist and psychiatrist Klaus Conrad to describe the finding of abnormal meaning or significance in random experiences by people experiencing the early stages of schizophrenia (an illness with which Bateson was also much concerned). The term has now been extended to describe not only the tendency of humans to find meaning and significance in random, coincidental, or impersonal data (and is one of the tendencies contributing to gambling, another of Bateson's primary objects of study) but also a tendency in neural networks to 'see' patterns that are not 'really' there. This tendency leads to the identification of what statisticians call false patterns in data but might also be considered a kind of positivity since it may be compared with finding a so-called false positive in other test situations.

While Bateson proposes that most transcontextual syndromes are not pathological, and should rather be understood as 'double takes' of a variety of kinds, he is also concerned with the pathological consequences of being trapped in transcontextualism: when, for example, double takes become double binds. And being trapped or captured is now, given the growing role accorded to participation as part of platformization, an increasingly commonplace experience. In a now classic essay, Philip Agre (1994) identified two models of privacy: surveillance and capture, with the latter, he suggested, acquiring a new prominence with the rise of applied computing. The capture model is one in which 'human activities are systematically reorganized to allow computers to track them in real time' (1994: 101): 'In addition to the continual updating of a representation, each tracking system is capable of closing a causal link between the entity [being tracked] and the computer' (1994: 105).

The implications of being captured can be more or less serious. Miller (2000) describes personal websites as 'aesthetic traps that express the social efficacy of their creators and attempt to draw others into social or commercial exchange with those who have objectified themselves through the internet' (2000: 6). Michael Dieter and David Gauthier (2019) identify the importance of chrono-design: the deliberate shaping of experiences of temporality and time through contemporary software techniques and digital technologies, not only in behavioural tracking, but also in practices of network optimization and user experience design. They suggest that contemporary user interfaces complicate conventional notions of the rational, self-reflexive subject by 'operating beyond consciousness at vast environmental dimensions and accelerated micro-temporal speeds, providing opportunities for new forms of behavioural suspense and captivation exemplified in the figure of the trap' (2019: 61).

Trapping can also happen 'in the wild': Ravi Sundaram (2015) describes how the use of 'circulation engines'; that

is, the widespread use of informal media, lead to unanticipated media ecologies in which the spread and storage
of data, documents, files and recordings of various kinds
of media outputs outstrip the means to control or understand what is happening. The resulting artefactualism of
media events is part of 'a generative loop or movement,
where practices, objects and people attach themselves to
changing assemblages' (2015: 298).

Sundaram observes that expanding media infrastructures have come in the wake of fragile postcolonial
sovereignties and informal economies of circulation:

> This process has linked up to new subaltern expan-
> sions of existing infrastructure, which are redeployed
> for creative uses ... This loop shapes much of contem-
> porary media circulation, wherein media objects move
> in and out of infrastructures, attach themselves to new
> platforms of political-aesthetic action, and are drawn
> to or depart from the spectacular time of media events.
> This drive marks the turbulent, dynamic ecology of
> entrapment, with changing combinations of protago-
> nists, technologies, and spaces: television newsrooms,
> online platforms, police stations, government offices,
> courts, enquiry commissions, demonstrations, and
> activist forums. (Sundaram 2015: 299)

In this field of entrapment, he says, truth does not exist
in contradistinction to the false, but simultaneously in
parallel with the fake and the politically (in)correct. As
Achille Mbembe and Janet Roitman foresaw:

> Fraudulent identity cards; fake policemen dressed
> in official uniform; ... forged enrollment for exams;
> illegal withdrawal of money orders; fake banknotes;
> the circulation and sale of falsified school reports,
> medical certificates and damaged commodities ...
> [This] is also a manifestation of the fact that, here,
> things no longer exist without their parallel. Every law

enacted is submerged by an ensemble of techniques of avoidance, circumvention and envelopment which in the end, neutralize and invert the legislation. There is hardly a reality here without its double. (Mbembe and Roitman 1995: 340)

For Sundaram, the materiality of contemporary media is what enables this kind of capture. He notes that in colonial India, paper-based databases (electoral rolls, ration cards, land lists) produced by state functionaries intersected with political mobilizations at local and city levels. In the informal media ecology that characterizes post-colonial India, new actors emerge. The example he gives is that of video 'stings' of phenomena as various as corruption and police atrocities. He says:

As a field, entrapment suggests a shifting set of forces, a world where we witness what the philosopher Keith Ansell Pearson refers to as "experience enlarged and gone beyond" ... In this milieu, the sting becomes a vehicle to enter a larger forensic laboratory, be it the palpable, visceral mood of the media event or the minor theater of the courtroom. (Sundaram 2015: 304)

The emergence of this field of entrapment is held to be a consequence of what happens when, 'public discourse abandons the security of given audiences'. To do so, he says, '"puts at risk the concrete world that constitutes its condition of possibility"' (Warner 2002: 109 in Sundaram 2015: 304).

In a discussion of the history of recommendation algorithms, Seaver records the setting up of B. J. Fogg's Persuasive Technology Lab at Stanford. He says, 'Fogg founded the lab in 1998 to develop the field he called "captology", a name derived from the acronym for "computers as persuasive technologies"' (Seaver 2019: 424). But by drawing on anthropological literature, Seaver aims to describe the trap as being not simply about brute capture but also captivation (as does Miller); that is, as embodying a scenario, a nexus of intentionalities, operating as 'agentic tangles in the broader ecologies of knowledge and technology' (2019: 427). This is a vocabulary that speaks to the compulsion of composition that is recognized by Isabelle Stengers who describes inquiry as a process of 'reciprocal capture' (see also Chow 2012). This can be spoken of, Stengers says, 'whenever a dual process of identity construction is produced: regardless of the manner, and usually in ways that are completely different, identities that coinvent one another each integrate a reference to the other for their own benefit' (Stengers 2010: 36).

For Stengers, reciprocal capture is a transversal concept that shifts attention away from the kinds of legitimacy afforded by methodology, paradigm or concept and 'emphasizes the event, an "It works!" that belongs to the register of creation' (Stengers 2010: 42; see also Michael 2017). Savransky (2016), drawing on Stengers, argues that the moment of reciprocal capture may be tied to ethical creativity in terms of practices of care, producing 'new modes of existence and thus adding something to the world in a way that is more democratic, and more ethical, than the modern, all too modern, social scientific knowledge practice'. This is, he says, a move from '"affirming productivity" to "actually producing" – from ideas to practices'.

In conclusion to this discussion of the cognitive tangles of transcontextualism, it is worth noting that Seaver describes an infrastructure as 'a trap in slow motion', and describes traps as 'agents of environmentalism (quoting Corsín Jiménez), making worlds for the entities they trap' (2019: 432). Corsín Jiménez and Nahum-Claudel propose that: 'The conceptual creativity of the trap lies in its duplex identity as a noun and a verb. A trap refers simultaneously to a specific material interface (a trap) and to an analytical description of mutuality (entrapment)' (2019: 384). To recognize as much is to point to the importance of (re-)capturing traps for our thinking and living' (Seaver 2019: 432), and the need to consider the relationship between habits, habitus and habitats in the composition of problem spaces.

Conclusion

This chapter has suggested that the double force of methods has acquired new methodological potential with platformization. As an increasingly important characteristic of the epistemic infrastructure, platformization builds on and extends the vectors of change identified in Chapter 2: explicitation, the changing semiotics of the epistemic infrastructure, the acknowledgement of the constitutive role of the observer, the recalibration of the geo-politics of methodology, and the increasing role of participation. In doing so, it transforms and redirects these vectors without leading to their convergence. It intensifies specific formal properties of circulation, most importantly, the ability of recursion to amplify the techniques of queuing, sorting, contexting and capturing, to provide both new opportunities and new dilemmas for the becoming topological of problems in circulation. With the possibilities of a more various articulation of the relation between physical copy and epistemical object, the double force of methods is multiplied, diversified and diverted, such that problem spaces are, for better and for worse, 'more than circular' (Bateson 1972).

While the use of the term trouble to describe these opportunities and dilemmas might seem to indicate difficulties that need to be overcome, the proposal made here, following Haraway (2016) is that we need to stay with the trouble(s). Helen Verran advocates something similar when she describes the need to 'stay true to laughter' in moments of disconcertment:

It is easy to ignore and pass by these moments – part of the problem is their fleeting subtlety – yet it is possible to become acutely sensitized to them. Interruptions, small and large, are what we, as theorists must learn to value and use. (2001: 5)

As the discussion in the previous chapter suggests, one way to do so is to focus on the figurative capacities of platforms, and to consider the double troubles described above as the inevitable consequence of figures 'seen twice' (Riles 2000: 91). This is the phrase that Annelise Riles uses to consider how the ontological and epistemic dimensions of 'network' operate together and apart as they inevitably do in the platform sequencing of recursion across a problem space. Staying with the trouble requires specifying the compulsion of composition, the work that needs to be done for the auto-spatialization of a problem to be inventive in a constantly transforming infra-ontology. But as the discussion above suggests, this is not easy: seeing double can as easily confuse as captivate.

The next chapter will further explore the implications of platformization for the composition of problem spaces, and proposes that while platforms increasingly configure the compulsion of composition for know-ability they can also serve answer-ability.

– 6 –

Know-ability and
Answer-ability

> I suppose this ought to seem quite an unremarkable
> epiphany: that knowledge does rather than simply is,
> it is by now very routine to discover.

Eve Kosofsky Sedgwick (2003: 4)

In the previous chapter, I described the configuration of
the compulsion of composition in plat-forms of circulation, emphasizing the significance of the formal property
of recursion. In this chapter, I consider the implications of
platformization for the composition of problem spaces,
including for the creation of topologies of knowledge and
power, for what knowledge does rather than simply is, as
Sedgwick (2003) puts it, by interrogating the thesis that
we are witnessing the internalization of science by society.

This thesis is the influential proposal made by Helga
Nowotny, Peter Gibbons, Michael Scott and others in their
elaboration of a distinction between Mode 1 and Mode 2
knowledge (Gibbons et al. 1994; Nowotny et al. 2001).
'In "traditional society"', they say, 'science was "external"
to society; society was, or could be, hostile to scientific

values and methods, and, in turn, scientists saw their task as "the benign" reconstitution of society according to "modern" principles which they were largely responsible for determining' (Nowotny et al. 2001: 2). This is Mode 1 knowledge. In Mode 2, science is internalized in processes of contextualization and socialization. By creating new knowledge, science continually introduces elements of uncertainty to the world, while at the same time being itself evaluated in relation to societal imperatives. Indeed, it is sometimes claimed that in Mode 2 the autonomy of scientific knowledge production is restricted by societal demands, exacerbating the tension between the scientific values of autonomy and accountability. While not assuming these values are mutually exclusive, this chapter explores some of the changes in their inter-relationship by describing the emergence of a cultural imaginary of know-ability linked to platformization. To do this I draw on the concept of interface. The chapter ends with a discussion of answer-ability and the values of response-ability.[1]

The internalization of science?

The thesis of a shift from Mode 1 to Mode 2 knowledge, as it was first developed, was criticized for a variety of reasons, including concerns about: its empirical validity (is enough evidence provided for either Mode existing, or for a shift happening?); conceptual strength (are the characteristics of either Mode clearly enough established and distinguished?); and political value (is the description of Mode 2 prescriptive rather than descriptive?) (Hessels and Van Lente, 2008). In response to these criticisms, the authors made significant refinements to their argument, elaborating the twin notions of 'science speaking to society' and 'society speaking back to science'. In doing so, they emphasize that Mode 2 knowledge production – in which society has internalized science – developed in the context of a Mode 2 Society.

To describe Mode 2 society, Nowotny et al. draw significantly on two influential accounts of recent societal change in the West: the emergence of a knowledge society (by reference to Bell, 1973, 1976) and the emergence of a risk society (authors include Beck, 1986 and Giddens, 1990). In relation to the first, they say:

> The growth of the 'knowledge' industries has not only led to an increase in 'knowledge' workers and a prolif- eration of sites of 'knowledge' production, but has also tended to erode the demarcation between tradi- tional 'knowledge' institutions such as universities and research institutes and other kinds of organi- zation. Novel 'knowledge' institutions are arising in small and medium-sized high-technology companies, for example, or management consultancies and think- tanks ... But even more radical change is underway; many, perhaps most, organizations in a Knowledge Society have to become learning organizations, in order to develop their human and intellectual capital, and have also to become increasingly dependent on the 'knowledge' systems to operate efficiently – or at all. (Nowotny et al. 2001: 25)

In relation to the second, 'industrial society and modernity have become antagonistic ... [In Beck's] scenario of the 'normalization of the abnormal' – that is, the self-made production and uncontrollable diffusion of risks – the dominant logic of the industrial age, namely that it can control the risks it produces, is breaking down in an irreversible way' (2001: 14). This second account is associated with the use of environment as an alternative to context (a term that is sometimes assumed to be social and exclude the natural). 'Environment' is a helpful addition insofar as it recognizes the existence of a plurality of 'regimes of nature' (Escobar 2008, 2019), inviting acknowledgement of the Anthropocene, as well as calling attention to processes of de- and re-territorialization, and the politics of the nation state, migration and security. As Brighenti puts it:

> An environment is not a territory, but a milieu where territories can be created and installed. Actors, practices, formats, dynamics, transformations and resistances are the analytical elements that compose measure–value environments ... [environment] is that invisible medium from which measure comes and to which it incessantly returns. (Brighenti 2018: 39)

While acknowledging the value of these accounts for understanding the epistemic infrastructure, I have given more significance to a third thesis that Nowotny et al. mention but do not discuss in detail: the emergence of an information society. This is the thesis that 'analyses the implications of information and communication technologies for services related to final users (who, by this definition are already drawn in and hence, part of the system and its evolving infrastructure)' (2001: 10). Theories of information society emphasize that 'people have been allowed a place in our knowledge' and thus, 'the context (can and does) speak back' (Nowotny 1999: 253).

> Pre-existing contexts, and deep social substructures, influence science-before-the-event, just as its future impacts anticipate science-after-the event. The setting of priorities and the patterns of funding are not self-evident or self-referential; rather they are the result of complex negotiations in a variety of contexts, where expectations and vested interests, unproven promises and mere potentials play a role. (Nowotny et al. 2001: 20)

In the account put forward here, emphasis has been placed on how the genres of participation associated with platformization are transforming the scope, scale and nature of processes of what Nowotny et al. call socialization. While their emphasis on the involvement of people is important it is only part of what is at stake: technologies of information and communication are not intermediaries, in Bruno Latour's terms (2005), but mediators. People are the context for technology as well as technology being a context for people. I have highlighted this by emphasizing that environments can capture the activities of people, contributing to an expanded sense of society as milieu or environment.

In the discussion of the changing geo-politics of methodology, a fourth account of social change, also introduced but not discussed in detail by Nowotny et al. (2001), was acknowledged: the globalization of knowledge. Here I drew on a range of analyses, but especially on the work of Arjun Appadurai: first, on his description of flows of disjuncture and difference in which people, things and ideas circulate (1990) and, second, on his identification of the importance for knowledge of the relationship between the circulation of forms and forms of circulation (2013). This latter conceptualization was drawn on to inform an account of the significance of platformization for the articulation of the double force of methods, highlighting the ways in which platforms exploit the formal property of recursion to reconfigure the compulsion of composition of problem spaces in a variety of ways. The methodological opportunities and dilemmas afforded by the exploitation of the property of recursion were summarized in a description of 'double troubles'. What also needs to be acknowledged are that such processes of contextualization are simultaneously issues of socialization, and that practices of contexting in, for example, a *sociedad abigarrada* or a 'motley society' (as employed in Botero-Mesa and Rocat-Servat 2019, for example) or a post-social knowledge society (Knorr Cetina 1997), will be very different in their consequences to practices of contexting in a 'Mode 2 society'. Indeed, it may be that the changing geo-politics of methodology described in earlier chapters are such that the value of any ideal type of society is necessarily limited.

Nowotny et al. suggest that science has always had to engage with the issue of contextualization, but say the issue of how to 'do' context has now become more pressing: 'the reflexive articulation of science and society induces a process of continued contextualization of knowledge. The articulation is reflexive because a pervasive discourse is developed which becomes constitutive of the social life it seeks to portray' (2001: 109). Indeed, they further suggest that the time between knowing and doing – what Ian Hacking (2012) describes as the looping between representation and intervention – 'has been radically shortened':

> ... the largely blind variation of what is possible has been greatly enlarged by the success of science, but it has become more difficult to devise mechanisms for selecting what should be retained, accepted, rejected, modified or incorporated. (2001: 112)

In consequence:

> ... the direction taken by research cannot be determined in advance but only *en route* ... choices emerge in the course of a project because of many different factors, scientific, economic, political and even cultural. These choices then suggest further choices in a dynamic and interactive process, opening the way for strategies of variation upon whose further development ultimately the selection through success will decide. (2001: 115–16)

The changing processual, or routing, dynamics of research were described here too: the formal properties of platformization as a form of circulation enable strategies of varying relations between a physical copy and the epistemological object more easily than model systems, enabling claims to be made in relation to ontologically multiple epistemological objects and ensuring that such claims are always less than final.

In short, the description of the methodological implications of the platformization of the epistemic infrastructure that has been presented here does not suggest that the boundary between society and science can be drawn permanently, or that either science or society are unified or coherent wholes, or that either contains the other. In the previous chapter, for example, the many ways in which the recursive properties of platform circulation introduce twists and tangles, traps, net(work)s and knots into problem spaces was described, introducing affects as various as paranoia, scepticism and hope. In such twists, science cannot be said to be in any simple sense, 'inside' society, or to be 'contained'. Instead, so it has been consistently argued, problems always become topologically, with-in and out-with problem spaces. But this does not mean that the composition of a problem space does not involve relations between science and society, or that those relations do not involve relations of power and control. Indeed, the thesis to be developed in this chapter is that the becoming topological of problem spaces supported by platformization contributes to an imaginary of knowability, an imaginary in which it seems everywhere there is a capacity to know (Thrift 2005; Hayles 2017), and everywhere the grounds for truth are disputed.[2] A different way of putting this is to say that the topologies of knowledge and power associated with platformization are interface effects.

Interface effects

The concept of interface deployed here is that put forward by Branden Hookway (2014; but see also Galloway 2012; and Ash 2015). Hookway defines the interface as a 'form of relation'; he says, 'what is essential to a description of the interface [is] the qualities of relation between entities':

... the interface is a form of relation that obtains between two or more distinct entities, conditions or states such that it only comes into being as these distinct entities enter into an active relation with one another; such that it actively maintains, polices and draws on the separation that renders these entities as distinct at the same time as it selectively allows a transmission or communication of force or information from one entity to the other; and such that its overall activity brings about the production of a unified condition or system that is mutually defined through the regulated and specified interrelations of these distinct entities. (2014: 4)

Hookway records that the term 'interface' was coined in the nineteenth century by the engineer James Thomson in his influential study of fluid dynamics. For Thomson, the interface, or dividing surface, denoted 'a dynamic boundary condition describing fluidity according to its separation of one distinct fluid body from another', and characterizing the properties of fluidity as differences of velocity, viscosity, and directionality of flow. In other words, for Thomson, fluidity is not pre-given or assumed, but rather emerges in relation to an interface understood as a dynamic boundary condition. Hookway says:

In effect, the emergence of the sciences of hydrodynamics and thermodynamics in the nineteenth century brought with it the positing of a boundary condition as requisite to the very possibility of the fluid as a state of being, and to that set of properties and behaviors collected under the concept of fluidity. In its defining of the fluid, the interface provides far more than a criterion for classification; rather, the boundary condition demarcated by the interface is held to describe the moment from which the state of being a fluid and the onset of performances of fluidity are generated. The installation of this boundary condition within the fluid then, did not constitute a kind of conceptual channeling of the notion of fluidity, as if imposed from without, but rather is given to emerge within the notion of fluidity as that which defines it, as that from which it springs. In this way, the interface would come to be installed as both the source and site of the genesis of fluidity, and the threshold of that which is fluid. (2014: 67)

In Hookway's account, as a boundary condition, the interface is inherently active; while imperceptible, it is inferable according to its effects.

It is this understanding of the interface as the boundary condition that activates fluidity, understood as the generic form of circulation that I am using here to address the organization of relations between science and society. Understood as the activity of an interface, the compulsion of composition is not a mechanism by which society internalizes science; instead the fluidity (the flows or circulation) of knowledge is an interface effect of the expansive force that is the compulsion of composition. Problem spaces are not the result of either the externalization or the internalization of science by society, but emerge, compulsively, across constantly dividing surfaces.

While obviating the language of internal and external, the interface vocabulary that Hookway provides nonetheless enables an acknowledgement of issues of power and control in relations between science and society. He says that at an interface, power is situational, and is typically directed to establishing and maintaining the conditions of its own existence. These conditions are those by which control becomes possible, with such control governing the change from one state to the next. Hookway further says that the interface possesses 'a tendency to come into being, operate within, and express its character with reference to the transformative or the transitional' (2014: 6). In relation to compositional methodology, this speaks to the ways in which the compulsion of composition emerges in the organization of continuity in transformation.

Hookway's account of how control is exercised at an interface helps an understanding of the issues at stake. He says, the interface 'both defines a system and determines the means by which it may be known':

> It takes its place as the zone across which all activity must occur in order to possess meaning, force, or power. It demarcates the site from which the parameters that define a system may be measured ... It is the generative source from which work may be extracted from the system, and the entryway into the system from which influence and control over that system may be exerted. (2014: 43)

To develop his analysis, Hookway introduces the idea of the *contre-rolle*. Historically, a *contre-rolle* was a duplicate account document created as a verification of an original document and a check against tampering. In this use, the *contre-rolle* does not carry content or produce meaning itself, but 'rather exists in a tracking and scanning of the original carrier of content, following the path of its trajectory and testing it at critical points identified along that trajectory' (2014: 25). That is, the control operated by an interface involves a doubling of the process that is controlled: 'What exists in a first reading is now not only doubly read, but has brought into its reading a supplemental activity of checking or testing.'

Hookway identifies the test and the simulation as contemporary derivatives of the interface but it will not have escaped the reader that just as Hookway describes the control exercised at an interface in terms of a doubling, in fact as a 'more than circular' doubling, the methodological opportunities and dilemmas of platformization have been described here as double trouble; that is, as to do with the doubled force of methods in forms of circulation that are recursive or 'more than circular'. In short,

it is through the exercise of interface control – not just
the test or the simulation but all sorts of recursive experimentation and interpretation that epistemological values
such as rigour and inventiveness may be effected. They are
consequences of the ways in which the circulation of forms
of problems interface with forms of circulation as events
of contestation.[3]

Know-ability

Despite the emphasis on contestation, my use of the
concept of the interface to describe relations between
science and society might be seen to naturalize issues of
power and control. But, if its history is acknowledged in
its use (Rheinberger 2010), it is also a way to acknowledge
the politics of the becoming topological of problem spaces
in the new empire of truth.

Developed in the context of thermodynamics as
described above, the concept of the interface was adopted
and adapted in cybernetic theory.[4] For example, Hookway
suggests that the first account of a purposeful machine
operating with an interface was a 'torpedo with a target-
seeking mechanism', as outlined by Rosenblueth, Wiener
and Bigelow (1943). In this paper, Hookway says, the
authors propose teleological as a technical term, specifically referring to goal-seeking by means of negative
feedback: '"Teleological behavior thus becomes synon-
ymous with behavior controlled by negative feedback"'
(2014: 106). Unlike positive feedback, which would
produce an overall amplification, negative feedback was
to be used to operate upon a discrepancy to produce a
behavior 'controlled by the margin of error at which the
object starts at a given time with reference to a relatively
specific goal'. Teleological behavior would then be defined
by 'a continuous feedback from the goal that modifies
and guides the behaving object'. As Hookway says, 'If the
term teleology once belonged to philosophical discussions

of causality or determinism, Rosenblueth, Wiener and Bigelow sought to define it as an instrumental term, "quite independent of causality, initial or final", and concerned "merely with an investigation of purpose"' (2014: 107).

Since these uses, the concept of an interface able to control the behaviour of an object or system by continuous negative feedback has informed very many practical developments in computational and digital media across a range of domains, including not only the military but also the economy and politics. As Hookway says, 'The contemporary proliferation of interfaces, whether by military-industrial projection or market preference, in this way constitutes an unprecedented regime of testing and development' (2014: 147). As an example, take the case of some of the uses of recursive functions described in the last chapter: as they are implemented in many platforms, such functions provide the basis on which rankings, techniques of 'continuous assessment' and 'continuous improvement', optimizing (and satisficing) activities and many of the knowledge claims made in operations science and management acquire epistemological credibility. Recursion has also become increasingly central to a variety of forms of prediction: Adrian Mackenzie (2019) identifies a shift from programmability to prediction, while Luciana Parisi suggests that 'with machine learning, automation has involved the creation of training activities that generalize the function of prediction to future cases – a sort of inductive parable that, from particulars, aims to establish general rules' (2019: 93).

But, rather than naturalizing such practices, a use of the term interface to describe relations between science and society that acknowledges the history of the term enables an acknowledgement of the ways in which the detachment of purpose from both cause and intent (so leaving behind both mechanistic and phenomenological accounts) has contributed, across a range of domains, to practices of weaponization in war and social media, for example, and gamification, be this in video games or the application of game theory in economics and elsewhere. Seltzer's (2009) analysis of game space, of self-enclosing spaces that model a self-modelling world illustrates this. He starts by observing that 'modern game theory, and the game-theoretical worldview that goes with it, takes off from John von Neumann's 1928 essay "On the Theory of Parlor Games" ("Zur Theorie der Gesellschaftsspiele")'. He writes:

> The attempt, in von Neumann's account, is to put on a mathematical basis the little games in which (unlike, say, playing dice) one is not merely playing against the odds but playing against others. This is a game, like poker or chess, in which we move against opponents whose intentions, or what look like them (bluffs), enter into the form of the game. This is a complex game in that one must observe and measure and misinform self-observing observers who are doing the same; that is, one must observe what and how the observed observer can't observe – and whether he can observe that or not. In short, the effects of playing the game must be included in it. (2009: 101)

He says that what defines the game form is its contingency, its self-conditioning, and its deliberate or purposive self-complication:

> It's contingent in the sense that the rules of the game are neither necessary nor impossible. It's self-conditioned in that rules, measure, and outcome are defined by the "sort of game" chosen and by what's possible or impossible in it. It's deliberately complicated to relieve the boredom of that self-conditioning. These are the sandbox elements that prolong the play – the gratuitous difficulties that keep it going, that seduce players to continue to play. (2009: 105–6)

As game space, 'training, educating, correcting, grading,

and self-realizing institutions' are, he says, 'the small worlds that calibrate and compare and measure and individualize individuals and socially distribute the possibilities of personally attributable reflection, action, and evaluation' (2009: 106–7).

In a related line of argument, Hayles (2014) suggests that the use of automated systems of feedback control mean that governmentality is no longer constituted by the law, the norm and reason but by control functions, reiterative loops, and self-regulating auto-poietic agencies. Stephen Collier describes such contemporary methodologies as topologies of power, by which he means to describe '"the patterns of correlations" in which heterogeneous elements – techniques, material forms, institutional structures and technologies of power – are configured, as well as the "redeployments" and "recombinations" through which these patterns are transformed' (Collier 2009: 80). It is through such practices, Collier suggests, that new bio-political formations of government are being assembled while John Allen's use of the phrase 'topologies of power' is intended to describe a 'composed spatiality where proximity and distance play across one another to form new spatial arrangements of power' (2016: 151).

Collier proposes that the most significant feature of these contemporary methodological practices is that they operate without recourse to the assumption of any inner necessity or coherence. The exploitation of this lack of inner necessity contributes to an imaginary of know-ability.[5] Without inner necessity, the epistemological object may be put into relation to multiple regimes of value, including not only epistemological values[6] but also a variety of operational values of decision-making, use-ability or action-ability: as Boellstorff puts it, 'emergent paradigms of algorithmic living pose the possibility that pragmatics and semantics might converge, that "use" will be the "meaning" that matters in what is claimed to be a new age of big data' (Boellstorff 2015: 91).[7] As part of a condition of know-ability, knowledge does not simply provide the basis for 'continuous action' (Bartlett and Tkacz 2017; Rouvroy and Berns 2013), but is the justification for it (Boltanski and Thévenot 2006). Recursion is implemented in a 'virtuous/vicious' circle: more can be known so more can be done (better): more can be done (better) so more can be known.[8]

These tendencies, stemming from the entanglement of social and epistemic control, may be especially acute in collaborative research. Indeed, Herberg and Vilsmaier (2020) suggest that 'collaborative research is epistemically embedded in control regimes' (by which they mean Deleuze's societies of control) and that while many meanings of control originate in the sciences, concepts of experimentation, care and learning are also being translated into decentralized governance concepts. They say:

> Reconfiguring control ... involves reflecting, reconnecting, and constantly balancing the social and epistemic facets of research. If successful, collaborative research approaches, for instance the newly emerging approaches of transdisciplinary research can – ever so slightly – shift the existing forms of authority and privilege. Nonetheless, they are very likely to co-produce some of the established or newly altered forms of control. (Herberg and Vilsmaier, 2020)

In short, in the pursuit of know-ability, it is all too easy for us all to become functionaries of method (Flusser 2014). As an example of the complexities of the balancing required by the entanglement of the social and the epistemic, consider Luciana Parisi's claim that the indeterminacy in contemporary conditions of knowledge allows for the possibility that the introduction of abductive logic in automated thinking provide the basis for critical computation (2019).[9] She suggests that the 'use-meaning of data refers not simply to a mere functional use, but to the dynamic reassessment of the social meaning (and not the truth) embedded in the computational abstraction of the social use of data' (2019: 97).

Interface control

As Hookway describes, in control theory a feedback loop defines a relationship where a past state of a system is harnessed in control of its future state.[10] A derivation of the output of the system is fed back into the system as input, forming a loop. As such, the feedback loop encloses a spatio-temporal discontinuity:

> [The feedback loop] draws into relation past state and future projection, measurement and desire. It proceeds from one discrete moment of measurement to another, as separated by a cycle of evaluation and response. The gap or discrepancy is as much the delay between measurement and reaction as it is the difference between an event as it occurs and as it is modeled or projected. (2014: 101)

Importantly, while control within the feedback loop at an interface remains an operation upon a discrepancy, it is not an act or event specifically located in space and time. It is, rather, a general condition that defines the problem space as being under control across a range of possible states:

> Here the loop diagram and the interface may be viewed as distinct modes of representing control. In the loop diagram, control is a general condition or accomplished state. Within the system described by the loop diagram, control is just now occurring, has already occurred and will continue to occur. The event of its contestation exists abstractly as a set of possible measured and desired values available for calibrated response. In the interface, as the site of control, control is a specific engagement or contested event. (2014: 101)

In short, what is key to issues of control at the interface operated by a feedback loop and their relation to topologies of power and knowledge are issues of temporality as discussed in the previous chapter, of how to interrupt what is 'just now occurring, has already occurred and will continue to occur' (2014: 101).

These issues are precisely what are at stake in the becoming topological of problem spaces in processes of platformization. Like the terms explicitation, literalization and datafication described in Chapter 2, platformization simultaneously conjures up an ongoing process and an already accomplished state of affairs. In their use of –ion, a suffix denoting both action and condition, the terms suggest that the processes they describe and the spatio-temporalities they employ are both already stopped and unstoppable. But this need not be so: feedback loops can be and are employed, in and out of platforms, to enable the operation of multiple temporalities – as in method as *gerund*, the activation of the present, and micro-teleologies of purpose – in the composition of problem spaces. Interfaces can be configured so that feedback loops can be used to feed-back and to feed-forward, to accelerate and decelerate circulation, to create pauses as well as stops, to feed 'elsewhere' and 'else-when', to enable what Haraway calls 'halting voices' (1991: 196) to be heard, to call and respond, to interrupt, resume, invert, and regress.[11]

In addition, interfaces can be designed so that the active adaptation, as Dewey describes it, of a line of inquiry across a problem space does not maintain equilibrium, so that there is no assimilation (of science) to the environment (to society) but instead a process of divergence. Interfaces can contribute to and make visible the making of continuities and discontinuities in the becoming topological of problem spaces. In addition, in the recursive activity of pausing, the feedback loop can enable a stopping and starting – a cutting – that repetitively gathers different kinds of collectivity. As pointed out in previous chapters, in the variety of assemblages of observers and observed, pausing can allow for both observation and the observation of the observing. And while there are many questions as to whether and how observation is rendered opaque or transparent (Kaldrack and Röhle, 2014; Lury and Day 2019; Esposito and Stark 2019), who or what can be held accountable, for what and how (Marres 2012), both observers and the observed can, to different degrees, acquire agency as operators or spect-actors[12] rather than spectators in such problem spaces.

Importantly then, the recursion made possible by interfaces can contribute to a (re-)turn to the 're-', rather than the 'de-' prefix (Felski 2015; Hughes and Lury 2013), to a generative circulation of the around-ness and about-ness of problem spaces rather than for- or against-ness.[13] Recognizing the many meanings of re-, a compositional methodology can articulate the values of autonomy and accountability together as answer-ability rather than know-ability.

Answer-ability

As noted in the Introduction, in the collection *Inventive Methods*, Nina Wakeford and I propose that a problem emerges in the relation between two moments: the addressing of a method (or methods) to a specific problem, and the capacity of what emerges in the use of the method(s) to change or transform the problem (Rheinberger 1997). This relation, we suggested, is what makes a method or methods answerable to a problem. Our use of the term answerable was informed by Matt Fuller and Olga Goriunova's explication of Mikhail Bakhtin's philosophy of the act (1999) to describe the relation between theory and experience as answer-ability. They quote Bakhtin who says:

... the answerability of the actually performed act is the taking-into-account in it of all the factors – a taking into account of the sense validity as well as of its factual performance in all its concrete historicity and individuality. (Bakhtin 1993, quoted in Fuller and Goriunova 2012: 166)

But even as the concern is with a taking-into-account of all the factors, while know-ability reinvigorates a sense of mastery (everything can be known), answer-ability is guided, more doubtfully, by and with the problem space, as it happens.[14] In the Foreword to *Toward a Philosophy of the Act*, Michael Holquist writes: 'For Bakhtin, the unity of an act and its account, a deed and its meaning, if you will, is something that is never *a priori*, but must always and everywhere be achieved' (1999: xii).

And in this respect a more-than-human doubtfulness [15] can temper the demand for know-ability. In a discussion of doubt, Louise Amoore (2019) suggests that the doubtful subject should no longer be considered a unified human subject but 'a composite subject in whom the doubts of human and non-human beings dwell together, opening onto an undecidable future, where one is permitted to ask new questions on the political landscape' (2019: 149). She says:

> In my refiguring of posthuman doubt I envisage the unfolding algorithm itself as straying from calculable paths. The hesitant and non-linear temporality of the etymology of doubt, from the Latin *dubitare*, suggests precisely a straying from other potential pathways. To be doubtful could be to be full of doubt, in the sense of a fullness and a plenitude of other possible incalculable pathways. (2019: 156)

Amoore finds that, in an inquiry into the decision to launch the NASA Space Shuttle Challenger which broke up over the Atlantic Ocean in 1986, 73 seconds after its launch, the scientists who had worked on the components of Challenger gave probabilities of failure that came from their 'particular and situated relationship to a material component and its properties' (2019: 157). Refusing accountability as such, she says, these partial accounts are closer to what Karen Barad describes as the 'condensation of responsibility' in matter, wherein the multiple past decisions are lodged as residue within the object, engaging us in 'a felt sense of causality' (Barad 2012: 208, quoted in Amoore 2019: 158). She affirms, 'It is precisely this mode of intuitive causality and embodied doubtfulness that I am seeking as a resistant and critical form of responsibility' (2019: 158).

In many other feminist accounts, the doubtfulness that is inherent to a more-than-human answer-ability is also expressed as responsibility/response-ability, a term Katherina Hoppe (2019) argues has gained a powerful but not exclusive relevance in relation to the Anthropocene. Hoppe describes a whole variety of ways in which this term has been developed, including Donna Haraway's advocacy of an ethos of curiosity and a practice of responding with otherness (1997), Karen Barad's (2007, 2012) plea for an ethics of entanglement that acknowledges the inherent ethical dimension of all worlding; Anna Tsing's (2015) emphasis on the transformative character of relating and of responding with the world due to its indeterminacy; Deborah Bird Rose's (2017) formulation of response as an ability to care; Alexis Shotwell's explication of compromise and constitutive impurity as a practice of response (2016); and Isabelle Stengers' concern with an ethics of exposure, by which she means the bringing of the other into the space of decision-making (Stengers 2010). In a similar vein to Amoore, Maria Puig de la Bellacasa argues for the need to de-centre the human subject in more-than-human webs of care that have the potential to re-organize human-nonhuman relations Bellacasa on-exploitive forms of co-existence' (2017: 24). She says:

> Care is everything that is done (rather than everything that 'we' do) to maintain, continue, and re-pair 'the world' so that all (rather than 'we') can live in it as well as possible. That world includes... all that we seek to interweave in a complex, life-sustaining web. (Puig de la Bellacasa 2017: 161).

All these approaches, Hoppe points out, share the idea that there is a need to go beyond individualizing notions of responsibility in addressing the multiple, never fully graspable interdependencies of a situation. In these understandings, there is, as Amoore suggests, a recognition of the cruel optimism (Berlant 2011) of optimization, and a re-evaluation of the 'good enough'.[16]

In her analysis, Puig de la Bellacasa invokes the concept of reparation, the act of repairing, mending or making ready again. Eve Kosofsky Sedgwick also employs this term in her discussion of the method of close reading (2003). She comes to it via a discussion of paranoia, an affect, she suggests, follows from the adoption of the hermeneutics of suspicion. To the question: '"How ... is knowledge performative, and how best does one move among its causes and effects?"', she gives the answer that she wants to open a space for 'moving from the rather fixated question, "Is a particular piece of knowledge true, and how can we know?" to the further questions, "What does knowledge do – the pursuit of it, the having and exposing of it, the receiving-again of knowledge of what one already knows?"' (2003: 124). She suggests that equating hermeneutics of suspicion with critical thinking *tout court* 'may have made it less rather than more possible to unpack the local, contingent relations between any given piece of knowledge and its narrative/epistemological entailments for the seeker, knower, or teller', and seeks instead to situate paranoia as one epistemological practice among others, including reparation. The desire of a reparative impulse, she says, is 'additive and accretive ...; it wants to assemble and confer plenitude on an object' (2003: 149). Perhaps, hopefully, in both paranoid and reparative practices in compositional methodology, autonomy and accountability may be, if not reconciled, subjected to the needs of answer-ability rather than the demands of know-ability.

Conclusion

This chapter has drawn on the history of the concept of the interface to move beyond the assumption of internal and external that informs an understanding of the internalization of science by society. The aim in drawing on the concept of interface to describe the topological organization of problem spaces, especially as enabled by platformization, was to enable issues of power and control to be addressed while also making it possible to see that autonomy and accountability need not be opposed, with one subordinate to the other, but may come together in practices of answer-ability and response-ability.

Conclusion: How and Why Methodology Matters

A performing science continually supplies
and defines its own contexts and resources in
the practical attempt to grasp and extend a
research situation.

Karin Knorr Cetina (2007: 363)

The conventional definition of problem space is a space
that contains problems by making them manageable or
amenable to being solved by establishing fixed relations
between three components: givens, goals and operators.
In place of this understanding, this book proposes that
problem spaces are spaces of methodological potential,
specifically spaces of potential that can be realized in
relations of continuity in transformation. Compositional
methodology is introduced as a methodology for the
realization of this potential to grasp and extend a research
situation as Knorr Cetina (2007) says. A problem space
does not contain problems but emerges with them.

Put simply, the aim of compositional methodology is
not to fix an inside or an outside to a problem, but to
twist a problem repeatedly into a process of problematization across a problem space. It informs the compulsive

composition of problems, the ways in which problems transform and are transformed in the operation of limits with-in and out-with a problem space. More specifically, to accomplish epistemological values, compositional methodology engages the becoming of a problem in relations of continuity and connection while providing limit conditions for generalization. These values are what are at stake in what Kelly and McGoey (2018) describe as 'the shifting relationships between knowledge, ignorance and power today'; they are why and how methodology matters.

The book has proposed that significant shifts in the epistemic infrastructure are underway, suggesting that they can be conceptualized in terms of changes in the inter-relationship of the circulation of problems and the changing formal properties of circulation. While describing a diversity of changes in the epistemic infrastructure, their different histories, locations and motivations, platformization was identified as a key dynamic of this change insofar as it enables a reconfiguration of the epistemic infrastructure as a boundary infrastructure (Bowker and Star 2000). The further suggestion was that, as a boundary infrastructure enabled by platformization, there are novel opportunities for infrastructural inversion in the contemporary epistemic infrastructure. Central to this claim was an exploration of the significance of the exploitation of the circulatory property of recursion for methodological purposes, including its ability to enhance the making of the 'active adaptive response ... made in carrying forward a course of behavior' (Dewey 1938: 7–8 in Brown 2012: 269).

Through the discussion of a variety of examples, the formal property of recursion was described as enabling problems to be transformed in circulation in diverse ways, including by:

1. varying the scale and speed of circulation (accelerating, decelerating, interrupting, sequencing, pausing,

interval-ing and so on) and diversifying ways to act on problems by amplifying capacities for queuing, sorting, and capturing, and multiplying possible actors;

2. supporting the assembly of more and different publics or collectivities of (participant) observation in the transformation of problems and equipping (participant) observers with a greater variety of ways to engage problems, precipitating a move – for at least some actors – from being spectators to being operators or spect-actors;

3. supporting a variety of modes of contexting, including the multiplication of the contexts in which the composition of a problem leads to interventions of many kinds, enabling a problem to be transformed in response to constantly changing contexts, and activating or radicalizing contexts and environments in a kind of perpetual re-purposing.

It was argued that a combination of these capacities contributes to a 'more than circular' compounding of the epistemic infrastructure, contributing to the generative circulation of problems in ways that are re-distributive of cognitive agency.

A series of methodological double troubles associated with the emergence of this infra-ontology were described, including: the natively artificial character of the empirical; the ontological multiplicity of the epistemological object; and transcontextualism. In staying with these troubles, the book argues for the importance of reflection on non-linear temporalities for the auto-spatialization of problem spaces. More specifically, it suggests that compositional methodology must be concerned with the (changing) ways in which the compulsive composition of problem spaces may be purpose-ful, informed by an 'intent toward' (Hayles 2014), a way of 'being for' or matter-ing while simultaneously acknowledging that epistemological value derives from the consequences of a situation. As a formal property of platformization, recursion was identified as playing a significant role in this regard since it amplifies the ability of platforms to enable indexically enabled feedback loops to feed backwards and forwards, complexifying the present (Uprichard 2011).

While the intention has been to emphasize the methodological opportunities associated with changes in the epistemic infrastructure, and the enhanced abilities they offer for making use of the property of recursion to realize methodological potential, it was also argued that the platformization of recursion enhances the weaponization and gamification of methods. Indeed, it was suggested that both weaponization and gamification contribute to the creation of a world in which, in pursuit of survival, distinguishing between truth or falsehood 'does not matter anymore' (Arendt 1972; Davies 2020), a world of pathological cognitive disorders such as 'doublethink', 'thinking without thinking', and 'believe it *and* not'.[1] However, it was also suggested that compositional methodology need not be complicit with an imaginary of know-ability, and might instead be informed by a care-ful concern with the needs of answer-ability.

An important aspect of the argument made in this book is that methodology – the twisting of the form of problems into forms of circulation – needs to be understood as a Mobius strip of topological sense-making (Lury 2013; Watkins and Stark 2018). To reflect (again) on how this is so, consider Matthew Spencer's (2019) description of methods research in computer science. Methods research, he says, is a form of recursive looping in which scientists act upon the purposeful structures of their practices, a looping that forms, at the level of the laboratory, 'an intrinsic motor of the historicity of experimental systems', or in my terms, the auto-spatialization of problem spaces. Spencer observes:

> We are familiar with the idea that methods are performative; they create objects and worlds. But when methods are themselves the object, this performativity

loops back to the wider structure of research itself. (2019: 314)

What this book has suggested is that all methodology is – unavoidably – methods research, the study *and* practice (study-as-practice and practice-as-study) of methods, a recursively purposeful way of doing, taking methods themselves as objects as well as means of research, as workings that matter, practices of infrastructural inversion (Bowker 2016), always operating the tension between laterality and hierarchy in the transversal meta-physics of the epistemic infrastructure.

With this understanding of *how* methodology matters comes a renewed sense of *why* it matters. The recognition of the performativity of methods brings an awareness of the capacity of methods to enact worlds, the practice of participatory methods acknowledges issues of inclusion, exclusion, and belonging. But an understanding of methodology as the exploration of the study-and-practice of methods inspires a recognition of its significance of and for the habitability (Simone 2018) of problem spaces. And, at least for now, it seems that habitability might be a way of introducing criteria for decisions as to which epistemological values are to be prioritized, how methodology can be put to the test of the present (Stengers 2019), the basis on which the tension between answer-ability and response-ability can be negotiated, and act as a guide to 'composition attaining worth for itself' (Whitehead 1968: 119).

Notes

Introduction

1 This approach is thus very different from what has been called solutionism (Morozov 2013), in which problems are identified in relation to solutions that are already available. However, it has similarities with the consideration of problems as wicked (Rittel and Webber 1973; Buchanan 1992). In this approach, problems are wicked because they are indeterminate; that is, they have no definitive conditions or limits. Problem definition is considered a design space just as the solution is, with progress towards a solution affecting the progress of defining the problem. There are no inherent stopping criteria. This understanding of wicked problems has many affinities with the analysis of problem spaces proposed here. However, the emphasis here is on methodology rather than design as such. This is to enable a more open-ended discussion of the issues involved. Perhaps most importantly, however, the focus on problem spaces, rather than problems, even if they are qualified as wicked, draws attention to how problems are made, their becoming, rather than seeing them as having inherent characteristics.

2 Drawing on Whitehead, both Bruno Latour (2010) and Isabelle Stengers (2010) also use the term composition in relation to issues of methodology and politics. While sympathetic to these approaches, my use has a more strongly aesthetic emphasis, indicated by the discussion of form.

3 I hope to avoid the charge of formalism: the understanding of form proposed here is a dynamic social category; that is, it is a modality of social making.

4 I would like to thank Emma Uprichard for this formulation.

5 Roy Wagner says, 'time is the difference between itself and space; space is the similarity between the two. Hence (*pace* Einstein) the nature of perception itself forbids a conflation of space and time as a single continuum' (2019: xiii).

6 Compare with the definition given by Edwards et al.: 'knowledge infrastructures comprise robust networks of people, artifacts, and institutions that generate, share and maintain specific knowledge about the human and natural worlds' (2010: 17; see also: http://pne.people.si.umich.edu/ PDF/Edwards_etal_2013_Knowledge_Infrastructures.pdf). Bowker defines knowledge infrastructures as: 'the network of institutions, people, buildings and information resources which enable us to turn observation and contemplation of the world into a standardized set of knowledge objects: journal articles and monographs' (2016: 391).

7 In most early uses of the term in the humanities and social sciences, infrastructure was used to refer to whatever assemblage of technologies, procedures, and people (hardware, software and people) was robust, stable or solid enough to facilitate a set of organized practices, but the recognition of the mutability of such assemblages has been gradually built into the working definition. There is now a concern with the doing of infrastructures; that is, with infrastructuring as a material-semiotic practice (Bossen and Markussen 2010; Simone 2015; Michael 2020).

8 Law, Ruppert and Savage (2011) describe this understanding of methods – that is, methods as tools – as 'the methodological complex' (presumably in an analogy to the 'patriarchal- military- capitalist complex') or 'the methods machine'. The problem with such an approach they say is the separation it introduces and enforces between theory, substance, and method.

1 What is a Problem Space?

1 Bachelard (1970) identifies the importance of what he calls

'applied doubt' for the identification of a problematic, in contradistinction to 'universal doubt' which, so he proposes, only destroys the world it seeks to investigate. As noted below, Donna Haraway uses the term 'generative doubt'.

2 Simon holds design to be a ubiquitous practice: 'Everyone designs who devises courses of action aimed at changing existing situations into preferred ones' (1996: 111).

3 There is considerable debate as to what it means to 'represent' a problem. A compositional methodology, as described in the Introduction, does not consider a problem space to be a representation of a problem, in the sense of re-presenting an external referent, but a relational process of composition, the transformation of a situation.

4 Other writers insist on the importance of re-presentation too, including for example Whitehead, who provides a powerful critique of the limitations of perception in the mode of 'presentational immediacy'.

5 The criticism of instrumentalism might also be levelled at pragmatism, although most commentators would distinguish between pragmatism's ethical concern with the difference an idea makes to the world from the instrumental design of problem spaces for predetermined purposes or goals.

6 As will be discussed in the next chapter, the equipping of a situation or environment with a variety of forms of cognition is one of the key transformations in the contemporary epistemic infrastructure.

7 Situated knowledges, she says, are neither totalizing nor relativizing. Indeed, in dismissing both, Haraway sees relativism as the 'perfect mirror twin of totalization ...: both deny the stakes in location, embodiment and partial perspective, both make it impossible to see well' (1991: 191).

8 She says that this promise arises in conversation, one of the few of Haraway's terms that has not been widely taken up, but which I draw attention to here because of its resonance with the term correspondence that Dewey uses (and which has recently elaborated upon by Tim Ingold 2016).

9 In this respect, there is a link to the understanding of the methodological potential of pattern, both in the sense in which Dewey discusses, and also in the understanding of figure-ground that has been powerfully developed in anthropology,

including, for example, in the work of Alfred Gell (1998; see also Küchler and Were 2005). His *Anthropology of Art* is an anthropology of agency, in that it shows how art objects index complex collective intentionalities as they circulate. In this sense, they are a form of embodied cognition, what he describes as a form of abductive reasoning.

10 As Karel van der Leeuw says, 'Comparison between different traditions can show which particular form is assumed by problems under different presuppositions, or how a particular answer to a question can make another problem invisible or insoluble ... Some aspects of a problem remain invisible, either because the tradition simply ignores the problematic side, or because it poses no problem to it, given its specific outlook on reality. Some solutions remain untouched, because they do not fit in with the expectations of the tradition, or because they are at variance with basic assumptions concerning the nature of reality. Thus we gain an insight into why a particular tradition is haunted by problems that seem to play no role at all in another tradition' (1997: 323).

11 In a discussion of the use of the concept 'reflex arc' in psychology, Dewey criticizes what he calls its patchwork of stimulus response and proposes instead the term sensori-motor circuits, by which he means the continual reconstitution and adjustment of organisms-in-environments. Begin, he says, not with the specious 'stimulus' (for example, 'seeing'), but with 'sensori-motor co-ordinations', such as 'seeing-for reaching' (https://pdfs.semanticscholar.org/a7ab/dafa9cc a3547d8f441ee9dc3b5ad19ee7f59.pdf). The 'response' that follows is not just 'reaching', it is 'reaching-guided-by-seeing'. He says, 'the arc is virtually a circuit, a continual reconstitution' (1896: 360), and 'It is the circuit within which fall distinctions of stimulus and response as functional phases of its own mediation or completion' (1896: 370). This description provides a vocabulary – phase, co-ordination and continual reconstitution – with which to address the partial continuities that can be established in relation to the properties of different forms of circulation.

12 Importantly for the understanding of problem space being developed here, while the dictionary declares that 'across' can be used as a preposition to refer to relations between

fixed points (from one side of a river to another for example), it can also mean to pass through, throughout or intersect at an angle, a crossing, to find or meet, and it is these meanings of the word that are enrolled here.

A paradigmatic example of how 'across' may be accomplished is the method of chiasmus (the dictionary definition of which is a rhetorical or literary figure in which words, grammatical constructions, or concepts are repeated in reverse order, as if across each other) or double proportional comparison as described by Roy Wagner (2019). This is a practice in which the comparisons do not result in an equivalence but a reversed doubling of sameness that results in difference. For Wagner, metaphor is the primary technique of double proportional comparison, 'the automatic reflex of [the] reinversion [of language] out of itself': '"a metaphor is two words, each dividing the significance of the other between them"' (2019: xvi). An apt example is Appadurai's 'the circulation of forms' and 'forms of circulation'.

2 The Parasite and the Octopus

1 Despite the apparent rejection of representation, it is argued by some commentators that non-representational theory is interested in representation, even if it does sometimes appear otherwise: '[n]on-representational theory takes representations seriously; representations not as a code to be broken or as an illusion to be dispelled rather representations are apprehended as performative in themselves; as doings' (Dewsbury et al. 2002: 438).
2 Among many others – Anzaldúa 1987; Hill Collins 2009; Braidotti 1994; Hughes and Lury 2013; Chow 2006; Barad 2007; Verran 2001; Kenney 2015. Haraway herself explicitly refuses 'self-vision as a cure for self-invisibility' (1997: 33).
3 Haraway writes: 'The tentacular are also nets and networks, it critters, in and out of clouds. Tentacularity is about life lived along lines – and such a wealth of lines – not at points, not in spheres' (2016: 31).
4 Verran (2001) compares herself collecting the Yoruba number system to Captain Cook collecting 'spears, axes, carrying

baskets, flutes, fans, and hats' (2001: 74) from the Pacific islands for display in European museums. She observes that while she initially presented her object, like Cook, as found, it is the collecting process (including wonder as a mode of attention) that comes to define the contours of the objects (number systems or carrying baskets). As an alternative to wonder, she proposes disconcertment.

5 The concept of infra-ontology will be taken up in later chapters.

6 They say, 'Definitions of the term "participation" in Indo-European languages are generally anchored in the idea of shared action, invoking notions of taking part or effecting an action with something or someone else. For instance, the French definition of the verb *participer* reads as *prendre ou avoir part à*, and finds a direct equivalent in the German verb *teilnehmen*, which literally means to take (*nehmen*) part (*teil*), while the verb's synonym, *mitmachen*, transliterates in English as "doing with"' (Barney et al. 2016: xxxi).

3 Indexing the Human (with Ana Gross)

1 Most of the research described in this chapter was carried out by Ana Gross, and is discussed in her PhD thesis (2015) as well as appearing in a co-authored article (Gross and Lury 2014). As indicated below the controversy continued beyond the period of our research.

2 Daniel and Lanata Briones note: 'The Argentine economy has experienced inflation since the nineteenth century ... . However, it was after the Second World War that continuous price rises became a crucial concern ... Since then, governments' performances and their policies began to be judged socially on the basis of their ability to control inflation, particularly given the periodically high inflation rates of the 1970s onwards ... Since its creation and until 2007, inflation as measured by the INDEC was a widely used and reliable representation of reality' (2019: 113).

3 According to Bruno, Didier and Vitale (2014) stat-activism is a broad concept that encompasses a wide variety of practices that put statistics at the heart of projects of political emancipation.

4 The Decree 55/2016 states that the National Institute for Statistics and Census (INDEC) suffers from an anomalous situation in its internal organization, hindering the production of sufficient and reliable statistical information related to consumer prices, gross domestic product, and trade.

5 Daniel and Lanata Briones suggest that in its origins the Argentine CPI was an economic indicator rather than a socio-labour index like its contemporaries in, for example, the US, the UK and Germany. This changed in the 1930s when the aim of the indicator changed due to '"political concern anchored in workers' living conditions and in their relationship with employers"' (2019: 128).

6 As Daniel and Lanata Briones note, 'The doubts concerning the INDEC CPI encouraged the proliferation of alternative, unofficial indices, something unusual within Argentina's statistical tradition. Provincial statistical agencies continued to publish their own provincial CPIs. But, the main novelty was that economic consultancy firms and research centres, once users of INDEC data, became 'factories' that collected information on prices and produced their own price indicators. Some of them sold their index as a private good' (2019: 139). They describe this as contributing to a 'mercantilization' of information that had previously been considered a public good.

7 The concern with accuracy does not, of course, disappear: it returns, for example, in relation to the question of which websites are identified for scraping.

8 In 2016, Premise was described as having 'data-gatherers situated across 34 countries, ... raised $66.5 million (£45m) in VC funding and ... paid out $3 million to its contributors on the ground' (https://www.wired.co.uk/article/premise-app-food-tracking-brazil-philippines). Since Ana Gross and I conducted the study for the above analysis, the BPP project has added a 'participative' methodological element. On the website as accessed on 2 August 2019, viewers were invited to help measure inflation in Venezuela. There were three ways identified for those wishing to 'help': visit stores and take photos of the prices, using the True Inflation app for Android phones; look at the images received and verify that the price that the volunteers entered is correct; promote the website via social media.

9 Savage observes that the 'critical incubator' of the sample survey was the Royal Statistical Society, and that 'economic and military examples provided the key precedents for its practice' (2010: 199, 200).

10 The Premise website identifies four streams of potential clients: international development, global security, and government as well as business. A magazine article in 2016 reports, 'The company charges customers a subscription to its indices and for individual annual contracts, which are in the six-figure dollar range' (https://www.wired.co.uk/article/premise-app-food-tracking-brazil-philippines).

11 The significance of staples was identified in the Staple Thesis, a theory formulated in the 1920s by economic historians Harold A. Innis and W. A. Mackintosh. It asserted that the export of natural resources, or staples, from Canada to more advanced economies had a pervasive impact on the economy and social and political systems (Innis 1967 [1930]; Mackintosh (1967 [1923]). Different staples (for example, fur, fish, lumber, agricultural products, oil) were held to have differing impacts on rates of settlement, and federal-provincial conflicts. Both Innis and Mackintosh argued that the nation of Canada was shaped by its emergence as a staple economy, but while Mackintosh projected an evolution toward a more autonomous industrialized economy based on the production of staples, Innis suggested that Canada would become permanently locked into dependency as a resource hinterland. Innis' prediction is thought to have been proved more accurate.

4 Platforms and the Epistemic Infrastructure

1 Fuller and Mazurov write: 'DRM [Digital Rights Management] constitutes a broad 'effort to impose power through technology' ... such as via the imposition of video playback control mechanisms into web standards ... . Watermarking and DRM can both be said to function as '[v]ideo protection techniques' which are in turn 'technological tools that enforce excludability of information goods, which otherwise would be public goods' ... Techniques such as DRM, which aim to technologically block the

unauthorized distribution of content are augmented in the contemporary forensic landscape with tactics reminiscent of isotopic tracking which focus on identifying the source of a leak so as to deter future leaks; namely, the forensic practice now often known as traitor tracing' (2019: 178).

2 Paradoxically both responses are part of the divinatory turn described by Elena Esposito (2012). As evidence of such a turn Esposito gives the example of financial markets: these are places, she says, where rationality alone is incapable of providing reliable guidance, as past crises have shown: 'In searching for a new model better able to capture circularities, reflexive mechanism and non-random irregularities, theories involving alternative forms of rationality are being explicitly formulated in this domain' (2012: 1–2).

She also highlights the spread of Web 2.0 and cloud computing, arguing that their use both requires a move away from the 'linear logic of the Western tradition' and a search to find connections, analogies and more complex correlations in which effect precedes cause, in which 'one must deal, even if vaguely and incompletely, with a higher intelligence and a perfect memory' (2011: 2).

3 She says, 'The figure of the 'centaur' in the algorithmic system is a posthuman body with a capacity to reach an unsupervised algorithmic judgement ('this event is critical') but also to display 'a human readable motivation for that judgement' so that action can be authorized against a threat' (2019: 162).

4 The methodological politics of platform figuration are only poorly addressed in most discussions of consent, since most such practices rely on the methodological politics of representationalism that is being displaced by a politics of participation. One initiative that attempts to remedy this problem in relation to the digital is being carried out by the Technoscience Salon (https://technosalon.wordpress.com): a series of events on the theme of 'Consent and its Discontents'. The aim is 'to expand visions of consent praxis beyond the narrow scope that structures conventional digital activities, such as terms of service, university ethics protocols, and developer-led community consultations'. Moving outside this paradigm, the Salon asks: What practices of permission and processual consent have communities *already* built

that can be brought to bear on digital practices? How can we learn across different protocols and efforts to create communities of meaningful and ongoing consent?'

5 More than Circular

1 As Scott Wark (2019) notes, the concept of circulation is widely used, but rarely theorized.
2 Creager et al. (2007) sometimes use the term platform as an alternative to model system. I distinguish between them to draw out the distinctive characteristics of contemporary forms of circulation. The term bio-medical platform was also used by Keating and Cambrosio (2003) to describe the transformation of medicine into biomedicine they associate with a specific configuration of instruments, individuals and programmes of action. They say, 'insofar as they embody regulations and conventions of equivalence, exchange, and circulation ... platforms are not simply one among many forms of coordination that include networks; rather, they account for the generation of networks or, at the very least, they are a condition of possibility for the very existence and transformation of networks' (2003: 324).
3 A case in point is the claim that genres have been 'broken' by the operation of recommendation systems operating across platforms (Cohen 2017).
4 Among other observers of science, Karin Knorr Cetina identifies 'contextual contingency as a principle of change' in science, old and new (1997: 10), referring to the fact that the context-dependence of scientific practice is not at odds with successful innovation. Indeed, she describes the laboratory as an environment that is deliberately enhanced to improve the possibilities such context-dependence affords for innovation. Bruno Latour argues 'that the very difference between the "inside" and the "outside" and the difference of scale between "micro" and "macro" levels, is precisely what laboratories are built to destabilize or undo' (1982: 143). The argument being developed here is that this undoing is happening in new ways because of platformization.
5 In a description of rankings as second-order observations, Stark and Esposito distinguish their effects from objectivity.

They say, 'The distinction of first-order and second-order observation has been introduced by Heinz von Foerster ... to distinguish the condition in which observers focus on objective data from the one in which they turn to the perspective of other observers. As von Foerster argues, in the shift to second-order observation reality does not disappear, but does not coincide with objectivity any more. Reality is not the starting point, it is the result of observation, produced by the reciprocal reference of observers to the perspective of others. This is the most reliable reference in a world that has become too complex for univocal determinations. Even if not objective, this multiple reality is by no means arbitrary. What observers observe is contingent (in the sense that it would be different from another perspective) but cannot be changed at will. Once a reference has been chosen and shared, the perspective is binding, effectively excluding any arbitrariness' (2019: 12). In emphasizing the 'binding' qualities of second order-observation, they draw attention to the onto-epistemological politics of problem spaces that will be addressed more directly in Chapter 6.

6   As argued in the previous chapter, platformization contributes to the emergence of what Bowker and Star describe as a boundary infrastructure. They write, 'the institutionalization of categorical work across multiple communities of practice, over time, produces the structure of our lives, from clothing to houses. The parts that are sunk into the built environment are called here boundary infrastructures – objects that cross larger levels of scale than boundary objects' (2000: 287).

7   This list of the techniques of recursion, queueing, sorting and capture is taken from Fuller and Goffey's (2012) description of algorithms. I have added contexting to the list, while identifying recursion as the 'meta' formal property of the plat-formization of the epistemic infrastructure.

8   In a blog post Nicholas Carr writes: 'In discussing the appeal of the News Feed in [an] interview with Kirkpatrick, [Mark] Zuckerberg observed: "A squirrel dying in front of your house may be more relevant to your interests right now than people dying in Africa." The statement is grotesque not because it's false – it's true, actually – but because it's a category error. It yokes together in an obscene comparison two events of radically different scale and import. And yet,

in his tone-deaf way, Zuckerberg managed to express the reality of content collapse. When it comes to information, social media renders category errors obsolete' (http://www. roughtype.com/?p=8724).

9 These concerns will be returned to in Chapter 6 in a discussion of response-ability, and in the Conclusion in relation to a concern with the habit-ability of problem spaces.

10 *Adobe After Effects* is a digital visual effects motion graphics application developed by Adobe Systems. It is used in the post-production process of filmmaking and television production. It can be used for keying, tracking, rotoscoping, compositing and animation as well as functioning as a non-linear editor, audio editor and media transcoder.

11 To repeat: the claim is not that recursion itself is new, but rather that platformization makes recursion and the sequencing of recursion easier to do, for more and more varied actors, and in doing so makes recursion a shared characteristic of more and more different kinds of inquiry.

12 This is a key aspect of double hermeneutics (Giddens 1993).

13 Of course, as Guggenheim and Krause make clear, challenges to standards have always occurred, as when new sources appeared or 'when scholars widened the pool of sources; examples include the interpretation of French history from the perspective of the provinces ... or from women's point of view' (2012: 111). But platformization not only makes challenges to this or that standard much easier, it also means that addressing the challenges of standardization becomes a site of innovation in methodologically informed practice.

14 He writes: 'In fact, the category [of the disappeared] is now a sensation. It has multiplied and become transnational. It has even been officially recognized through an international convention. It has succeeded, been naturalized, and taken the form of evidence. And it expands and grows, colonizing territories that are farther and farther away from its birth-place. It was born in Argentina in the 1970s, and today it sails with the abducted across the Mediterranean, it rides with those banished from all logic, it lies beside the slain women in Juárez ... bad lives ..., *vie sans* (lifeless) ... : unformed, unsupported, unseen' (2020: 26).

15 To develop his analysis, Spencer suggests that it is helpful

to consider Ruth Millikan's naturalist theory of 'proper functions' (organs, instincts, artefacts *being for* some purpose)'. He writes: 'Millikan relies on a rejection of the conceptual analysis of 'in principle' causal mechanisms, emphasizing instead the observation that all actual purposes arise out of specific (and indeed overwhelmingly specific) histories of (re)production (Millikan 1989). If methods become epistemic as ways of working that matter, these micro-teleologies, what Pickering called "vectors of cultural extension" (Pickering 1995) are not effects of their internal causal structure alone. Nor are they effects of being represented as such by an agent, or of being designed from scratch as such. They are an effect of historicity, the actuality of their emergence within historical sociotechnical assemblages, conditioned in their various ways by the relative persistence of that laboratory, wider experimental systems, their unique trajectories, and the modes of transformation in science' (2019: 319–20).

16 For Serres an engagement with an expanded vocabulary of prepositions is necessary at a time when 'the milieu [the middle or the in-between] arises in every place' (Serres 1994: 128 in http://stevenconnor.com/milieux/). For Serres, like many other contemporary thinkers, milieu does not just refer to media, but speaks instead to the ways in which the occupation of in-between has become a defining characteristic of contemporary life.

17 In using the term auto-construction, Corsín Jiménez is also explicitly concerned with the fact that many accounts speaking about a place (geographical or epistemic) pay little or no attention to how such places must themselves be drawn together as empirical and pragmatic problems. He says, 'The empirical problems of this or that place cover up the very operation of problematization as method' (2017: 454). In contrast, he considers the heuristic of auto-construction leads to an understanding of the city itself as a method: a method of design, theory and problematizations. In this regard, the city is an infra-ontology. There is a parallel here with the case of 'Asia as method' and the method of district-ing as described by Simone (2018), both discussed in Chapter 2.

18 The use of –ing here is one of the things distinguishing the

practice of Forensic Architecture from that of Premise, as described in Chapter 3.

19 In a discussion of visualization design, Miriah Meyer and Jason Dykes (2019) propose six criteria to guide researchers in constructing, communicating, and assessing rigorous knowledge claims. Rigour should be evident in how a visualization is: *informed* by existing designs to inspire and understand candidate solutions; *abundant* in observations, designs, and descriptions; expresses *plausible* designs and interpretations of design processes; generates *resonant* designs and claims; and expresses knowledge claims explicitly through *transparent* description and evidence.

20 Knorr Cetina describes the importance of what she calls synthetic situations; that is 'situations that include electronically transmitted on–screen projections that add informational depth and new response requirements to the "ecological huddle" ... of the natural situation' (2011: 61).

6 Know-ability and Answer-ability

1 In using the terms 'know-ability', 'answer-ability', and response-ability, I draw on Samuel Weber's discussion of Walter Benjamin's '–abilities', a set of terms including communicability and reproducibility. Weber explicates these terms by reference to Jacques Derrida's concept of iterability or 'structural possibilities' (1988), 'the necessity of which does not depend on actual fact or probable implementation' (Weber 2010: 116). That is, an –ability refers to 'a possibility or a potentiality, to a capacity rather than to an actually existing reality' (Weber 2010: 116).

2 In 2016, the *Oxford Dictionary*'s Word of the Year was 'post-truth'.

3 I am thinking here of Jullien's explication of a concept of efficacy that 'teaches one to learn how to allow an effect to come about: not to aim for it (directly) but to implicate it (as a consequence), in other words, not to seek it, but simply to welcome it – to allow it to result' (Jullien 2004: vii). Perhaps alongside explicitation we should also acknowledge 'implicitation'.

4 Other histories of the use of the term interface provide other

resources with which to critically interrogate the implications of platformization for the becoming topological of problem spaces and its dependence on forms of participation. So, for example, Stephen Monteiro (2017) draws attention to the many historical connections between textiles, gendered practices of domestic labour, craft-based activity and the development of computer code and understandings of the interface. His discussion of the relationship between digital labour practices such as liking, linking and tagging and earlier forms of collective labour such as quilting bees and textile industry piecework provides a salutary reminder of the inequalities perpetuated in many contemporary participatory data practices (see also Terranova, 2000; Watkins and Stark 2018; Wark and Wark 2019).

5 According to Weber, for Benjamin, it was important to maintain the distinction between knowability and knowledge: '"knowability" is not, for Benjamin at least, simply a preface to its realization as full-fledged knowledge. It has its own dignity, precisely as potentiality, and above all, it has its distinctive structure. It is this structure alone, which is that of *awakening* as distinguished both from consciousness and from unconsciousness, that explains how and why knowability, whose manifestation is inseparable from its vanishing, cannot be reduced to the positive knowledge it both makes possible and relativizes' (2010: 168–9). My proposal is that the Benjaminian 'now' of know-ability is so frequently subsumed by action-ability in the contemporary epistemic infrastructure that the concept of answer-ability is better able to acknowledge the potentiality of knowing that Benjamin wishes to recognize.

6 There is no single widely shared criterion for the quality of an explanation, but rather, several criteria that may come into mutual conflict.

7 It is also revealing to think about the different ways in which inductive and abductive forms of reasoning contribute to forms of planning and governance. Schurz says, 'Inductions and abductions can be distinguished by their different targets. Both serve the target of extending our knowledge beyond observation but in rather different respects. Inductions serve the goal of inferring something about the future course of events, which is important for planning; that is, adapting

our wishful actions to the course of events. In contrast, abductions serve the goal of inferring something about the unobserved causes or explanatory reasons of the observed events – which is of central importance for manipulating the course of events; that is, adapting the course of events to our wishes' (2008: 202).

 8 Steven Connor describes Serres' notion of ichnography, or the absolute maximum of all variations, as 'a suffocating nightmare of omnicompetence'. He says, 'What such a vision seems to lack is precisely lack itself – the possibility of exposure to chance, mischance, error, weakness, exhaustion, forgetting, death. Or rather, insofar as it includes and operationalizes all these things, as continuous, but homogenous possibility, it lacks the deficiency, the falling short, which have previously represented the limits of all systems' (http://www.stevenconnor.com/topologies/).

 9 She says, 'My attempt to re-theorize automated intelligence ... argues that the crisis of deductive logic is mediated by new meanings of artificial thinking stemming from the scientific image of experimental axiomatics, which has indeterminacy at its core' (2019: 95).

10 Hookway says, 'Yet the interface ... does not require such a teleology. The interface attends only to the specific interrelation in which it comes into being. While the activity of the interface may on occasion be described as equilibrium seeking or goal-directed, the end state of the interface is only ever the condition of its own existence. The interface constitutes the zone within and through which the activity of otherwise distinct entities may be translated into an equivalence, through which they may meaningfully and effectively contest, communicate with, or *mutually define one another*. Through this mediated interrelation, mutually directed formations or actions are made possible' (2014: 108).

11 For an example, consider the practices of the self-described 'multidisciplinary research and curatorial platform' Slow Research Lab: https://www.slowlab.net/ABOUT.

12 This is a term created by the Brazilian theatre practitioner Augusto Boal, who was influenced by Paulo Freire; it refers to the dual role of those involved as spectator and actor, as they both observe and create dramatic meaning and action in any performance.

13 Rita Felski says, 'We shortchange the significance of art by focusing on the "de" prefix (its power to demystify, destabilize, denaturalize) at the expense of the "re" prefix: its ability to recontextualize, reconfigure, or recharge perception' (2015: 17).

14 The acknowledgement of historicity points to the importance of the building up of active memory in any platform, of cognitive failure and cognitive success.

15 For Bakhtin, answerability was actualized in the individual person but he also cautions against conflating psychic being and unitary Being (1999: 17).

16 Weber writes of the structure of awakening, 'The (person) awakening never wakes up in general, but always in and with respect to a determinate place. The locality in turn is never closed upon itself or self-contained, but opened to further relationships by the iterations that take place "in" it. To be sure, such iterations are never infinite, they will always *stop*, but that stopping will never amount to a conclusion or a closure. Rather, it will be more like an interruption or a suspension. A cut' (2010: 171).

Conclusion

1 In a discussion of the political deception that was revealed with the leaking of *The Pentagon Papers* in 1971, Hannah Arendt describes what she terms defactualization, or the inability to discern fact from fiction. Arguing that factual truths are inherently contingent and 'never compellingly true', she writes: 'There always comes the point beyond which lying becomes counterproductive. This point is reached when the audience to which the lies are addressed is forced to disregard altogether the distinguishing line between truth and falsehood in order to be able to survive. Truth or falsehood – it does not matter which anymore, if your life depends on your acting as though you trusted; truth that can be relied on disappears entirely from public life, and with it the chief stabilizing factor in the ever-changing affairs of men' (1972).

References

Adkins, L. and Lury, C. (2011) Introduction: special measures, *Sociological Review*, 59(2): 5–23.

Agamben, G. (2002). *What is a Paradigm?*, transcribed by Max van Manen, Lecture, European Graduate School, August.

Agrawal, A. (2002) Indigenous knowledge and the politics of classification, *International Social Science Journal*, 54(173): 277–81.

Agre, P. E. (1994) Surveillance and capture: two models of privacy, *The Information Society*, 10: 101–27.

Albuquerque, J. Porto de and Almeida, A. A. (2020) Modes of engagement: reframing 'sensing' and data generation in citizen science for empowering relationships, in A. Mah and T. Davies (eds) *Toxic Truths: Environmental Justice and Citizen Science in a Post Truth Age*, Manchester: Manchester University Press, pp. 267–81.

Allen, J. (2016) *Topologies of Power: Beyond Territory and Networks*, London and New York: Routledge.

Amoore, L. (2013) *The Politics of Possibility: Risk and Security Beyond Probability*, Durham, NC: Duke University Press.

Amoore, L. (2019) Doubt and the algorithm: on the partial accounts of machine learning, *Theory, Culture and Society*, 36(6): 147–69.

Amoore, L. and Piotukh, V. (2015) Life beyond big data: governing with little analytics, *Economy and Society*, 44(3): 341–66.

Anzaldúa, G. (1987) *Borderlands = La Frontera: The New Mestiza*, San Francisco: Spinsters/Aunt Lute.

Appadurai, A. (1990) Disjuncture and difference in the global economy, *Theory, Culture and Society*, 7(2–3): 295–310.

Appadurai, A. (2013) *The Future as Cultural Fact: Essays on the Global Condition*, London: Verso Books.

Aradau, C., Blanke, T. and Greenway, G. (2019) Acts of digital parasitism: hacking, humanitarianism and platformization, *New Media and Society*, 21(11–12): 2548–65.

Arendt, H. (1972) Lying in politics: reflections on the Pentagon Papers, *The New York Review of Books*, 18 November. https://www.tramuntalegria.com/wp-content/uploads/2018/08/Lying-in-Politics-Reflections-on-The-Pentagon-Papers-by-Hannah-Arendt-The-New-York-Review-of-Books.pdf

Asdal K. and Moser I. (2012) Experiments in context and contexting, *Science, Technology and Human Values*, 37(4): 291–306.

Ash, J. (2015) *The Interface Envelope: Gaming, Technology, Power*, London: Bloomsbury Academic.

Bachelard, G. (1970) The role of epistemology in the sciences, trans. Theodore Kisiel, in J. J. Kockelmans and T. J. Kisiel (eds) *Phenomenology and the Natural Sciences: Essays and Translations*, Evanston: Northwestern University Press.

Back, L. and Puwar, N. (eds) (2012) *Live Methods*, Oxford: Wiley-Blackwell.

Bakhtin, M. M. (1999) *Toward a Philosophy of the Act*, trans. and notes by V. Liapumov, Austin: University of Texas Press.

Barad, K. (2007) *Meeting the Universe Halfway: Quantum Physics and the Entanglement of Matter and Meaning*, Durham, NC: Duke University Press.

Barad, K. (2012) On touching: The inhuman that therefore I am, *Differences: A Journal of Feminist Cultural Studies*, 23(3): 206–23.

Barocas, S. and Levy, K. (2019) Equivocal measures, paper delivered at Algorithmic Prediction vs. Shared Uncertainty: social consequences of individualized forecast, Society for the Advancement of Socio-Economics Annual Meeting, 27 June.

Barney, D., Coleman, G., Ross, C., Stern, J. and Tembek, T. (2016) (eds) *The Participatory Condition in the Digital Age*, Minneapolis: University of Minnesota Press.

Bartlett, J. and Tkacz, N. (2017) *Governance by Dashboard. A Policy Paper*, DEMOS; https://www.demos.co.uk/wp-content/uploads/2017/04/Demos-Governance-by-Dashboard.pdf

Bateson, G. (1972) *Steps to an Ecology of Mind*, Chicago: University of Chicago Press.

Beck, U. (1986) *Risk Society*, London: Sage.

Beck, U. and Sznaider, N. (2010) Unpacking cosmopolitanism for the social sciences: a research agenda, *British Journal of Sociology*, 57(1): 381–403.

Beer, D. (2018) *The Data Gaze*, London and New York: Sage.

Bell, D. (1973) *The Coming of Post-Industrial Society: A Venture in Social Forecasting*, New York: Basic Books.

Bell, D. (1976) *The Cultural Contradictions of Capitalism*, New York: Basic Books.

Bennett, T. (2007) The work of culture, *Cultural Sociology*, 1(1): 31–47.

Berlant, L. (2008) Thinking about feeling historical, *Emotion, Space and Society*, 1(1): 4–9.

Berlant, L. (2011) *Cruel Optimism*, Durham, NC: Duke University Press.

Bhambra, G. K. (2017) Brexit, Trump and 'methodological whiteness': on the misrecognition of race and class, *British Journal of Sociology*, 67(S1): S214–32.

Bhambra, G. K. and de Sousa Santos, B. (2017) Introduction: global challenges for sociology, *Sociology*, 51(1): 3–10.

Birch, K. and Muniesa, F. (eds) (2020) *Assetization: Turning Things into Assets in Technoscientific Capitalism*, Cambridge, MA and London: MIT Press.

Bochner, M. (2008) *Solar System and Rest Rooms: Writings and Interviews, 1965–2007*, Cambridge, MA and London: MIT Press.

Boellstorff, T. (2015) Making big data, in theory, in T. Boellstorff and B. Maurer (eds) *Data, Now Bigger and Better!*, Prickly Paradigm Press, pp. 87–108.

Boltanski, L. and Thévenot, L. (2006) *On Justification: Economies of Worth*, trans. C. Porter, Princeton, NJ: Princeton University Press.

Borgman, C. L. (2019) The lives and after lives of data, *Harvard Data Science Review*,1(1).

Bossen, C. and Markussen, R. (2010) Infrastructuring and ordering devices in health care: medication plans and practices on a hospital ward, *Computer Supported Cooperative Work*, 19(6): 615–37.

Botero-Mesa, M. and Roca-Servat, D. (2019) Water rights and

everyday Ch'ixi practices in the Barrio El Faro in Medellín, Colombia, *Water*, 11(10): 2062; doi.org/10.3390/w11102062

Bowker, G. (2016) How knowledge infrastructures learn, in P. Harvey et al. (eds) *Infrastructures and Social Complexity*, London: Routledge, pp. 391–403.

Bowker, G. C. and Star, S. L. (2000) *Sorting Things Out: Classification and its Consequences*, Cambridge, MA: MIT Press.

boyd, D. and Crawford, K. (2012) Critical questions for big data, *Information, Communication and Society*, 15(5): 662–79.

Braidotti, R. (1994) *Nomadic Subjects*, Columbia University Press.

Brighenti, A. M. (2018) The social life of measures: conceptualizing measure-value environments, *Theory, Culture and Society*, 35(1): 23–44.

Brown, M. J. (2012) John Dewey's logic of science, *Hopos: The Journal of the International Society for the History of Philosophy of Science*, 2(2): 258–306.

Bruno I., Didier E. and Vitale, T. (2014) (eds) Statactivism: forms of action between disclosure and affirmation, *Partecipazione e conflitto. The Open Journal of Sociopolitical Studies*, 7(2).

Buchanan, I. (1992) Wicked problems in design thinking, *Design Issues*, 7(2): 5–21.

Calkins, S. and Rottenburg, R. (2016) Evidence, infrastructure and worth, in P. Harvey et al. (eds) *Infrastructures and Social Complexity*, London: Routledge, pp. 253–65.

Calvillo, N. (2012) The affective mesh: air components 3D visualizations as a research and communication tool, *Parsons Journal for Information Mapping*, 4(2): 1–8.

Cardon, D. (2019) Society2Vec. From categorical prediction to behavioral traces, paper delivered at Algorithmic Prediction vs. Shared Uncertainty: Social consequences of individualized forecast, Society for the Advancement of Socio-Economics Annual Meeting, 27 June.

Cavallo, A. (2010) *Scraped Data and Sticky Prices*, PhD thesis, MIT Sloan.

Chen, K-H. (2010) *Asia as Method: Toward Deimperialization*, Durham, NC: Duke University Press.

Chen, K-H. (2012) Takeuchi Yoshimi's 1960 'Asia as method' lecture, *Inter-Asia Cultural Studies*, 13(2): 317–24.

Chow, R. (2006) *The Age of the World Target: Self-Referentiality in War, Theory and Comparative Work*, Durham, NC: Duke University Press.

Chow, R. (2012) *Entanglements, or Transmedial Thinking about Capture*, Durham, NC: Duke University Press.

Chua, Beng Huat (1998) Culture, multiracialism and national identity in Singapore, in K-H. Chen (ed.) *Trajectories: Inter-Asia Cultural Studies*, London: Routledge, pp. 186–205.

Clough, P. Ticineto, Gregory, K., Haber, B., and Scannell, J. R. (2018) The datalogical turn, in P. Clough, *The User Unconscious: On Affect, Media and Measure*, Minneapolis: University of Minnesota Press, pp. 94–114.

Cohen, K. (2017) *Never Alone, Except For Now*, Durham, NC: Duke University Press.

Coleman, R. (2019) https://maifeminism.com/glitter-a-methodology-of-following-the-material

Collier, J. H. (2005) (ed.) *The Future of Social Epistemology: A Collective Vision*, Rowman and Littlefield.

Collier, S. (2009) Topologies of power: Foucault's analysis of political government beyond 'governmentality', *Theory, Culture and Society*, 10(6): 78–108.

Connolly, W. (2000) *Why I am Not a Secularist*, Minneapolis: University of Minnesota Press.

Connor, S. (1994) http://www.stevenconnor.com/topologies

Cooley, C. H. (1897) The process of social change, in J. D. Peters and P. Simonson (eds) *Mass Communication and American Social Thought Key Texts 1919–1968*, London: Rowman & Littlefield.

Corsín Jiménez, A. (2014) The right to infrastructure: a prototype for open source urbanism, *Environment and Planning D: Society and Space*, 32: 342–62.

Corsín Jiménez, A. (2017) Auto-construction redux: the city as method, *Cultural Anthropology*, 32(3): 450–78.

Corsín Jiménez, A. and Nahum-Claudel, C. (2019) The anthropology of traps: concrete technologies and theoretical interfaces, *Journal of Material Culture*, 24 (4).

Couldry, N. and Mejias, U. A. (2019) Data colonialism: rethinking big data's relation to the contemporary subject, *Television & New Media*, 20(4): 336–49.

Creager, A. N. H., Lunbeck, E., and Wise, M. N. (2007) *Science*

Without Laws: Model Systems, Cases, Exemplary Narratives, Durham, NC: Duke University Press.

Dagiral, E. and Peerbaye, A. (2016) Making knowledge in boundary infrastructures: inside and beyond a database for rare diseases, *Science and Technology Studies*, 29(2): 44-61.

Dalsgaard, S. (2016) Carbon valuation: alternatives, alternations and lateral measures, *Valuation Studies*, 4(1): 67–91.

Daniel, C. J. and Lanata Briones, C. T. (2019) Battles over numbers: the case of the Argentine consumer price index (2007–15), *Economy and Society*, 47(1): 127–51.

Davies, W. (2020) Post-liberal competitions?: Pragmatics of gamification and weaponization, in D. Stark (ed.) *The Performance Complex: Competitions and Valuations in Social Life*, Oxford: Oxford University Press, pp. 187–207.

Davis, J. and Jurgenson, N. (2014) Context collapse: theorizing context collusions and collisions, *Information, Communication and Society*, 17: 4, 476–85, doi:10.1080/1369118X.2014.888458

Day, S. and Lury, C. (2017) New technologies of the observer: #BringBack, visualization and disappearance, *Theory, Culture and Society*, 34(7–8): 51–74.

De Sousa Santos, B. (2014) *Epistemologies of the South: Justice Against Epistemicide*, London and New York: Routledge.

De Sousa Santos, B. (2019) *The End of the Cognitive Empire: The Coming of Age of Epistemologies of the South*, Durham, NC: Duke University Press.

Derrida, J. (1988) *Limited Inc*, Illinois: Northwestern University Press.

Desrosières, A. (1998) *The Politics of Large Numbers: A History of Statistical Reasoning*, Cambridge, MA: Harvard University Press.

Dewey, J. (1896) The reflex arc concept in psychology, *Psychological Review*, 3(4): 357-370.

Dewey, J. (1922) *Human Nature and Conduct: An Introduction to Social Psychology*, Oxford: Henry Holt.

Dewey, J. (1938) *Logic: The Theory of Inquiry*, Oxford: Henry Holt.

Dewsbury, J. D. (2003) Witnessing space: 'knowledge without contemplation', *Environment and Planning A*, 35(11): 1907–32.

Dewsbury, J. D., Harrison, P., Rose, M. and Wylie, J. (2002) Enacting geographies, *Geoforum* 33(4): 437–40.

Didier, E. (2005) Releasing market statistics, in B. Latour and P. Weibel (eds) *Making Things Public: Atmospheres of Democracy*, Cambridge, MA: MIT Press.

Dieter, M. and Gauthier, D. (2019) On the politics of chrono-design: capture, time and the interface, *Theory, Culture and Society*, 36(2): 61–87.

Dieter, M., Gerlitz, C., Helmond, A., Tkacz, N., van der Vlist, F. and Weltevrede, E. (2019) Multi-situated apps studies: methods and propositions, *Social Media and Society*.

Dilley, R. M. (1999) *The Problem of Context*, New York: Berghan Books.

Drucker, J. (2018) Non-representational approaches to modeling interpretation in a graphical environment, *Digital Scholarship in the Humanities*, 33(2): 248–63.

Edwards, P. N. (2010) *A Vast Machine: Computer Models, Climate Data and the Politics of Global Warming*, Cambridge, MA: MIT Press.

Edwards, P. N., Jackson, S. J., Chalmers, M. K., Bowker, G. C., Borgman, C. L., Ribes, D., Burton, M. and Calvert, S. (2013) *Knowledge Infrastructures: Intellectual Frameworks and Research Challenges*, Ann Arbor: Deep Blue. http://hdl.handle.net/2027.42/97552

Erikson, S. (2015) Secrets from whom? Following the money in global health finance, *Current Anthropology*, 56: S12, S306–16.

Escobar, A. (2008) *Territories of Difference: Place, Movement, Life, Redes*, Durham, NC: Duke University Press.

Escobar, A. (2019) *Designs for the Pluriverse*, Durham, NC: Duke University Press.

Espeland, W. and Sauder, M. (2007) Rankings and reactivity: how public measures recreate social worlds, *American Journal of Sociology*, 113(1): 1–40.

Espeland, W. and Sauder, M. (2016) *Engines of Anxiety: Academic Rankings, Reputation and Accountability*, New York: Russell Sage Foundation.

Esposito, E. (2012) A time of divination and a time of risk: social preconditions for prophecy and prediction, *Selected Lectures of FATE*, International Consortium for Research in the Humanities, Friedrich-Alexander-University Erlangen Nuremberg.

Esposito, E (2013) Economic circularities and second-order observation: The reality of ratings, *Sociologica*, 2: 1–20.

Esposito, E. (2017) Artificial communication? The production of contingency by algorithms, *Zeitschrift für Soziologie*, 46(4): 249–65.

Esposito, E. and Stark, D. (2019) What's observed in a rating? Rankings as orientation in the face of uncertainty, *Theory, Culture and Society*, 36(4): 3–26.

Felski, R. (2015) *The Limits of Critique*, Chicago: Chicago University Press.

Flusser, V. (2014) *Gestures*, trans. N. A. Roth, Minneapolis: University of Minnesota Press.

Fourcade, M. and Healy, K. (2013) Classification situations: life-chances in the neoliberal era, *Accounting, Organizations and Society*, 38: 559–72.

Fourcade, M. and Healy, K. (2017) Seeing like a market, *Socio-Economic Review*, 15(1): 9–29.

Freire, P. (1970) *Pedagogy of the Oppressed*, trans. Myra Bergman Ramos, London: Continuum.

Fuller, M. and Goffey, A. (2012) *Evil Media*, Cambridge, MA: MIT Press.

Fuller, M. and Goriunova, O. (2012) Phrase, in C. Lury and N. Wakeford (eds) *Inventive Methods: The Happening of the Social*, London: Routledge, pp. 163–71.

Fuller, M. and Mazurov, N. (2019) A counter-forensic audit trail: disassembling the case of *The Hateful Eight*, *Theory, Culture and Society*, 36(6): 171–96.

Gabrys, J. (2016) *Program Earth: Environmental Sensing Technology and the Making of a Computational Planet*, Minneapolis: University of Minnesota Press.

Gal, S. (2002) A semiotics of the public/private distinction, *differences: A Journal of Feminist Cultural Studies*, 13(1): 77–95.

Galloway, A. (2012) *The Interface Effect*, Cambridge: Polity.

Gatti, G. (2020) The social disappeared: genealogy, global circulations, and (possible) uses of a category for a bad life, *Public Culture*, 32(1): 25–43.

Gell, A. (1998) *Art and Agency: An Anthropological Theory*, Oxford: Oxford University Press.

Gerlitz, C. and Lury, C. (2014) Social media and self-evaluating assemblages: on numbers, orderings and values, *Distinktion: Journal of Social Theory*, 15(2): 174–188.

Gibbons, M., Limoges, C., Nowotny, H., Schwartzman, S., Scott, P. and Trow, M. (1994) *The New Production of Knowledge. The Dynamics of Science and Research in Contemporary Societies*, London: Sage.

Gibbs, M., Meese, J., Arnold, M., Nansen, B. and Carter, M. (2015) #Funeral and Instagram: death, social media, and platform vernacular, *Information, Communication and Society*, 17(3): 255–68. doi:10.1080/13 69118X.2014.987152.

Giddens, A. (1987) *Social Theory and Modern Society*, Cambridge: Polity.

Giddens, A. (1990) *The Consequences of Modernity*, Cambridge: Polity.

Giddens, A. (1993) *New Rules of Sociological Method: A Positive Critique of Interpretative Sociologies*, Stanford, CA: Stanford University Press.

Gieryn, T. (1999) *Cultural Boundaries of Science: Credibility on the Line*, Chicago: University of Chicago Press.

Gillespie T. (2010) The politics of 'platforms', *New Media and Society*, 12(3): 347–64.

Gitelman, L. (2013) (ed.) *'Raw Data' is an Oxymoron*, Cambridge, MA: MIT Press.

Goriunova, O. (2017) The lurker and the politics of knowledge in data culture, *International Journal of Communication*, 11: 3917–33.

Griffiths, H. (2019) *Smart City Demonstrators: A Global Review of Challenges and Lessons Learned*, Future Cities Catapult, https://cp.catapult.org.uk

Gromme, F. and Ruppert, E. (2019) Population geometries of Europe: the topologies of data cubes and grids, *Science, Technology and Human Values*, 45(2): 235–61.

Gross, A. (2015) Data types and functions: a study of framing devices and techniques, PhD thesis, Warwick University.

Gross, A. and Lury, C. (2014) The downs and ups of the consumer price index in Argentina: from national statistics to big data, *Statactivism: State Restructuring, Financial Capitalism and Statistical Mobilizations*, Special Issue, *Partecipazione e Conflitto – Rivista Scientifica di Studi Sociali e Politici*, pp. 258–77.

Guggenheim, M. and Krause, M. (2012) How facts travel: the model systems of sociology, *Poetics*, 40: 101–17.

Guyer, J. I. (2004) *Marginal Gains: Monetary Transactions in Atlantic Africa*, Chicago: University of Chicago Press.

Guyer, J. I. (2016) *Legacies, Logics, Logistics: Essays in the Anthropology of the Platform Economy*, Chicago: University of Chicago Press.

Hacking, I. (2006) *The Emergence of Probability: A Philosophical Study of Early Ideas about Probability, Induction and Statistical Inference*, Cambridge: Cambridge University Press.

Hacking, I. (2012) *Representing and Intervening*, Cambridge: Cambridge University Press.

Halpern, O. (2015) *Beautiful Data: A History of Vision and Reason Since 1945*, Durham, NC: Duke University Press.

Halpern, O., LeCavalier, J., Calvillo, N. and Pietsch, W. (2013) Test-bed urbanism, *Public Culture*, 25(2): 272–306.

Hansen, M. B. N. (2015) *Feed-Forward: On the Future of Twenty-First-Century Media*, Chicago: University of Chicago Press.

Haraway, D. J. (1991) *Simians, Cyborgs and Women: The Reinvention of Nature*, London: Free Association Books.

Haraway, D. J. (1997). *Modest_Witness@Second_Millennium. Femaleman_Meets_Oncomouse: Feminism and Technoscience*, London: Routledge.

Haraway, D. (2003) *The Companion Species Manifesto: Dogs, People and Significant Otherness*, Chicago: University of Chicago Press.

Haraway, D. J. (2016) *Staying with the Trouble*, Durham, NC: Duke University Press.

Haraway, D. J., and Goodeve, T. N. (2000) *How Like a Leaf: An Interview with Thyrza Nichols Goodeve*, Hove: Psychology Press.

Hart, K. (2000) *The Memory Bank: Money in an Unequal World*, London: Profile Books.

Harvey, P., Bruun Jensen, C. and Morita, A. (2016) (eds) *Infrastructures and Social Complexity: A Companion*, London: Routledge.

Hayles, N. K. (2014) Cognition everywhere: the rise of the cognitive nonconscious and the costs of consciousness, *New Literary History*, 45(2): 199–220.

Hayles, N. K. (2016) Cognitive assemblages: technical agency and human interactions, *Critical Inquiry*, 43(1): 32–55.

Hayles, N. K. (2017) *Unthought: The Power of the Cognitive Nonconscious*, Chicago: University of Chicago Press.

Helmond, A. (2015) The platformization of the web: making web data platform ready, *Social Media and Society*, 1(2): 260–75.

Herberg, J. and Vilsmaier, U. (2020) Social and epistemic control in collaborative research: reconfiguring the interplay of politics and methodology, *Social Epistemology*, doi:10.108 0/02691728.2019.1706115.

Hessels, L. K. and van Lente, H. (2008) Re-thinking new knowledge production: a literature review and a research agenda, *Research Policy*, 37(4): 740–60.

Hill Collins, P. (2009) *Black Feminist Thought: Knowledge, Consciousness, and the Politics of Empowerment*, New York: Routledge.

Hind, S. and Lammes, S. (2016) Digital mapping as double-tap: cartographic modes, calculations and failures, *Global Discourse*, 6(1–2): 79–97.

Holquist, M. (1999) Foreword, in M. M. Bakhtin, *Toward a Philosophy of the Act*, trans. and notes by V. Liapunov and ed. by V. Liapunov and M. Holquist, Austin: University of Texas Press, pp.vii–xvi.

Hoppe, K. (2019) Responding as composing: towards a post-anthropocentric feminist ethics for the Anthropocene, *Distinktion: Journal of Social Theory*, 21(2): 125–42.

Hookway, B. (2014) *Interface*, Cambridge, MA: MIT Press.

Hughes, C. and Lury, C. (2013) Re-turning feminist methodologies: from a social to an ecological epistemology, *Gender and Education*, 25(6): 786–99.

Hui, Y. (2019) *Recursivity and Contingency*, Lanham: Rowman and Littlefield International.

Ingold, T. (2016) On human correspondence, *Journal of the Royal Anthropological Institute*, 23(1): 9–27.

Innis, H. A. (1967) The importance of staple products, in W. T. Easterbrook and M. H. Watkins (eds) *Approaches to Canadian Economic History*, Toronto: McClelland and Stewart.

Jullien, F. (2004) *A Treatise on Efficacy: Between Western and Chinese Thinking*, trans. J. Lloyd, Honolulu: University of Hawaii Press.

Kaldrak, I. and Röhle, T. (2014) Divide and share: taxonomies, orders and masses in Facebook's Open Graph, *Computational Culture* 4.

Keating, P. and Cambrosio, A. (2003) *Biomedical Platforms: Realigning the Normal and the Pathological in Late Twentieth-Century Medicine*, Cambridge, MA: MIT Press.

Kelly, A. H. and McGoey, L. (2018) Facts, power and global evidence: a new empire of truth, *Economy and Society*, 47(1): 1–26.

Kelty, C. (2020) *The Participant: A Century of Participation in Four Stories*, Chicago: University of Chicago Press.

Kenney, M. (2015) Counting, accounting, and accountability: Helen Verran's relational empiricism, *Social Studies of Science*, 45(5): 749–71.

King, K. (2011) *Networked Reenactments: Stories Trans-disciplinary Knowledges Tell*, Durham, NC: Duke University Press.

Kitchin, R. (2014) *The Data Revolution*, London: Sage.

Knorr Cetina, K. (1997) Sociality with objects: social relations in postsocial knowledge societies, *Theory, Culture and Society*, 14(4): 1–30.

Knorr Cetina, K. (2007) Culture in global knowledge societies: knowledge cultures and epistemic cultures, *Interdisciplinary Science Reviews*, 32(4): 361–75.

Knorr Cetina, K. (2011) The synthetic situation: interactionism for a global world, *Symbolic Interaction*, 32(1): 61–87.

Koed Madsen, A. (2013) *Web-Visions: Repurposing Digital Traces to Organize Social Attention*, Copenhagen: Copenhagen Business School.

Kopytoff, I. (1986) The cultural biography of things: commoditization as process, in A. Appadurai (ed.) *The Social Life of Things: Commodities in Cultural Perspective*, Cambridge: Cambridge University Press, pp. 64–91.

Krause, M. (2016) Comparative research: beyond linear-casual explanation, in J. Deville, M. Guggenheim and Z. Hrdličková (eds) *Practising Comparison: Logics, Relations, Collaborations*, London: Mattering Press, pp. 45–67.

Krauss, R. (1976) Video: The aesthetics of narcissism, *October*, 1, Spring: 50–64.

Krauss, R. (2010) *Perpetual Inventory*, Cambridge, MA: MIT Press.

Krikorian, G. and Kapczynski, A. (eds) (2010) *Access to*

Knowledge in the Age of Intellectual Property, Cambridge, MA: Zone Books, MIT Press.

Küchler, S. and Were, G. (2005) *Pacific Pattern*, London: Thames and Hudson.

Kurgan. L. (2013) *Close Up at a Distance: Mapping, Technology and Politics*, Cambridge, MA: MIT Press.

Kwon, M. (1997) One place after another: notes on site specificity, *October* 80: 85–110.

Langlois, G., Elmer, G., McKelvey, F. and Devereaux, Z. (2009) Networked publics: the double articulation of code and politics on Facebook, *Canadian Journal of Communication*, 34(3): 415–34.

Lash, S. and Lury, C. (2007) *Global Culture Industry: The Mediation of Things*, Cambridge: Polity.

Last, A. (2018) Of interdisciplinarity, in C. Lury et al. (eds) *Routledge International Handbook of Interdisciplinary Research Methods*, London and New York: Routledge, pp. 197–208.

Latour, B. (2005) *Reassembling the Social – An Introduction to Actor-Network-Theory*, Oxford: Oxford University Press.

Latour, B. (2007) A plea for earthly sciences, http://www.bruno-latour.fr/sites/default/files/102-BSA-GB_0.pdf

Latour, B. (2010) An attempt at a 'Compositional Manifesto', *New Literary History*, 41: 471–90.

Lave, J. and Wenger, E. (1991) *Situated Learning: Legitimate Peripheral Participation*, Cambridge: Cambridge University Press.

Law, J. (2004) *After Method: Mess in Social Science Research*, London and New York: Routledge.

Law, J. and Mol, A-M. (1994) Regions, networks and fluids: anaemia and social topology, *Social Studies of Science*, 24(4): 641–71.

Law, J. and Mol, A-M. (eds) (2002) *Complexities: Social Studies of Knowledge Practices*, Durham, NC: Duke University Press.

Law, J., Ruppert, E. and M. Savage (2011) The double social life of methods, CRESC Working Paper, no. 95, http://www.open.ac.uk/researchprojects/iccm/files/iccm/Law%20Savage%20Ruppert.pdf

Law, J. and Urry, J. (2003) Enacting the social, https://www.lancaster.ac.uk/fass/resources/sociology-online-papers/papers/law-urry-enacting-the-social.pdf

LeCun, Y., Bengio, Y. and Hinton, G. (2015) Deep learning, *Nature*, 521, May, pp. 436–44.

Lentin, A. (2019) Charlie Hebdo: white context and black analytics, *Public Culture*, 31(1): 45–67.

Leonelli, S. (2015) What counts as scientific data? A relational framework, *Philosophy of Science*, 82(5): 810–21.

Levin, N., Leonelli, S., Weckowska, D., Castle, D. and Dupré, J. (2016) How do scientists define openness? Exploring the relationship between open science policies and research practice, *Bulletin of Science, Technology and Society*, 36(2): 128–41.

Lezaun, J. (2012) The pragmatic sanction of materials: notes for an ethnography of legal substances, *Journal of Law and Society*, 39(1): 20–38.

Lezaun, J., Marres, N. and Tironi, M. (2017) Experiments in participation, in C. Miller, E. Smitt-Doer, U. Felt and R. Fouche (eds) *Handbook of Science and Technology Studies*, vol. 4, Cambridge, MA: MIT Press, pp. 195–222.

Lury, C. (2012) 'Bringing the world into the world': the material semiotics of contemporary culture, *Distinktion: Journal of Social Theory*, 13(3): 247–60.

Lury, C. (2013) Topological sense-making: walking the mobius strip from cultural topology to topological culture, *Space and Culture*, 16(2): 128–32.

Lury, C. (2020) Shifters, in N. Bonder Thylstrup, D. Agostinho, A. Ring, C. D'Ignazio and K. Veel (eds) *Uncertain Archives: Critical Keywords for Big Data*, Cambridge, MA: MIT Press.

Lury, C., Parisi, L. and T. Terranova (2012) Introduction: The becoming topological of culture, *Theory, Culture and Society*, 29(4–5): 3–35.

Lury, C. and Wakeford, N. (eds) (2012) *Inventive Methods: The Happening of the Social*, London: Routledge.

Lury, C. and Marres, N. (2015) Notes on objectual valuation, in M. Kornberger, L. Justesen, A. Koed Madsen and J. Mouritsen (eds) *Making Things Valuable*, Oxford: Oxford University Press, pp. 232–56.

Lury, C., Fensham, R., Heller Nicholas, A., Lammes, S., Last, A., Michael, M. and Uprichard, E. (eds) (2018) *Routledge Handbook of Interdisciplinary Research Methods*, London and New York: Routledge.

Lury, C. and Day, S. (2019) Algorithmic personalization as a mode of individuation, *Theory, Culture and Society*, 36(2): 17–37.

Lynch, M. (1993) *Scientific Practice and Ordinary Action: Ethnomethodology and Social Studies of Science*, Cambridge: Cambridge University Press.

McInerny, G. J. (2018) Visualising data – a view from design space, in C. Lury et al. (eds) *Routledge International Handbook of Interdisciplinary Research Methods*, London: Routledge, pp. 133–41.

Mackenzie, A. (2016) Infrastructures in name only? Identifying effects of depth and scale, in P. Harvey, C. Bruun Jensen and A. Morita (eds) *Infrastructures and Social Complexity: A Companion*, London: Routledge, pp. 379–90.

Mackenzie, A. (2017) *Machine Learners: Archaeology of a Data Practice*, Cambridge, MA: MIT Press.

Mackenzie, A. (2018) Personalization and probabilities: impersonal propensities in online grocery shopping, *Big Data and Society*, 5(1): 1–15.

Mackenzie, A. (2019) From API to AI: platforms and their opacities, *Information, Communication and Society*, 22(13): 1989–2006.

Mackenzie, A. and Munster, A. (2019) Platform seeing: image ensembles and their invisualities, *Theory, Culture and Society*, 36(5): 3–22.

Mackintosh, W. A. (1967) Economic factors in Canadian economic history, in W. T. Easterbrook and M. H. Watkins (eds) *Approaches to Canadian Economic History*, Toronto: McClelland and Stewart.

McQuillan, D. (2015) Algorithmic states of exception, *European Journal of Cultural Studies*, 17(4–5): 564–76.

Magnani, L. (2001) *Abduction, Reason and Science: Processes of Discovery and Explanation*, New York: Springer.

Marcus, G. E. (1995) Ethnography in/of the world system: the emergence of multi-sited ethnography, *Annual Review of Anthropology*, 24: 95–117.

Marres, N. (2012a) The redistribution of methods: on intervention in digital social research, broadly conceived, *The Sociological Review*, 60(S1): 139–65

Marres, N. (2012b) *Material Participation: Technology, the Environment and Everyday Publics*, London: Palgrave Macmillan.

Marres, N. (2018) Why we can't have our facts back, *Engaging Science, Technology, and Society*, 4: 423–43.

Maurer, B. (2005) *Mutual Life, Limited: Islamic Banking, Alternative Currencies, Lateral Reason*, Princeton, NJ: Princeton University Press.

Maurer, B. (2008) Resocializing finance? or dressing it in mufti? Calculating alternatives for cultural economies, *Journal of Cultural Economy*, 1(1): 65–78.

Maurer, B. (2012) Payment. Forms and functions of value transfer in contemporary society, *Cambridge Anthropology*, 30(2): 15–35.

Maurer, B. (2015) Principles of descent and alliance for big data, in T. Boellstorff and B. Maurer (eds) *Data, Now Bigger and Better!*, Prickly Paradigm Press, pp. 67–86.

Mayer-Schönberger, V. and Cukier, K. (2013) *Big Data: A Revolution That Will Transform How We Live, Work, and Think*, London: John Murray.

Meier, N. and Dopson, S. (eds) (2019) *Context in Action and How to Study It: Illustrations from Health Care*, Oxford: Oxford University Press.

Merz, M. (2018) Epistemic innovation: how novelty comes about in science, in W. Rammert, A. Windeler, H. Knoblauch and M. Hutter (eds) *Innovation Society Today: Perspectives, Fields and Cases*, Wiesbaden, Springer VS, pp. 325–339.

Meyer, M. and Dykes, J. (2019) Criteria for rigor in visualization design study, *IEEE Transactions on Visualization and Computer Graphics*, 26: 87–97.

Michael, M. (2017) Walking, falling, telling: the anecdote and the mis-step as a 'research event', in C. Bates and A. Rhys-Taylor (eds) *Walking Through Social Research*, London: Routledge.

Michael, M. (2020) London's fatbergs and affective infrastructuring, *Social Studies of Science*, 50(3): 377–97.

Michael, M. and Rosengarten, M. (2012) HIV, globalization and topology: of prepositions and propositions, *Theory, Culture and Society*, 29(4–5): 93–115.

Mignolo, W. D. (2009) Epistemic disobedience: independent thought and decolonial freedom, *Theory, Culture and Society*, 26(7–8): 159–81.

Milan, S. and Treré, E. (2019) Big Data from the South(s):

beyond data universalism, *Television and New Media*, 20(4): 319–35.

Miller, D. (2000) The fame of Trinis: websites as traps, *Journal of Material Culture*, 5(1): 5–24.

Millikan, R. G. (1989) In defense of proper functions, *Philosophy of Science*, 56(2): 288–302.

Mbembe, A. and Roitman, J. (1995) Figures of the subject in times of crisis, *Public Culture*, 7(2): 323–52.

Monteiro, S. (2017) *The Fabric of Interface: Mobile Media, Design and Gender*, Cambridge, MA: MIT Press.

Moor, L. and Lury, C. (2011) Making and measuring value, *Journal of Cultural Economy*, 4(4): 439–54.

Moor, L. and Lury, C. (2018) Price and the person: markets, discrimination and personhood, *Journal of Cultural Economy*, 11(6): 501–513.

Moreno Figueroa, M. G. (2008) Looking emotionally: racism, photography and intimacies in research, *History of the Human Sciences*, 21(4): 66–83.

Morozov, E. (2013) *To Save Everything, Click Here: The Folly of Technological Solutionism*, New York: PublicAffairs, Hachette Book Group.

Motamedi Fraser, M. (2019) Dog words – or, how to think without language, *Sociological Review*, 67(2): 374–90.

Muniesa, F. (2007) Market technologies and the pragmatics of price, *Economy and Society*, 36(3): 377–395.

Murphy, M. (2017) *The Economization of Life*, Durham, NC: Duke University Press.

Nafus, D. (2014) Stuck data, dead data, and disloyal data: the stops and starts in making numbers into social practices, *Distinktion: Journal of Social Theory*, 15(2): 208–22.

Nakazora, M. (2016) Infrastructural inversion and reflexivity: a 'postcolonial' biodiversity databasing project in India, in P. Harvey, C. Bruun Jensen and A. Morita (eds) *Infrastructures and Social Complexity: A Companion*, London: Routledge, pp. 309–22.

Nash, C. (2000) Performativity in practice: some recent work in cultural geography, *Progress in Human Geography*, 24, 653–64.

Nature Publications (2014) Opening up communications, *Nature Communications*, 5, 5523.

Ndlovu, M. (2018) Coloniality of knowledge and the challenge of creating African futures, *Ufahamu: A Journal of African Studies*, 40(2): 95–112.

Neff, G. and Nafus, D. (2016) *Self-Tracking*, Cambridge, MA: MIT Press.

Ngai, S. (2012) *Our Aesthetic Categories: Zany, Cute, Interesting*, Cambridge, MA: Harvard University Press.

Nieborg, D. and Poell, T. (2018) The platformatization of cultural production, *New Media & Society*, 20(11): 4275–92.

Niranjana, T. (2015) Introduction to genealogies of the Asian present: situating Inter-Asia Cultural Studies, in T. Niranjana, X. Wang and N. Vasudevan (eds) *Genealogies of the Asian Present: Situating Inter-Asia Cultural Studies*, New Delhi: Orient Blackswan. https://www.academia.edu/14934670/Introduction_to_Genealogies_of_the_Asian_Present_Situating_Inter-Asia_Cultural_Studies

Nowotny, H. (1999) The place of people in our knowledge, *European Review*, 7(2): 247–62.

Nowotny, H., Scott, P. and Gibbons, M. (2001) *Re-Thinking Science: Knowledge and the Public in an Age of Uncertainty*, Cambridge: Polity.

Pape, H. (2008) Searching for traces: how to connect the sciences and the humanities by a Peircean theory of indexicality, *Transactions of the Charles S. Peirce Society*, 4(1): 1–25.

Pereira, M. do Mar (2018) Boundary-work that does not work: social inequalities and the non-performativity of scientific boundary-work, *Science, Technology and Human Values*, 44(2): 338–65.

Parisi, L. (2019) Critical computation: digital automata and general artificial thinking, *Theory, Culture and Society*, 36(2): 89–121.

Parker, M. and Kingori, P. (2016) Good and bad research collaborations: researchers' views on science and ethics in global health research, *PLoS ONE* 11(10): e0163579. doi.org/10.1371/journal.pone.0163579

Pasquale, F. (2015) *The Black Box Society: The Secret Algorithms that Control Money and Information*, Cambridge, MA: Harvard University Press.

Pasquinelli, M. (2019) How a machine learns and fails: a grammar of error for artificial intelligence, *Spheres: Journal for Digital Cultures*, November, http://spheres-journal.org/

how-a-machine-learns-and-fails-a-grammar-of-error-for-artificial-intelligence

Pearce, W., Özkula, S. M., Greene, A. K., Teeling, L., Bansard, J. S., Joceli Omena, J. and Teixeira Rabello, E. (2020) Visual cross-platform analysis: digital methods to research social media images, *Information, Communication and Society*, 23(2): 161–80.

Peirce, C. S. (1931–5) *Collected Papers of Charles Sanders Peirce*, vols. 1–6, ed. C. Hartshorne and P. Weiss, Cambridge, MA: Harvard University Press.

Perkins, C. (2003) Cartography: mapping theory, *Progress in Human Geography* 27: 325–35.

Phillips, J. W. P. (2013) On topology, *Theory, Culture and Society*, 30(5): 122–152.

Pickering, A. (1995) *The Mangle of Practice: Time, Agency and Science*, Chicago: University of Chicago Press.

Picot, A. and Hopf, S. (2018) Innovation by the numbers: crowdsourcing in the innovation process, in W. Rammert, A. Windeler, H. Knoblauch and M. Hutter (eds) *Innovation Society Today: Perspectives, Fields and Cases*, Wiesbaden, Springer VS, pp. 183–206.

Pina-Cabral, J. de (2018) Modes of participation, *Anthropological Theory*, 17(4): 435–55.

Plantin, J-C. and Powell, A. (2016) http://blogs.oii.ox.ac.uk/ipp-conference/2016/programme-2016/track-b-governance/platform-studies/jean-christophe-plantin-alison-powell.html

Plantin, J-C., Lagoze, C., Edwards, P. N. and Sandvig, C. (2016) Infrastructure studies meets platform studies in the age of Google and Facebook, *New Media & Society*, 20(1): 293–310.

Poell, T., Nieborg, D. and van Dijck, J. (2019) Platformisation, *Internet Policy Review*, 8(4).

Pötzsch, H. and Hayles, N. K. (2014) Posthumanism, technogenesis and digital cultures: a conversation with N. Katherine Hayles, *The Fibreculture Journal*, 23: 95–107.

Porter, T. (1996) *Trust in Numbers: The Pursuit of Objectivity in Science and Public Life*, Princeton, NJ: Princeton University Press.

Power, M. (1999) *The Audit Society: Rituals of Verification*, Oxford: Oxford University Press.

Puig de la Bellacasa, M. (2017) *Matters of Care: Speculative*

Ethics in More Than Human Worlds, Minneapolis: University of Minnesota Press.

Rabinow, P. (2009) *Marking Time: On the Anthropology of the Contemporary*, Princeton, NJ: Princeton University Press.

Rabinow, P., Marcus, G. E., Fabion, J. D. and T. Rees (2008) *Designs for an Anthropology of the Contemporary*, Durham, NC: Duke University Press.

Rai, S. M., Hoskyns, C. and Thomas, D. (2013) Depletion, *International Feminist Journal of Politics*, 16(1): 86-105.

Research Councils UK (2013) https://www.ukri.org/funding/information-for-award-holders/open-access/open-access-policy

Rheinberger, H-J. (1997) *Toward a History of Epistemic Things*, Stanford, CA: Stanford University Press.

Rheinberger, H-J. (2010) *On Historicizing Epistemology: An Essay*, trans. D. Fernbach, Stanford, CA: Stanford University Press.

Ricaurte, P. (2019) Data epistemologies, the coloniality of power, and resistance, *Television & New Media*, 20(4): 350-65.

Riles, A. (2000) *The Network Inside Out*, Ann Arbor, Michigan: University of Michigan Press.

Rittel, H. W. J. and Webber, M. (1973) Dilemmas in a general theory of planning, *Policy Sciences*, 4(2): 155–69.

Rose, D. Bird (2017) *Reports from a Wild Country: Ethics of Decolonisation*, Sydney: UNSW Press.

Rosenblueth, A. Wiener, N. and Bigelow, J. (1943) Behavior, purpose and teleology, *Philosophy of Science*, 10(1): 18–24.

Rouvroy, A. (2013) The end(s) of critique: data behaviourism versus due process, in M. Hildebrandt and K. de Vries (eds) *Privacy Due Process and the Computational Turn: The Philosophy of Law Meets the Philosophy of Technology*, London: Routledge, pp. 143–67.

Rouvroy, A. and T. Berns (2013) Algorithmic governmentality and prospects of emancipation, *Reseaux*, 177: 163–96.

Ruppert, E., Isin, E. and Bigo, D. 2017 Data Politics, *Big Data and Society*, 4(2); https://journals.sagepub.com/doi/full/10.1177/2053951717717749

Savage, M. (2010) *Identities and Social Change in Britain since 1940: The Politics of Method*, Oxford: Oxford University Press.

Savransky, M. (2016) *The Adventure of Relevance: An Ethics of Social Inquiry*, London: Palgrave Macmillan.

Savransky, M. (2018) The social and its problems: on problematic sociology, in N. Marres, M. Guggenheim and A. Wilkie (eds) *Inventing the Social,* London: Mattering Press, pp. 212–33.

Schurz, R. (2008) Patterns of abduction, *Synthese*, 164: 201–34.

Seaver, N. (2015a) The nice thing about context is that everyone has it, *Media, Culture and Society*, 37(7): 1101–9.

Seaver, N. (2015b) Bastard algebra, in T. Boellstorff and B. Maurer (eds) *Data, Now Bigger and Better!,* Prickly Paradigm Press, pp. 27–47.

Seaver, N. (2019) Captivating algorithms: recommender systems as traps, *Journal of Material Culture*, 24(4): 421–36.

Sedgwick, E. Kosofsky (2003) *Touching Feeling: Affect, Pedagogy, Performativity*, Durham, NC: Duke University Press.

Seltzer, M. (2009) Parlor games: the apriorization of the media, *Critical Inquiry*, 36(1): 100–33.

Serra, R. and L. Borden (1994) About drawing: an interview, in R. Serra, *Writings/Interviews*, Chicago: University of Chicago Press.

Serres, M. (2007) *The Parasite*, trans. L. R. Schehr, Minneapolis: University of Minnesota Press.

Shah, N., Sneya, P. P. and Chattapadhyay, S. (eds) (2016) *Digital Activism in Asia Reader*, Leuphana: Meson Press.

Shields, R. (2013) *Spatial Questions: Cultural Topologies and Social Spatializations*, London, New York and Delhi: Sage.

Shiva, V. (1993) *Monocultures of the Mind: Perspectives on Biodiversity and Biotechnology*, London: Zed Press.

Shotwell, A. (2016) *Against Purity: Living Ethically in Compromised Times*, Minneapolis: University of Minnesota Press.

Simon, H. (1990) Invariants of human behavior, *Annual Review of Psychology*, 41: 1–19.

Simon, H. (1996) *The Sciences of the Artificial*, Cambridge, MA: MIT Press.

Simone, T. A. (1996) *In Whose Image?: Political Islam and Urban Practices in Sudan*, Chicago: University of Chicago Press.

Simone, A. (2004) *For the City Yet to Come: Changing African Life in Four Cities*, Durham, NC: Duke University Press.

Simone, A. (2015) Relational infrastructures in postcolonial urban worlds, in S. Graham and C. McFarlane (eds) *Infrastructural Lives: Urban Infrastructure in Context*, Abingdon and New York: Routledge, pp. 17–39.

Simone, A. (2018) *Improvised Lives: Rhythms of Endurance in an Urban South*, Cambridge: Polity.

Sloterdijk, P. (2009) *Terror from the Air*, Cambridge, MA: MIT Press.

Snickars, P. (2017) More of the same – On Spotify Radio, *Culture Unbound*, 9(2): 184–211.

Spencer, M. (2019) The difference a method makes: methods as epistemic objects in computational science, *Distinktion: Journal of Social Theory*, 20(3): 313–27.

Spivak, G. Chakravorty (2012) Forward: cosmopolitanisms and the cosmopolitical, *Cultural Dynamics*, 24(2–3): 107–14.

Stark, D. (2011) *The Sense of Dissonance: Accounts of Worth in Economic Life*, Princeton, NJ: Princeton University Press.

Stengers, I. (2005) The cosmopolitical proposal, in B. Latour and P. Weibel (eds) *Making Things Public*, Cambridge, MA: MIT Press, pp. 994-1003.

Stengers, I. (2009) William James: an ethics of thought?, *Radical Philosophy*, 157: 9–19.

Stengers, I. (2010) *Cosmopolitics*, vol. 1, trans. R. Bononno, Minneapolis: University of Minnesota Press.

Stengers, I. (2019) Putting problematization to the test of our present, *Theory, Culture and Society*, doi. org/10.1177/0263276419848061

Steyerl, H. (2013) Too much world: is the Internet dead?, *e-Flux*, 49.

Steyerl, H. and Poitras, L. (2015) Techniques of the observer: Hito Steyerl and Laura Poitras in conversation, *Artforum*, May, pp. 306–17.

Strathern, M. (1991) *Partial Connections*, London: Rowman and Littlefield.

Strathern, M. (1992) *After Nature: English Kinship in the Late Twentieth Century*, Cambridge: Cambridge University Press.

Strathern, M. (2003) *Commons and Borderlands: Working Papers on Interdisciplinarity, Accountability and the Flow of Knowledge*, Sean Kingston Publishing.

Suchman, L. (2012) Configuration, in C. Lury and N. Wakeford (eds) *Inventive Methods: The Happening of the Social*, London: Routledge, pp. 48–58.

Sundaram, R. (2015) Publicity, transparency and the circulation engine: the media sting in India, *Current Anthropology*, 56(12): 297–305.

Terranova, T. (2000) Free labor: producing culture for the digital economy, *Social Text*, 18(2): 33–58.

Thévenot, L. (1984) Rules and implements: investment in forms, *Social Science Information*, 23(1): 1-45.

Thévenot, L. (2009) Postscript to the Special Issue 'Governing Life by Standards: A View from Engagements', *Social Studies of Science*, 39(5): 793–813.

Thrift, N. (2005) *Knowing Capitalism*, London: Sage.

Thrift, N. (2007) *Non-Representational Theory: Space, Politics, Affect*, London: Routledge.

Thrift, N. (2008) Movement-space: the changing domain of thinking resulting from the development of new kinds of spatial awareness, *Economy and Society*, 33(4): 582–604.

Tironi, M. (2018) Speculative prototyping, frictions and counter-participation: a civic intervention with homeless individuals, *Design Studies*, 59: 117–38.

Tkacz, N. (2014) *Wikipedia and the Politics of Openness*, Chicago: Chicago University Press.

Tooker, L. (2014) Conversation with Bill Maurer, *Exchanges: Warwick Research Journal*, 2(1).

Totaro, P. and Ninno, D. (2014) The concept of algorithm as an interpretive key of modern rationality, *Theory, Culture and Society*, 31(4): 29–49.

Tsing, A. Lowenhaupt (2015) *The Mushroom at the End of the World: On the Possibility of Life in Capitalist Ruins*, Princeton, NJ: Princeton University Press.

Uprichard, E. (2011) Dirty data: longitudinal classification systems, *Sociological Review*, 59(2): 93–112.

Uprichard, E. (2013) Describing description (and keeping causality): the case of academic articles on food and eating, *Sociology*, 47(2): 368–82.

Uprichard, E. (2016) Reply to Smith and Atkinson, *International Journal of Social Research Methodology*, 19(1): 131–6.

Uprichard, E., Burrows, R. and Byrne, D. (2008) SPSS as an

inscription device: from causality to description, *Sociological Review*, 56(4): 606–22.

Uprichard, E. and Dawney, L. (2016) Data diffraction: Challenging data integration in mixed methods research, *Journal of Mixed Methods Research*, 13(1): 19–32.

Verran, H. (2001) *Science and an African Logic*, Chicago: University of Chicago Press.

Verran, H. (2005) Knowledge traditions of Aboriginal Australians: questions and answers arising in a databasing project, draft published by Making Collective Memory with Computers, School of Australian Indigenous Knowledge Systems, Charles Darwin University, Darwin, NT 0909, Australia, at http://www.cdu.edu.au/centres/ik/pdf/knowledgeanddatabasing.pdf

van der Leeuw, K. (1997) François Jullien: comparative thinking, *China Review International*, 4(2): 322–6.

von Neumann, J. (1928) Zur Theorie der Gesellschaftsspiele, *Mathematische Annalen*, 100: 295–300.

Wagner, R. (2019) *The Logic of Invention*, Chicago: Hau Books.

Walby, S. (2005) Improving the statistics on violence against women, *Statistical Journal of the United Nations ECE 22*: 193–216.

Walby, S. and Towers, J. S. (2017) Measuring violence to end violence: mainstreaming gender, *Journal of Gender-Based Violence*, 1(1): 11–31.

Wark, S. (2018) The subject of circulation: on the digital subject's technical individuations, *Subjectivity*, 12(2): 65–81.

Wark, S. (2019) *Meme Theory*, PhD thesis, Warwick University.

Wark, S. and Wark, M. (2019) Circulation and its discontents, in A. Brown and F. Russell (eds) *Post Memes: Seizing the Memes of Production*, Santa Barbara: punctum books.

Warner, M. (2002) *Publics and Counterpublics*, Durham, NC: Duke University Press.

Watkins, E. A. and Stark, D. (2018) The Möbius organizational form: make, buy, cooperate, or co-opt?, http://blogs.cim.warwick.ac.uk/diversityandperformance/wp-content/uploads/sites/157/2018/04/Stark-Watkins-Mobius.pdf

Weber, S. (2010) *Benjamin's –abilities*, Cambridge, MA: Harvard University Press.

Whatmore, S. J. and Landström, C. (2011) Flood apprentices:

an exercise in making things public, *Economy and Society*, 40(4): 582–610.

White, H. (1991) *Figural Realism: Studies in the Mimesis Effect*, Baltimore: Johns Hopkins University.

Whitehead, A. N. (1968) *Modes of Thought*, New York: The Free Press.

White House Office of Science and Technology Policy (2013) https://obamawhitehouse.archives.gov/sites/default/files/microsites/ostp/ostp_public_access_memo_2013.pdf

Wilkie, A., Savransky, M. and Rosengarten, M. (2019) (eds) *Speculative Research: The Lure of Possible Futures*, London: Routledge.

Won Yin Wong, W. (2017) Speculative authorship in the city of fakes, *Current Anthropology*, 58: S15, S103–S112.

World Health Organization (2014) https://www.who.int/publishing/openaccess/enArt

Artwork

Dorothea Rockburne, *Drawing Which Makes Itself* (1972–3).

Index

Page numbers in *italic* refer to Figures and Tables.